MW00574643

Our Data, Ourselves

Our Data, Ourselves

A Personal Guide to Digital Privacy

JACQUELINE D. LIPTON

UNIVERSITY OF CALIFORNIA PRESS

University of California Press
Oakland, California

© 2022 by Jacqueline Lipton

Library of Congress Cataloging-in-Publication Data

Names: Lipton, Jacqueline D., author.
Title: Our data, ourselves : a personal guide to
    digital privacy / Jacqueline D. Lipton.
Description: Oakland, California : University of
    California Press, [2022] | Includes bibliographical
    references and index.
Identifiers: LCCN 2021062823 (print) |
    LCCN 2021062824 (ebook) | ISBN 9780520379664
    (hardback) | ISBN 9780520390508 (paperback) |
    ISBN 9780520976849 (ebook)
Subjects: LCSH: Data privacy.
Classification: LCC HD30.3815 .L46 2022 (print) |
    LCC HD30.3815 (ebook) | DDC 323.44/8—dc23/
    eng/20220203
LC record available at https://lccn.loc
    .gov/2021062823
LC ebook record available at https://lccn.loc
    .gov/2021062824

Manufactured in the United States of America

31 30 29 28 27 26 25 24 23 22
10 9 8 7 6 5 4 3 2 1

CONTENTS

Introduction

What Is Data Privacy and Why Is It Important?

In February 2021, social media giant Facebook entered into a settlement agreement in a class action lawsuit brought by over 1.5 million of its users for infringements of an Illinois state law prohibiting the use of photo tags and other biometric data without the permission of those users.[1] The case was settled for $650 million to be distributed among any Facebook members who chose to participate in compensation, potentially providing at least $345 to each affected user. The law in question is the Illinois Biometric Information Privacy Act, which requires companies to get permission before harvesting and using people's biometric data, including digital "faceprints" and fingerprints. Facebook has routinely used facial recognition technology to find "friends" of its users for targeted advertising and other purposes. Since the litigation started in 2015, it has modified its practices on photo tagging.

This case is one of the more high-profile examples of increasing concerns by consumers about digital privacy in recent years. Amid the global COVID-19 pandemic, allegations of election interference, racial injustices, and identity theft, personal privacy concerns have bubbled to the forefront of the public imagination. Congress seems to be taking seriously the need for a comprehensive national privacy law for the first time since the dawn of the digital age. However, enacting, implementing, and enforcing such a law is fraught with technological and political challenges. This book attempts to explain these challenges, the genesis of privacy worries in the digital age, and the situations in our daily lives that most threaten our personal privacy.

The aim is not to be alarmist, but simply to explain, in user-friendly terms, when governments, businesses, and others may be harvesting your personal information, how they use it, and what you can do to monitor and protect your personal data. Each chapter relates to a different aspect of our lives where privacy concerns may arise: privacy at home, privacy at work, privacy on social media, privacy and the government, privacy at school, and so on. And each chapter concludes with some tips and tricks for monitoring and protecting your privacy in the relevant context. Throughout the text, particularly important and/or unfamiliar terms will be in bold at first use.

First, let's take a brief look at the background to some of the central concepts. What is personal data privacy and why does it matter? Let's start with a familiar scenario.

Have you ever gone to a store and admired, say, a designer pair of shoes that you think your best friend might like? You snap a photo on your smartphone and text it to her. When you get home, you turn on your computer and check Facebook, where an ad pops up for other items by the same designer. Facebook suggests you might want to connect with the friend you texted. When you curl up in bed, you log in to your favorite streaming service, which suggests you might like to watch a new documentary about the designer.

While this scenario seems pretty mild, and maybe quite useful (you may want to watch that documentary, after all, or share it with your friend), does it bother you that your online service providers seem to know so much about you—your hobbies, your favorite books and TV shows, your location, your friends and family, your professional connections?

What if the information is inaccurate?

What if it is embarrassing?

What if it could expose you, or your family, to harm?

You may remember the 2012 news report about a distraught man storming into a Target store to complain that his teen daughter had received personally addressed coupons for baby clothes and cribs. He accused the store manager of encouraging teen girls to get pregnant. He called back later to apologize for the outburst, admitting that there had been some activities in his house that he was not aware of. His daughter was indeed pregnant, and Target's directed marketing had outed her.[2]

Personal data is useful for more than just targeted marketing. Information about you can affect employment decisions, political decisions, and healthcare. Think about situations like the allegations of Russia hacking the 2016 presidential election, the Equifax data breach in 2017, or the government's use of data from home DNA tests to identify criminal suspects. All these activities rely on technology that collects and aggregates personal information.

Election hackers can target messages to voters likely to support a particular candidate, but who might not otherwise bother to vote, in order to galvanize them into action. To do so, the hacker must have access to information about how those people were likely to vote in the first place. The Equifax data breach implicated massive quantities of personal information that could be used for crimes like identity theft: using someone's credentials to engage in credit card fraud, tax fraud, or health fraud. The police can, and have, used aggregated databases of home-DNA-test results to identify criminal suspects, often without a warrant, which raises significant due process concerns.[3] And then there's the increased use of facial recognition technology (or FRT), which is discussed in some detail in chapter 11, and which formed the basis of the Facebook example at the beginning of this introduction.

These activities have one commonality: reliance on massive amounts of personal data that are now routinely collected and aggregated by governments and businesses around the world. Most of us are aware that some businesses, like Facebook, rely on aggregating personal data to support their entire business model, capitalizing on targeted advertising. We will talk more about how targeted marketing works in chapter 4.

Governments and businesses routinely harvest and use our personal information, sometimes harmfully and sometimes helpfully. Contact tracing for those who may have been exposed to COVID-19 is an obvious example where gathering and processing personal information may be immensely helpful to controlling the spread of the virus.

However, those of us concerned about how much data is gathered about us on a daily basis may feel confused and powerless against faceless database operators cataloguing the finer details of our lives. The law is not much comfort, especially in the United States, which has no comprehensive federal privacy-protection law. Congress continues to debate the need for such a law, particularly in the wake of the Mueller Report with its focus on manipulation of data collected through social media, like Facebook, to influence election outcomes, hitting at the heart of our democracy.[4] Some states, like

California, have moved forward in the absence of federal law to create their own comprehensive privacy laws, but these laws are limited to situations affecting residents of the state in question.

By contrast, most European countries have historically protected privacy as a basic human right. The **European Convention on Human Rights (ECHR)**, a treaty in force throughout Europe—or at least in those countries that signed it—accepts privacy as a fundamental human right that is to be protected in all walks of life, with respect to all types of information, including but not limited to social, political, health, and financial. European Union member countries have also traditionally taken a strong stance on the protection of personal privacy, initially under the **1995 Data Protection Directive**, and more recently under the **General Data Protection Regulation (GDPR)**, which came into force in May 2018. We will consider the GDPR in some detail in chapter 8.

This book focuses on the American position on individual privacy, with some reference to other countries where comparisons are useful to aid our understanding of what is, or isn't, possible in terms of privacy protection, as well as in regard to privacy issues that may arise across national borders. An obvious example is international travel: if one country's law prohibits air-lines from collecting certain data about passengers (like race, religion, polit-ical affiliation, or health information) and another country's law requires it, how can that be resolved as a legal or practical matter?

Further, this book focuses on the individual level—what you can do to help monitor and protect your privacy. The idea is to empower readers to understand their rights and responsibilities in relation to protecting their per-sonal information—and that of others—and to emphasize that sometimes you have more control than you might expect. Before we get into the meat of the discussion, we should also consider why, historically, privacy has been such a difficult issue for American lawmakers to embrace. Obviously, a big part of the explanation has to do with political priorities, but our history is very different from that of the European Union, both constitutionally and politically.

PRIVACY PROTECTION: THE LEGAL BACKGROUND

Unlike the situation in many other countries, the U.S. Constitution does not include any clear right to privacy. Additionally, our powerful First Amendment protections of free speech—that is, speech free from government interference—have been regarded as limiting laws that restrict what we can say about each other. Many other countries protect both speech and privacy as basic constitutional rights, so the courts and lawmakers in those countries are constitutionally required to balance the two. However, in the United States we have typically prioritized speech over privacy—because of the lack of a clear privacy right in our Constitution. This means that there is less protection here against the collection and use of personal information than in other countries.

In the absence of a clear constitutional right to privacy, lawmakers in the United States have developed the concept in a piecemeal way. The first major recognition of a general American need for a law on privacy dates back to the late nineteenth century, with the publication of a foundational law-review article by Samuel Warren and Louis Brandeis that attempted to define the concept.[5] Warren and Brandeis famously described privacy as "the right to be let alone."

That definition seems simplistic now. But it's interesting that in the many, many, *many* years since that article was published, American law has never really come to grips with what privacy means, which is one of the reasons we struggle so much to protect our privacy in the digital age. It was not until the 1950s and 1960s that there were any other serious attempts to create legal privacy rights, and those came in the form of disharmonized state privacy **torts**.

Torts are laws that impose obligations on members of society not to harm others. They include negligence, trespass, and defamation. We will look at the privacy torts in more detail in chapter 2. In parallel to the tort law discussions are criminal laws developed to protect suspects against unreasonable searches and seizures, based on the due process provisions in the Constitution. These laws are the focus of much of chapter 11, including the extent to which due process protects our privacy in the face of mass government surveillance initiatives.

In the latter part of the twentieth century, some federal laws came into play to protect privacy in specific contexts, including privacy in the workplace, privacy in healthcare settings, and financial and consumer privacy. We will discuss those laws in later chapters. However, the history of American privacy law suggests a "reactive" approach: courts and Congress have taken steps to address specific privacy problems when they arise, rather than tackling privacy in a comprehensive way.

TECHNOLOGY AND PRIVACY

While the law has struggled to keep pace with individual privacy, technology has charged ahead. The ability of computer networks to collect, organize, disseminate, and aggregate all kinds of information, including a lot of personal information, has, in recent years, been referred to under the label **Big Data**. Bernard Marr, in his *Beginner's Guide to Big Data*, points out that it is not just human interactions that enable the collection and collation of huge amounts of data about individuals; computers interact with each other, too. Marr puts it like this: "We generate data whenever we go online, when we carry our GPS-equipped smartphones, when we communicate with our friends through social media or chat applications, and when we shop. You could say we leave digital footprints with everything we do that involves a digital transaction, which is almost everything."[6] This explains the scenario described earlier—how our connected devices link information about a designer pair of shoes to other aspects of our lives.

Marr continues by noting that part of the data-aggregation equation involves our devices generating their own collections of data and analyzing the data automatically—based on their original programming, of course:

> On top of this, the amount of machine-generated data is rapidly growing too. Data is generated and shared when our "smart" home devices communicate with each other or with their home servers. Industrial machinery in plants and factories around the world is increasingly equipped with sensors that gather and transmit data. Soon, self-driving cars will take to the streets, beaming a real-time, four-dimensional maps [sic] of their surroundings back home from wherever they go.[7]

Sounds like science fiction, doesn't it? But the future is happening now. Self-driving cars are already in use in many cities, including Pittsburgh, where Lyft and Uber self-driving vehicles collect data about where customers are going and when. Big Brother really is watching us now, although it is not only one Big Brother (the government), but many, including companies, research labs, and nonprofit entities. Without necessarily realizing it, we often consent to data uses when we click "I agree" to access online services.

We are agreeing to contracts that include terms about what is done with our personal information. The fact that we don't read the terms doesn't mean they are not legally enforceable.

Big Data comprises more than names, addresses, email addresses, and telephone numbers. Today, Big Data—and the personal information from which it is aggregated—includes photographs, video, and location and voice data. It is also important to appreciate that Big Data, in and of itself, is neither good nor bad. Like most advances in technology, it has socially beneficial as well as potentially harmful uses, depending on who is using it and for what purposes. Remember that COVID-19 example? Knowing who has been exposed to the virus and being able to trace clusters and outbreaks is an essential part of addressing national and global health concerns.

The concept of Big Data is based on the idea that not only can an entity aggregate a lot of information, but that information can be used to predict social behaviors and gain new understandings of those behaviors. The more data you have, the more you can identify patterns of behavior and make predictions about the future. This could be as simple as figuring out which customers might be predisposed to buy which products, to enable more cost-effective marketing; or it could be as complex as ascertaining data about the universe to help NASA, and private companies like SpaceX, plan future space exploration missions.

As Marr points out, Big Data can serve many socially useful purposes, including research and development—for example, to help cure diseases like cancer by using demographic patient and genetic data; to prevent crime by analyzing patterns of where and when crimes are more likely to occur and deploying more resources to those areas; and to feed the hungry by aggregating agricultural data about crop yields at particular times in specific places.[8]

Of course, on the flip side, Big Data may impinge on an individual's privacy and the security of personal information, or manipulated to justify undesirable practices like racial or gender discrimination or election hacking. The harms to an individual from misuse of, or insecurity over, personal data can range from a general sense of unease—who knows what about me?—to actual harm like identity theft or damage to one's credit score.

Many real-world harms could be prevented by prohibiting the manipulation of so much personal data. For example, a lot of health, housing, education,

BIG DATA, MACHINE LEARNING, AND ARTIFICIAL INTELLIGENCE

Artificial intelligence (AI) and machine learning are often mentioned in conjunction with Big Data. This is because Big Data relies on self-learning computer programs (AIs) that can analyze data more efficiently, and at much greater speeds, than human analysts can manage.

Machine learning happens when computers are programmed to recognize certain patterns and automatically improve upon those patterns through experience. Machine learning is the basis of AI. Recently, the term *AI* has become more of a marketing ploy, when most references to AI really indicate machine learning. For example, the self-driving cars being developed by Tesla and Ford collect vast amounts of video data. They are programmed to recognize things like people, road signs, bicycles, and other vehicles. They are also programmed to identify the patterns these objects make and what to do when there is an anomaly in the pattern. The voluminous data points, when brought together, allow the program to make calculated predictions and safely navigate a vehicle through traffic that, to a human eye, seems random. Other uses of machine leaning include predictions about population growth, healthcare needs, environmental phenomena, land use, and space exploration.

and employment discrimination can be traced to the increased availability of applicants' personal information on social networks. Cyberstalking and cyberharassment—which statistically tend to target those groups who have less power (e.g., women, children, people of color, members of the LGBTQIA+ community)—have also led to tangible physical and emotional harms, including tragic events like suicides. We will discuss some of these real-world tragedies in chapters 4 and 6.

Researchers have suggested that when negative consequences occur because of undesirable uses of personal information, the best approach is for lawmakers to address the resulting harms (e.g., discrimination, physical attacks, or emotional abuse) rather than regulating the information itself.[9] In other words, the focus should be on dealing with the resulting damage rather than regulating the source of information that led to the damage.

This is an interesting idea, although discrimination and other harms, short of physical violence, are often notoriously difficult to prove, particularly in cases where those discriminating in areas like healthcare, employment, housing, and so on can shield the reasons for their decisions behind more reasonable-sounding explanations—for example, it wasn't that the applicant was African American, she simply wasn't the best-qualified person for the job.

Also, a focus on only particular real-world harms doesn't deal with the larger, underlying issue that makes many people uncomfortable: not knowing who holds what information about them—information that may even be inaccurate, and yet may impact their lives in tangible ways. Many dystopian novels and movies play on such fears. And those with this kind of power over information are not just in government. Today, we may be equally concerned about businesses that are collecting volumes of our personal information, and about what they may do with that information, for better or worse. George Orwell's Big Brother has multiplied into a family of Big Brothers and Sisters monitoring our daily lives. Think about the runaway success, a few years ago, of Dave Eggers's *The Circle*—a best-selling novel, adapted into a film starring Tom Hanks, in which a fictional company that resembles Facebook encourages its employees and customers to share all their information all the time, regardless of the consequences.

Despite many deep-seated real-world and fictional concerns about unbridled uses of our personal information, a lot of researchers and writers have suggested that we should, in fact, all be more transparent about our personal information. As dramatized in *The Circle*, one suggestion is that if we could all know everything about one another, this would level the playing field in many ways. The reasons for decisions on housing, employment, and other matters would be made clear and transparent. We would ultimately lose our fears about privacy and secrecy, because no one would have any significant expectations of privacy at all, in a world of transparency enforced for everyone.[10]

A significant problem with this approach comes down to aggregation of data. There is simply too much data for any human to process effectively at a

IS BIG BROTHER TRACKING ME?

Radio frequency identification (RFID) is a technology that uses electromagnetic fields to track digital tags attached to physical objects and devices. Unlike bar codes (those black and white codes affixed to products in the grocery store), RFID tags can be monitored at a distance. You do not need a digital reader in the proximity of the device to locate and "read" its information. RFID microchips are implanted in livestock and pets to help find them if they are lost. They are implanted into digital devices, notably automobiles, to find them if they become stolen or lost, or simply to track them for work or other purposes. Theme parks even use RFID tags to track where you are sitting in a restaurant in order to deliver food you preordered.

In terms of personal privacy concerns, it is, of course, possible to implant an RFID tag under a person's skin or in the clothes they wear or items they carry. Concerns with RFID have led to various agreements internationally about limiting uses of the technology in relation to tracking and release of personal information. RFID tags mainly track product information. However, the collection of product information in relation to a particular person has the potential to create personal data profiles without the knowledge of the individual.

Similar concerns arise with respect to the cell site location information that is triangulated from cell towers, which enables cell phone service providers like AT&T, Verizon, and Sprint to locate a specific cell phone. In 2018, the Supreme Court held in essence that it was a violation of the Fourth Amendment's constitutional guarantee against unreasonable searches and seizures for the government to search a suspect's cell phone location records without a warrant, at least in the particular circumstances that arose in the case. This was a landmark decision that overturned previous law on governmental use of cell phone location records. We will look more at government intrusions into personal life in chapter 11.

given time. Having access to voluminous amounts of data does not necessarily help anyone make better decisions, at least not without machine learning as an aid. Additionally, most of us simply do not want everyone else in the world to have access to all information about us all the time. Our actions may be embarrassing or damning, or maybe we just want to be left alone. That is a big problem with Big Data: we never know who has access to what information about us, or how and when it might be used to harm, embarrass, or simply annoy us.

The bottom line is that digital technology enables more collection, aggregation, and use of personal information than ever before. Again, this is neither good nor bad, in and of itself—data can be used for both beneficial and harmful purposes. We may like the beneficial aspects of Big Data and fear the potential harms. On one hand, we may be uncomfortable with the thought of large amounts of our personal information being collected by entities outside our control. On the other hand, we may be okay with our information being collected if it is anonymized—although, with modern technology, it is frighteningly easy to de-anonymize data and identify the subject of specific information.

So how do we proceed from here?

Each chapter of this book will target a particular area of daily life, highlighting when and how personal information may be collected and used and making suggestions about how best to monitor and protect that information. In our digital reality, it is simply not realistic to attempt to claw back absolute privacy rights to personal information. Privacy can never be an absolute right in any event. Even in countries that protect privacy as a constitutional or human right, that right has to be balanced against rights and concerns like national security, public health, and free speech. We will look at where those balances play out currently in the United States, and how the situation in this country differs from that in other countries (and why).

Whether you choose to read from cover to cover or dip in and out of chapters that interest you, the pages that follow will offer some explanations, and maybe even some comfort, about your data and how it is used, along with many useful tips and tricks. Chapter 1 sets the scene by explaining, in simple terms, the issue of who (if anyone) "owns" our data and in what contexts. The answers are not as obvious as you might think!

CHAPTER ONE

Who Owns Our Data?

+ Property and contract rights in personal data
+ Survey of laws protecting compilations of data
+ Data sharing between companies and other institutions
+ Legal restrictions on corporate data sharing

If you've bought a new car in the last decade or so, there's a good chance it came equipped with an event data recorder, also known as a "black box." These devices automatically record how the car is operating, its speed, and its location at any given time. Some cars also have cameras that record road and traffic conditions. These devices can be extremely useful in generating data about, say, road accidents: whether a driver was speeding, whether a car malfunctioned, and so on. They can also record driving habits and are often used to adjust insurance premiums to reward careful drivers.

Who owns the information these devices record? The driver? The insurance company? The car manufacturer? What about the data our other devices generate?

And who owns my health information? It is information about me, but it is actually created and compiled by my healthcare providers, and then much of it is shared with my insurance company. Do we jointly share ownership of this information?

This chapter looks at who owns our information, and in what contexts. It also explains the important difference between the *legal* concept of ownership and the ways we think about ownership on a more informal or social basis. A lot of things we think of as belonging to us are actually not legally classified as property. For example, you do not technically "own" your website (if you have one) or the domain name used to access it. You may hold copyright in your website design, and you have a contractual license to use your domain name, but that is not the same as owning those things as property in a legal sense. The issue of ownership is confusing because the way we use words like *own* and *property* colloquially is different from the way the law defines them.

Why does this difference matter? Because the law imposes rights and obligations with respect to the things we legally own. In particular, we can sell, license, or donate those things to others, and the transfer will have legal effect. In other words, we have a significant degree of legal *control* over our property. If I legally own my car, I can sell it or I can give it away, and then the person to whom I give or sell it will legally own it. On the other hand, if something is *not* my property in a legal sense, I may want to control it but there may not be a realistic way of doing so.

This is a big challenge with personal information. It may be about us, but it can be very difficult for us to control it in the way we might control, say, a computer, a car, or a house. I may feel proprietorial about my children, and I am definitely responsible for certain things they do, but I don't legally "own" them. Things we feel like we should control are not necessarily things we legally do control.

To make everything more complex with respect to our personal information, we may not be the only people who want to claim ownership of data about us. The companies that collect, organize, and use information about us may likewise want to claim ownership because they took the time and trouble to collect and compile all that information. They invested in its collection and so they should reap the rewards, or so the argument goes.

Of course, what is of value to them is the *collection*, not each individual piece of data. Lawmakers in many countries have, in fact, struggled about whether, how, and on what basis property rights might be created for those who compile commercially valuable databases. The European Union created a special regulation in 1996 to grant property rights to those who collate large compilations of digital and other data. We will come back to this law later in the chapter.

DO YOU OWN YOUR PERSONAL INFORMATION?

Questions about owning our own personal information are, at least legally speaking, quite similar to questions about whether we own parts of our own bodies. This is because our personal information—like our DNA, blood, and cells—is, in a sense, part of us, but it is not created by us. Legal ownership tends to attach to things people *make* or *create*. This includes physical property like computers, furniture, cars, and houses, as well as intellectual property like copyrights, patents, and trademarks (inventions of the human mind, broadly speaking). We can own land, of course, but that is generally because someone, at some point in history, consciously laid claim to the land, and often because that person developed the land. Legal property typically requires some actual, conscious human effort to create.

Things that organically, or automatically, come from us—like body parts and information about us—tend not to meet the bar required for legal property. This is quite an oversimplification of the idea of property, but for present purposes, let's take a look at ways in which the law has considered ownership of parts of the human body as an analogy to how the law regards our personal information.

In the landmark case of *Moore v. Regents of the University of California* in 1990, a patient, John Moore, sued hospital researchers for failing to obtain his permission to cultivate cell lines from cancer cells they extracted from his body. Moore claimed that he owned his cell lines (i.e., they were his property because they came from his body) and that the researchers had thus stolen or misappropriated his property when they took, and used, his cells for research purposes without his permission. The court disagreed. The upshot was that patients do not own the cells, blood, or other tissue samples that are extracted from them. This case does not stand alone—many subsequent courts have said the same thing.

Courts have held that physicians and medical researchers may have obligations to disclose any financial or other interests they have as a result of patient treatments, and should obtain consent from patients for further uses of biological material, but this is not a property issue. It is a contractual consent issue, for the most part. Lawmakers and legal scholars have made similar points about personal information: consent is often required to use particular kinds of sensitive information (health, financial, etc.), but not because the information is *property*. We will look at laws on health information in chapter 9, and credit and other financial information in chapter 10.

THE IMMORTAL LIFE OF HENRIETTA LACKS

One of the more high-profile and significant unauthorized uses of a person's biological material is the case of Henrietta Lacks, whose cells were taken and used, without her consent, to develop and propagate cell lines for cancer research, initially by Johns Hopkins Hospital in Baltimore, where Lacks died from the disease in 1951. The cell lines derived from Lacks's cells now form the basis of many patents for cancer research. Lacks's story was shared in Rebecca Skloot's best-selling nonfiction book of 2010, *The Immortal Life of Henrietta Lacks*, later made by HBO into a TV movie starring Oprah Winfrey as Deborah Lacks, Henrietta's daughter.

The book drew attention to the issue of unauthorized use of human biological material by medical researchers and focused public attention on the need for consent at the very least, and also for more precise rules about ownership of cell lines and other biological material. Some litigation has emerged involving the HeLa cell line, developed from Lacks's cells, but no clear legal rules have yet emerged.

Why does it matter whether body parts or personal information are *property* if consent is already required to use them? Largely because consent is required only in certain contexts, like sharing sensitive financial information with other financial service providers. Property rights apply in all circumstances and give a more complete sense of control. In simple terms, laws that protect property rights against theft and other kinds of misappropriation or misuse are stronger and broader than those that simply require consent for particular uses.

CAN A COMPANY OWN YOUR INFORMATION?

Regardless of whether we can own information about ourselves (and the consensus at the moment is that we cannot), the companies, hospitals, researchers, financial institutions, and others that collect our information often claim that *they* own our information. Is that true? How can they own information about us when we do not own the information ourselves?

To understand the difference between our claims to our own personal information and the claims of those who collect and collate it, we need to appreciate that companies like Target, Walmart, Facebook, and Amazon do not collect only one person's information. They collect information from many people about a variety of things. The value to those companies, and to researchers, financial institutions, and other private entities—not to mention the government—is having a lot of information about a lot of people. That way, they can make more informed decisions about resource allocation, marketing, research directions, and the like. When we talk about personal information in, say, Amazon's hands, it is a different kind of information, or at least a different amount of information, than each of our own personal slices of Amazon's big information pie.

Simply knowing a lot about *one person* is not all that useful to Amazon. What the company wants to know are things like how many people in which cities want to purchase which products. This helps with advertising, choosing locations for warehouses, and shipping/delivery logistics. For another example, medical research facilities may use a significant amount of data about many patients so that they have a better sense of where to put their resources in terms of researching cures for diseases.

If we accept that there are good reasons why companies, researchers, and other entities want to develop large-scale databases about us, there is still the question of whether those databases should be their legal *property*. A common justification for property ownership in Anglo-American law is a concept often referred to as the Lockean labor theory of property. Although this sounds highbrow, it actually relates to an often misquoted, or oversimplified, version of ideas about government and society suggested by the famous seventeenth-century English philosopher and physician John Locke.

Locke suggested that legal property rights should, to a large extent, be derived from a person's labor (work, effort, etc.). Back in the late seventeenth century, of course, he was talking about property in the sense of land ownership. He was not concerned about information or body parts. His idea, in a nutshell, was that if someone worked hard to cultivate land, the land and the results of his labor should belong to him (and it was typically a "him" in those days). If he cultivated an apple orchard, he should own the land and the apples grown on it.

LIMITATIONS ON THE EU DATABASE DIRECTIVE

One of the major cases in the European Union that limited the impact of the Database Directive was the case of *British Horseracing Board v. William Hill* in 2004. This was the first case where the court that interprets EU Directives and Regulations—known as the European Court of Justice (ECJ) at the time, now the Court of Justice of the European Union (CJEU)—held that a company wanting to claim a property right in a database had to have expended dedicated resources to developing the database outside its usual course of business.

The database in this case involved horseracing statistics compiled by the British Horseracing Board in the ordinary course of its business. When William Hill (a global sports betting organization) repurposed some of this data for its own commercial purposes, the Horseracing Board brought an action claiming unauthorized misappropriation and misuse of its database contents. The British court referred the matter to the ECJ for interpretation of the Directive to clarify which databases were covered as property. Because the ECJ interpreted the Directive narrowly, the British court was ultimately able to say that there was no infringement of the database protection law because the Board had not devoted specific resources to the development of the database, but rather compiled it in the ordinary course of its business, and therefore could not claim a property right in the database.

This view of property is logical given the era in which it was written. However, it does not cover everything about modern legal property rights. The theory does not explain why anyone should legally own intangible property, like a database of customer spending habits. Laboring over a field of wheat is different than setting up a computer program that records customers' purchases automatically. Of course, you have to hire someone to develop the database, but arguably that is a different kind of labor than tilling a field.

Who Owns Our Data?

In any event, for better or worse, companies all over the world have argued that they own, or at least *should* own, the voluminous databases of customer information they collect. In some countries, lawmakers have supported these claims by creating specific property rights. In the European Union, the Database Directive of 1996 creates a special property right in databases where a company has expended significant efforts in compiling the information. The Database Directive led to concerns in the United States that our lawmakers were not doing enough to protect databases as property in the hands of American businesses. Congress considered several suggestions for new laws in the late 1990s and early 2000s to create this kind of property right, but none came into being.

It turns out that the combination of technology and existing laws—like trade secret law—in the United States sufficiently protects a company's ability to gather and use consumer information without a legal "property" label attached to it. Subsequent reviews of the European Union's law also suggested that the Database Directive was not necessary there, either. Companies have not generally needed to rely on that law to protect their ability to collect, control, and use customer information. Additionally, courts have interpreted the Directive so narrowly that it is no longer of much practical use (see "Limitations on the EU Database Directive").

CONTRACTING AROUND PERSONAL INFORMATION OWNERSHIP AND USE

While it is difficult for us to claim legal property in our personal information, and it can be equally difficult for companies, researchers, and others to claim a property right in compilations of our personal information, there are other ways for companies and researchers to exert control over our personal data. The cell-line and tissue sample cases we looked at earlier in the chapter introduced the important idea of individual consent to collection and use of biological matter. This applies equally to personal data. Obtaining consent is one of the easiest, most effective, and most ubiquitous ways for governments, businesses, and researchers to gain the authority to access, collect, and use our personal information.

Consent can be easily implemented through a contract, which may be in a physical (paper) form or digital. Usually, some benefit is exchanged in return for the consent, so it is enforceable as part of a contract with a health-care provider, business, or educational/research institution.[1] You may scratch your head and think, "I don't remember entering into any contracts to sell my private information to anyone else." The reality is, we do it all the time. Every time we sign up for an online service like Amazon or iTunes or Netflix, we click on a button that says, "I agree."

What we "agree" to in these contracts—whether we've read them or not—is the company's **terms of service**—often referred to as **TOS**. If you have ever read a company's terms of service, you have seen that most include terms about privacy: notably, what you are giving up by signing up for the service in question. You typically agree to hand over your personal information for listed purposes in return for the service. We will look at some examples of these terms of service in more detail in chapter 4.

Under these contracts, you often agree to the terms of service being changed unilaterally (by the company) without any additional consent. Some laws in the United States, notably laws relating to financial institutions, require customers to be notified of changes to these contractual terms. We will talk more about these laws in chapter 10. Generally, however, retail companies and social networks can ask you to agree to whatever terms they want, including terms that allow them to change the terms without your consent, and sometimes even without giving you particular notice.

By way of example, let's look at the Google Privacy Policy. As of this writing, it allows Google to collect information about

+ terms you search for,
+ videos you watch,
+ your views/interactions with online ads,
+ voice/audio information when you use Google's audio features,
+ your purchasing activities,
+ people you communicate with or share content with online,
+ your activities on websites and apps (digital applications such as those on a smartphone) outside Google that use Google's services, and
+ your browsing history on Google's Chrome browser.[2]

Who Owns Our Data?

CONTRACTS OF ADHESION

There is nothing legally wrong with contracts, like the "I agree" contracts, that do not give you any chance to negotiate terms. If you remember the days before the internet, think about the types of contracts you agreed to without negotiating the terms: home loans, car loans, mortgages, insurance policies, and the like. When you enter a parking lot, you agree to the terms on the ticket. When you buy an airline ticket, there are tons of fine-print terms you agree to and probably don't bother reading.

If the law did not enforce these contracts—typically referred to as contracts of adhesion (or adhesion contracts)—think about what the result would be. If companies could not dictate standard terms and had to negotiate each term separately with each customer, those companies would go out of business. At the very least, they would pass on the significant costs of the bargaining and resulting additional insurance risks to their customers.

There are some circumstances in which preprinted contract terms are not enforced, notably if they are egregiously unfair or if they are presented in an unconscionable manner—for example, a significant term printed in especially tiny font and hidden in an unusual place in the contract. But generally, in the absence of unfair or fraudulent conduct, courts will enforce these contracts.

Additionally, Google may collect information about your location and travel that it can track from your personal digital devices, or obtain from publicly available sources like local newspaper articles about you, which it indexes as part of its search function.[3]

Google also explains—in somewhat vague terms—what it does with the information it collects, including testing and maintaining the quality of its products and services, providing targeted services to individuals, and developing new services.[4] The policy notes that Google does not use sensitive personal information (including information about race, religion, sexual orientation, or health) to create targeted advertising. However, that does not

Who Owns Our Data?

mean that Google will not *collect* this information or use it for purposes other than targeted advertising.

The uses that Google makes of this information may benefit or harm you. You may like some—such as targeted suggestions for movies you want to watch or games you want to play—but you may be wary of others, such as the collection of large-scale profiles about you that include your sensitive information. It may be that the collection of this information, in and of itself, is enough to make you uneasy, or it may be that the fear of what might be done with the information is more scary, but the fact is that Google and many other corporations now have access to huge volumes of your personal information. Often, they obtain permission to collect and use the information through "I agree" contracts, and often they simply monitor what you do online.

Google does a little of both. If you sign up for particular services, like Gmail, or open a YouTube account, you will contractually agree to Google's specific privacy policies for its members. If you simply use Google's free services (like online searching using Google's search engine or watching YouTube videos without an account), you have not contractually agreed to anything but Google may still track you on the basis of your IP address or other identifying information. Do you trust Google to do the "right" thing, whatever that means to you?

Could Congress do a better job of regulating what companies like Google, Amazon, and Facebook do with our personal information? They could, with sufficient political will and consensus. But there are certainly reasons why government action has been relatively slow. As April Falcon Doss notes in her 2020 book on digital privacy, "Government regulators in the United States and abroad have vacillated between wanting to encourage corporate growth and innovation and wondering when to rein them in."[5]

The Federal Trade Commission (FTC) has certainly played a role in regulating these companies in the United States, in terms of both privacy and antitrust concerns. We will look more closely at their powers and actions in later chapters. Additionally, Robert Mueller's Office of Special Counsel investigated Russian interference in the 2016 American presidential election, with an emphasis on manipulations of social media including Facebook, Instagram, and Twitter. We will look at the Cambridge Analytica

scandal in more detail in chapter 4. Federal and state legislators have continued to debate new, more comprehensive, privacy laws,[6] with some states
already having enacted versions of a comprehensive privacy law, like California's Consumer Privacy Act of 2018.[7]

European lawmakers have assertively regulated what corporations can
do with information about European residents. We will look at the European
position in more detail in chapter 8. In the United States, there has been
more of a struggle to protect privacy, largely because Congress must balance
a desire to protect personal privacy and data against the freedoms enshrined
in the Constitution, including free speech under the First Amendment.

The price of convenience in the modern digital world is, sadly, often the
loss of privacy. That does not mean we cannot be more aware of how our
information is used in the digital world and what options are available to
monitor or protect against some of the more problematic uses. Taking more
control may simply mean reading and understanding privacy policies before
using a company's services, or comparing one internet browser's privacy
policies to another's (e.g., Chrome vs. Firefox or Safari) before selecting an
internet browser. Being informed is often half the battle.

OTHER LAWS THAT PROTECT DATABASES
OF PERSONAL INFORMATION

Outside of contract law, there are some other laws that companies use to
bolster their ability to control or use your personal data. The most obvious
are trade secret law and copyright law. **Trade secret law**, as the name suggests, protects valuable trade secrets in the hands of the companies that
develop them. **Copyright law**, on the other hand, protects original works (as
defined in the copyright act) that are reduced to a tangible medium such as
paper records, electronic records, microfilm, or microfiche. *Works* typically
means books, songs, music, movies, and the like. However, in the digital
age, the definition has broadened to cover computer software—and digital
databases, which are the products of software programs.

Trade secret law protects information—originally things like industrial
processes and business methods—that companies develop in house and keep
secret from others: the "secret sauce" that gives the business an edge. KFC's

trade-secret-protected "eleven herbs and spices" is a good example of a famous trade secret, as is the Coca-Cola recipe.

Trade secret law also includes things like customer lists, supplier lists, and any other information kept secret by a business that may give the company a competitive edge. Customer databases are a form of customer list that have historically been protected by trade secret law, as long as reasonable measures are taken to keep them secure within the company—for example, using digital encryption so that no one can access the database without permission (e.g., needing a password for access).

Courts and legal scholars have gone back and forth over whether a trade secret should be regarded as *property* in the legal sense.[8] But even if trade secrets aren't "property," they can be protected as valuable corporate assets, and businesses can exercise significant control over them.

Copyright law is a less effective way for American companies to try to claim property rights in digital databases. American copyright law does protect copyrights in compilations to an extent, which might suggest that companies can own digital databases, including databases that contain large volumes of personal data. However, in 1991 the U.S. Supreme Court rejected an aspect of copyright law historically known as the "sweat of the brow" doctrine. This doctrine had allowed copyrights in any compilation of information that someone had expended resources collecting and compiling, like the position under the European Union's Database Directive, and not unlike the Lockean labor theory mentioned earlier.

In *Feist v. Rural Telephone Service* in 1991, however, the Supreme Court said that copyright, constitutionally speaking, is about protecting *original* works of authorship: works that originate from the creator's mind. A compilation that is the result of hard work, rather than original creativity, should not be protected by the law, according to *Feist*. The case itself was about a "white pages" telephone directory. Because there is no originality or creativity involved in compiling an alphabetical listing of telephone customers, Rural Telephone Service was unable to claim copyright in the directory. This meant that Feist could copy Rural's directory entries without infringing copyright, and without having to pay a license fee.

Interestingly, courts have not necessarily felt the same way about "yellow pages" telephone directories, whether in print or digital formats. Yellow pages are often protected by copyright because of the way they are organized and formatted. A degree of original thought goes into decisions about how to arrange the contents: what classifications and subclassifications to use, how to arrange entries within those classifications, and so on. According to the Supreme Court decision in *Feist*, the standard of originality required by American copyright law is not particularly high, but it is higher than simply "hard work."

Fast-forwarding to the digital world, most of the value in large-scale customer databases is not in their originality, but rather in their comprehensiveness. They contain a lot of information that is very useful when gathered and analyzed. These databases are not arranged or organized in a particularly creative way, but are keyed to categories of data (name, address, purchasing history, etc.) that enable easy searching and repurposing of records. For these reasons, in the United States at least, copyright is not a good fit for digital databases.

Another problem with businesses relying on copyright law to protect the contents of customer databases is that, at a more basic level, copyright law aims to protect the *expression* of original works, not the *ideas* behind those works. This distinction is often referred to as the **idea/expression dichotomy**. Copyright law was never intended to grant property rights in ideas, data, and facts, because those things are the building blocks of human knowledge. The point of copyright is to protect creative works made out of those building blocks, not to allow ownership of the building blocks themselves.

DATA SHARING WITH THIRD PARTIES

Many businesses make money from selling our personal data to other companies. That is how a lot of targeted marketing works. If, say, Amazon knows that I often purchase *Star Wars* memorabilia, it can sell this information to other companies that retail similar products. When we "agree" to those contracts with online businesses, we are often consenting to the sale or sharing of our data with other companies that want to market their wares to us.

Even where we do not specifically give our consent, or where the company promises it will not share or sell our personal data, their use of the data may tip off other companies about, say, our spending habits or other elements of our personal information. For example, Amazon's privacy policy

PATENT LAW AND DIGITAL DATABASES

For anyone wondering why patent law is not particularly relevant to the question of companies exercising control over databases of personal information, this is because, unlike copyright and trade secret law, the patent law requires a high degree of novelty and nonobviousness for the United States Patent and Trademark Office to grant a patent. Patents are usually granted for inventions, processes, and procedures that are new contributions to the state of play within a particular industry. The patenting process takes a lot of time and is typically much more expensive than registering a copyright or protecting a trade secret.

Like copyright law and trade secret law, patent law can, and does, protect digital developments. Computer software can be patented, as well as copyrighted and protected through trade secrecy. However, the standard for patent protection is much higher in terms of novelty than for copyright and trade secrets. Additionally, patent law requires a public disclosure of the original software innovation. Companies that can maintain the secrecy of their digital code in house may be more likely to rely on trade secret protection than to seek a patent. Patents last for only twenty years, whereas trade secrets can last indefinitely, provided they are kept secret.

Because the information in digital databases is not usually particularly novel or nonobvious, the databases themselves are not likely to qualify for patent protection. However, software innovations used to aggregate or analyze information in a database may be patentable.

states that Amazon does not directly sell customer information to third parties that are not affiliated Amazon companies. But Amazon has many affiliates! The policy also notes that advertisers and other third parties who contract with Amazon to serve advertisements to users may themselves be able to figure out which users are interested in certain items because of the advertisements they click on.[9] As a result, those third-party advertisers can effectively create a database of consumer spending profiles derived from Amazon's customer base without Amazon technically sharing any

Who Owns Our Data?

information with them. We will delve more into the details of how this works in chapter 4.

DOES THE GOVERNMENT OWN YOUR INFORMATION?

Prior to the rise of the digital age, most concerns about keeping our information private were directed at the government. Historically, citizens of many countries have been suspicious of what the government does with personal data. Those concerns have never really gone away. They have simply been compounded by worries about what other entities are doing with our data. Many of us now feel like we are fighting a privacy war on two fronts: the historical battle against the government, and the newer battle against others who collect our data for commercial and research purposes.

So far, this chapter has focused on the corporate side of data collection. A related question is whether the government can own information about us, and when or whether it matters. Given the uncertainty about information being property, it should not surprise anyone to know that the government probably cannot "own" our personal information in a legal sense any more than anyone else can. However, the government can, and certainly does, compile and use our information for all sorts of purposes, from the census to law enforcement and national security. The dispute in 2020 about including a citizenship question on the census is but one example of how serious American residents' concerns are about shielding their sensitive personal information from the government.[10]

There are some laws that regulate what information the government can collect about us, and from whom it can be collected. For example, governments generally need a warrant to search our private premises, and they need a subpoena to extract information about us from, say, our bank. We will consider some of those laws in more detail in chapter 10. However, typically, if the government wants information about you, there will be a way for them to get it.

As noted in the introduction, and unlike the situation in many other countries, the United States does not have a constitutional right to privacy. Some privacy rights have been read into certain sections of the Constitution, notably those dealing with due process in the criminal context. We will take a closer look at those in chapter 11. Most readers, at least anyone addicted to police procedurals, will be familiar with the distinction between legal and illegal searches and seizures. Constitutionally, we have reasonable expectations of privacy in our bodies, our homes, and, to a limited extent, in other private places like our offices and vehicles. This means that the police are limited, at least theoretically, in what kinds of searches they can make both with and without a warrant, but those limits are certainly tested by digital developments like facial recognition technology and cell site location information from cell phone services. We look more at the impacts of those technologies on our constitutional expectations of privacy in chapter 11.

WHO REGULATES PRIVACY?

Before turning to the specific chapters dealing with privacy in particular contexts (home, work, school, finance, health, etc.), it is worth briefly noting the American regulatory matrix involving privacy. The American position differs significantly from that in many other countries. Since the 1990s, and even earlier in some cases, a number of governments around the world have established dedicated privacy departments. All EU countries have Data Protection Offices: government departments designed to assist in the protection of consumer privacy and advocate to help consumers protect their privacy. Canada has the Office of the Privacy Commissioner of Canada. Australia has the Office of the Australian Information Commissioner (previously the Office of the Australian Privacy Commissioner).

Unlike these countries, the United States has never had a central government agency dedicated to consumer privacy protection. This is one reason why privacy often falls between the cracks. The task of protecting individual privacy is spread out between various government agencies, all of whose primary responsibilities are over other things. In other words, the American agencies that protect individual privacy typically do so as a subset of their other work, rather than as their main focus.

The closest we have to a government department dedicated to individual privacy is the Federal Trade Commission (whose role is discussed in more detail in chapter 4). As its name suggests, its main function is to promote effective and fair competition, rather than to protect consumer privacy. The FTC has taken on the role of protecting privacy from a sideways angle. One of its regulatory powers is to investigate and prevent unfair trade practices.

Where companies have not lived up to their own privacy policies, the FTC takes the view that this amounts to an unfair trade practice and has investigated, and sanctioned, many companies accordingly. Some of the companies that have been investigated by the FTC on privacy grounds are Target, ChoicePoint, Lenovo, Uber, and D-Link. In 2019, the FTC approved a historic $5 billion fine against Facebook for sharing personal information with third parties in the context of the 2016 presidential election. Another landmark fine was imposed on Google and YouTube in the same year, for failure to live up to their obligations under the Children's Online Privacy Protection Act, which is discussed in more detail in chapter 5.

The FTC does not handle individual consumer complaints about privacy, although consumers can complain to the FTC, and these complaints often trigger FTC investigations. Consumers themselves can take their own legal actions against companies that breach privacy policies. However, this is an expensive route and is often not particularly successful. It can be difficult for customers to prove they suffered any clear financial harm as a result of a privacy breach. We will talk more about the problems of individual court action in chapter 2.

Outside the FTC, government regulation of privacy in the United States is much more piecemeal. At the federal level, some of the organizations that regulate financial institutions protect customer privacy to an extent. This typically happens under laws that regulate banks and other financial institutions more broadly. For example, the Gramm-Leach-Bliley Act, which streamlined the banking and financial services industry in 1999, includes provisions on permissible issues of a bank customer's personally identifiable information (PII) in standard banking contexts.

The system largely relies on an "opt out" concept. Customers must have a reasonable opportunity to opt out of certain uses of their PII by a bank or financial institution. If they do opt out, however, they may not be able to avail themselves of the financial services they were seeking. These privacy protections—discussed in more detail in chapter 10—are weak at best. The regulators here include the Federal Reserve Board, the Federal Deposit Insurance Corporation (FDIC), and state financial regulators.

The Securities and Exchange Commission (SEC) and equivalent state regulators play a role in ensuring that companies trading on various stock exchanges do not engage in unfair and deceptive practices—which, again, may involve questionable uses of private information. However, the privacy protections are secondary to the larger questions of regulating stock markets more generally.

The challenge for American residents is to understand how our patchwork of laws works, what roles our array of regulators play in protecting privacy, and what specific strategies we might employ to monitor and control our information. Each of the following chapters tackles a particular privacy context (privacy at home, privacy at work, privacy at school, etc.), explains the privacy issues arising in that context, and details how current laws deal, or fail to deal, with those issues.

Additionally, each chapter provides simple suggestions for what you can do to help safeguard your own personal information in each context. Often, the choice comes down to a decision whether to trade a certain amount of privacy for the convenience of a particular service. If you want to be on Facebook, you take a lot of privacy-related risks. If you choose not to participate on Facebook, you miss out on a lot of social discourse. Are the risks worth the benefits? More people than ever are shying away from Facebook and other social networks for those reasons. However, before you make those choices, you should understand the nature of the trade-off and whether there are any other options open to you to protect your privacy while taking advantage of the services you require.

PRIVACY TIPS AND TRICKS

While most of the issues raised in this chapter are discussed in more detail in later chapters, it should already be clear that being informed about collection and use of our personal information in different contexts is half the battle. It is not possible to read every line of every agreement you enter into with an online service provider, bank, hospital, or educational institution, but to the extent that you are concerned about privacy, you should at least do the following:

+   Look at the terms of service on privacy, which are often presented separately from the rest of the contract you sign (in some cases, they may be displayed prominently on a website or in a physical office space).

+ If you cannot find a privacy policy, ask to see it.

+ Ask questions if you do not understand the privacy policy.

+ Check whether the policy allows for unilateral changes (i.e., changes by the company without requiring your specific consent) and familiarize yourself with whether and where those changes will be shared.

+ Check if there are any procedures for raising complaints about privacy collection practices, whether you can check the accuracy of your private information, whether there are procedures for correcting inaccurate information, and whether your information can be deleted on request.

+ Look for information about a privacy officer or contact number if you have privacy concerns.

+ If you have a choice between different service providers (e.g., different music, game, or movie downloading or streaming services), compare their privacy policies before you click on "I agree."

+ Make sure you understand that clicking on "I agree" creates a legally binding contract whether or not you read all, or any, of the terms of service.

+ Do not share particular information if there is any way around it and if you are concerned about how it might be used. This may mean forgoing a product or service (yes, there are people who don't use Twitter or Facebook), or perhaps sharing the least amount of information required to sign up for a service. If there are "mandatory" and "optional" or "suggested" information sharing requirements, stick with only the "mandatory" fields. Mandatory fields are typically indicated with an asterisk.

+ Work out your "bottom line" with respect to what information you are prepared to share with any particular company, bearing in mind that the company may share the information with others, so you should consider what might happen if the information is shared more generally.

Who Owns Our Data?

CHAPTER TWO

Our Data at Home

+ Rights to privacy at home vs. in public spaces
+ Tort, contract, and constitutional rights to privacy in the home
+ American privacy torts: intrusion into seclusion, misappropriation, public disclosure of private facts, and false light publicity
+ Limitations of contract and tort law privacy protections
+ Contracting away privacy when purchasing digital devices

One of the major advances in digital technology has been in the home security area. Now, people can protect their homes with sophisticated video cameras that have the capacity to send immediate notifications of suspicious activity to their smartphones. These systems can also arm or disarm security systems remotely to allow only trusted people to enter or leave a home. They can also regulate home heating and cooling units remotely. The technology itself also contains artificial intelligence that can analyze patterns of energy use and individual comings and goings, and suggest automatic programming based on that data.

This level of technological sophistication has its upsides and its downsides. Consider the story of Tara Thomas, who bought a Nest Cam, a home-camera system, to use as a baby monitor in her three-year-old daughter's bedroom. When her daughter complained of nightmares about monsters in her room, and pointed to the Nest Cam, Tara thought it was the product of a toddler's overactive imagination. Then she realized that the Nest Cam had been hacked, when she walked into the room one night and heard pornography playing over the camera's speaker. She was unable to learn who the hacker was, although it became clear that Google—the owner of the Nest Cam company—was aware of the simple hacks that could be performed on the cameras. Google had opted, prior to that time, not to patch the software that allowed for hacking because addressing the problem by updating the firmware (the permanent software used to run programs on a device) would have been costly and inconvenient.[1]

It is not only security cameras that allow intruders to virtually invade our private spaces. Think about all the devices you bring into your home that have the capacity to digitally spy on you. How many people own an Alexa or Google Home device? At the last count, it was hundreds of millions of people in the United States. It is easy to ask Alexa to play your music or set an oven timer, but what data is she (or rather Amazon) collecting about you at the same time?

This is not meant to scare you, although it is a little scary. In many ways, it is a lot scarier *not* to know how the technology works. The point of this chapter is to make you aware of how much privacy you legally and realistically have—and don't have—inside your home. One of the main challenges for American residents is that the handful of laws we do have to protect our privacy in personal spaces is largely outdated because it was created mostly

---

WHAT ABOUT THOSE PESKY ROBOCALLS?

Before we had digital devices in our houses that could track us, we had telephones. Early targeted marketing (including scams) involved collecting phone numbers, often targeting the elderly, and used call centers to seek additional personal information. Over time, these systems became more sophisticated. Now many of these calls are made robotically, through automatic dialing from large digital databases of telephone customers using programmed electronic voices.

Congress has enacted legislation to regulate robocalls, which is enforced by the Federal Communications Commission (FCC) and the Federal Trade Commission (FTC). The legislation limits when calls can be made, and the content of the calls, and includes a "Do Not Call" registry, where telephone customers can enter their names to prevent being called. These legal approaches have not been as effective as hoped, but the government, particularly the FCC, continues to monitor and attempt to control the problem.

BREACH OF PRIVACY—WHAT'S THE HARM?

A primary problem of the U.S. legal system in coming to terms with digital privacy is how to quantify harm: how to put a dollar amount on the damage done to a person as a result of privacy invasion. Historically, most laws related to personal harm (e.g., defamation, negligence, assault and battery) have required the showing of an objectively quantifiable harm—typically physical damage or property damage—in order for a court to provide a remedy. When the harm is a general feeling of being watched, how is a court supposed to evaluate that?

This problem has not stopped lawmakers in other countries from moving forward with privacy-protecting laws. The United Kingdom adopted its first significant privacy laws in the early years of the twenty-first century. Courts in Britain have often looked to breach of contract/breach of confidence law and defamation law as yardsticks to measure privacy damages. In a case involving a media publication of a story about Max Mosley, then president of the International Automobile Federation, engaging in a Nazi-themed orgy, several lawyers suggested defamation as a suitable yardstick for measuring privacy damages. The court ultimately awarded a record £60,000 for the privacy invasion.

in the mid-twentieth century, well before the rise of digital technology. These laws have not aged particularly well.

As a result, one of the most practical ways to protect privacy inside the home is to be aware, to the greatest extent possible, of how our devices work, whether the trade-offs between privacy and convenience are worthwhile, and whether we have any recourse for any harms caused in this setting. Be aware that not all privacy harms are as stark or obvious as the case of Tara Thomas and her daughter. Sometimes the damage is simply a general sense of unease or lack of control over things that, ideally, should be our own business. Home is where we let our guard down. The thought of being surveilled in our kitchens and bedrooms may be a cause of psychological unrest even in the absence of any particular identifiable harm.

In the United States, we have never had an absolute right to privacy in our homes, offices, vehicles, or other personal spaces. Digital technology further challenges our expectations of privacy. In legal terms, there are really three main avenues of law that impact our expectations of privacy at home: tort law, contract law, and constitutional due process doctrines relating to government searches and seizures. Each field of law, while arising in different contexts, raises similar issues.

Let's look at each of them in turn.

PRIVACY TORTS

One of the oldest, although perhaps least effective, avenues of American privacy law is tort law. A tort is a civil wrong. Tort law deals with damage caused by one person (or business) to another. Even though you may not have heard the term before, you will have heard terms like *defamation*, *negligence*, and *trespass*. These are all torts—situations where the law allows one person to sue another for causing harm, usually physical or property damage, although sometimes, as in defamation, injury to reputation.

America has a series of privacy torts, but, as with most tort law, each of the fifty states has its own version. In some states those laws are created by **legislation** (law made by the state legislature), and in some states they come from the **common law** (law developed by courts). Some states have a combination of both legislation and common law for privacy.

Because we do not have a general federal privacy law that applies to all states comprehensively, it is often difficult to know which state's law should apply to a particular privacy problem, especially for problems that arise online. Additionally, big corporations like Facebook or Google not only have greater legal resources, but include jurisdiction selection clauses in their contracts, which say that any lawsuits will be tried in court in their home state. Traveling to another state for a lawsuit increases the costs of the lawsuit and poses significant challenges for most people.

Those contract terms, like the privacy policies we talked about in chapter 1, are usually tucked away somewhere in the **clickwrap agreement** ("I agree" contract) you sign when you purchase your device or service. Contract terms that talk about where a case will be handled, and whose law will apply, are referred to legally as **forum selection clauses** and **choice of law clauses**: clauses about which forum (or court) will hear the matter and which law will be applied, respectively. Many of these contracts also include requirements that before you go to court, or instead of going to court, you agree to participate in an **alternative dispute resolution** process such as arbitration or mediation. These are private dispute settlement systems, outside the court system, that can be quite expensive. We will examine those clauses in more detail in chapter 4 when we look at social network privacy contracts.

MODELS FOR PRIVACY TORT LAW

There have been attempts over the years to harmonize state laws on privacy, among other torts, to make the national application of those laws more uniform and predictable. The most well-known and successful approach has been spearheaded by the **American Law Institute (ALI)**, an independent organization of legal experts established in 1923 to help codify and unify state laws. The ALI regularly issues **Restatements** of various areas of law. State lawmakers use these Restatements, and associated comments written by experts, to help harmonize the laws.

The Restatement that deals with privacy law is the Second Restatement on Torts, developed in the 1960s and 1970s. There is a later Third Restatement on Torts that covers other areas of tort law, but not privacy. The Second Restatement includes four independent privacy torts: intrusion into seclusion, appropriation of name or likeness, public disclosure of private facts, and false light publicity.

When we think about privacy in the home, the most important of these torts is the first: intrusion into seclusion. This is the tort that deals with encroachments into a person's private space. The other three privacy torts focus more on what happens to private information once it has been collected (e.g., publication or other sharing of the information). Of course, some conduct implicates more than one tort simultaneously. For example, **doxing** (or doxxing) involves gathering and publishing private information, which may be aggregated from publicly available websites or require physical and/or digital incursions into a person's private space (e.g., home, work, IP address).

DOXING AND PRIVATE SPACES

People have doxed others to expose them to embarrassment, ridicule, litigation, physical harm, or threats of harm. This is obviously problematic,
but even more so in cases of mistaken identity, like the 2017 doxing of a
biomedical researcher at the University of Arkansas who was erroneously
identified as a white nationalist marching in the Charlottesville demonstra-
tion that year. Details of his work life, private life, family members, and
home address were leaked online, resulting in death threats and other
harassment of himself and his family. He had to take measures to protect
his family and his research team and was lucky to have the resources of the
university to support him. Other people subject to doxing attacks may not
have similar resources.

Let's briefly consider how each of the four privacy torts works.

Intrusion into Seclusion

Because it is the law aimed most closely at encroachments into private
spaces, it is useful to understand the scope and limitations of the intrusion
tort. According to the Restatement, intrusion into seclusion is described as
follows: "One who intentionally intrudes, physically or otherwise, upon the
solitude or seclusion of another or his private affairs or concerns, is subject to
liability to the other for invasion of his privacy, if the intrusion would be
highly offensive to a reasonable person."[2]

To explain the legalese, basically intrusion into seclusion means that if
you intrude (physically or otherwise) into another person's private space or
private affairs, you may have broken this law, *if*—and this is a big if—the
intrusion would be *highly offensive to a reasonable person*. Many of the devices
we bring into our private homes may well intrude into our private affairs, not
dissimilar to the way Peeping Toms or paparazzi may intrude by taking photos of a person in a fenced backyard or using a long-range microphone to
record private conversations.

But how many of these intrusions are *highly offensive to a reasonable
person?* They sound offensive, don't they? Who wants to be spied on in their

own home? However, courts have generally interpreted the "highly offensive" standard quite narrowly. Maybe if someone took topless photos of you in your yard, that would cross the line, but simply listening in and collecting data via, say, an Amazon Echo device probably does not meet the legal standard.

With digital devices, we also face challenges related to contractual consent (via the terms of service) that allows the devices to surveil us in our homes. Even without the consent problem, how would we prove to a judge or jury that we have suffered compensable damage at the hands of the intruder—that we can quantify a harm to us in a way a court considers meaningful?

Of course, there is a big difference between a consensual and a nonconsensual intrusion (like use of a long-distance, telephoto lens to photograph you in your house), but the problem of proving legally recognizable damage remains, no matter the presence or absence of consent.

The Misappropriation Tort

The misappropriation tort, while classified as a privacy tort, is more about making an unauthorized commercial profit from someone else's identity than about intruding into a private space. It typically comes up when someone, say, takes a photo of someone else in a public space and uses the image in an advertisement or media story. For example, in 2009, Virgin Mobile was sued by a teenager in Texas (Alison Chang) because the company had downloaded her picture from Flickr and used it in a series of advertisements in bus shelters in Australia. If the case had proceeded in the Texas courts, Chang would have had a strong claim for misappropriation. However, the Texas court decided that the appropriate court to hear the case was the Australian court (because that was where the ads were released), and Australia does not have a similar misappropriation law, so Chang was out of luck.

Public Disclosure of Private Facts

The public disclosure and false light publicity torts are two separate laws that deal with similar things. Neither of them deals with an actual physical intrusion into a private space. Instead, they both revolve around public sharing of private information. As with the intrusion into seclusion tort, you can make a successful case for public disclosure of private facts only if the disclosure would be *highly offensive to a reasonable person*. In addition, it must not be *of legitimate concern to the public*.

Many gratuitous releases of a person's information on the internet, like doxing, are not of legitimate concern to the public, so that is generally not an issue under public disclosure or false light. However, like the intrusion tort, many of these disclosures are not highly offensive to a reasonable person, at least not in the sense required to satisfy the legal standard. This tort is not useful where the problem is not technically public disclosure, but rather in-house use of personal information by large corporations like Google or Amazon. Even unauthorized sharing of your personal information with another company is not likely sufficiently "public" to attract liability under this tort.

False Light Publicity
This tort is similar to the public disclosure tort in many respects. It prohibits publicly sharing information about another person if the publication would portray the person in a false light. For example, if a news story about a local restaurant owner named Bradley Pitt were illustrated with a photograph of the actor Brad Pitt, it might place either of the Pitts in a false light—people might think, say, that the actor had opened the restaurant. Usually, when this tort is claimed, the circumstances are more sinister than this example because the tort can succeed only where the publication of the information would be *highly offensive to a reasonable person*. For a claim to succeed, the person who published the information must also know that she was creating a false impression or being otherwise reckless about publishing it. Again, this tort does not require an intrusion into a private space, although information taken from a private space and shared publicly may portray a person in a false light.

CONTRACTING OUT OF PRIVACY AT HOME
As already noted, usually when we purchase digital devices to bring into our homes, we contract out of many of the privacy rights we might otherwise have enjoyed. For example, when a Nest Cam device and associated services (thermostat, security services, etc.) are sold to a customer, the customer agrees to the Privacy Statement and Privacy Policy for Nest Web Services.[3] Nest's privacy policies describe the types of information it collects from

users and their devices, including personal information about the users, such as name, address, billing information, email addresses, and potentially video and other content shared on Nest services. Additionally, while the contract says that information will not be shared without permission, Nest users automatically grant permission when they sign up for associated services such as the Rush Hour Rewards or Safety Rewards programs.

The Rush Hour Rewards program allows users to earn credits for saving energy during peak periods by automatically tuning thermostats to comfortable temperatures during peak times to put less strain on power grids. The Safety Rewards program gives extra credits to Nest customers who sign up with one of Nest's insurance company partners. While these programs create benefits to users, they also feed into the concerns many of us have about increasing aggregations of data falling into private hands.

While Nest's privacy policies—like those of many companies—are written in responsible-sounding terms ("we will not share your data without your permission"), those companies do end up with a lot of personal data, and no one really monitors what they do with it. Even if they comply with their own policies, their customers will still likely have a hard time tracking what is being done with the data. If a company fails to comply with its data privacy policies, it may not face many legal or practical consequences. If enough customers complain, the Federal Trade Commission (FTC) may investigate (a possibility considered in more detail in chapter 4). A group of customers could attempt to sue the company by way of a class action lawsuit. However, that would be expensive and time consuming, and often those customers are faced with contract terms that require them to go to court in the company's state or agree to arbitration rather than litigation, as noted previously. Terms of service may also attempt to prevent class actions altogether.

The bottom line with contracts like these is that you should try to read them and compare terms between similar products. As digital technology develops, there will be more players in each marketplace: more competing home security devices and other home conveniences. If consumers pay more attention to the contract terms, it may be that companies will take their privacy policies more seriously. Facing the threat of losing customers to competitors with more desirable privacy policies may encourage businesses to rethink their own approaches to personal privacy.

A HOME FREE FROM GOVERNMENT INTRUSION

Even though chapter 11 focuses on government intrusions into personal privacy, it is worth briefly touching here on the American law that deals with how intrusively the government can investigate you and your private spaces, largely in the course of criminal investigations. This is one area of American law where the Constitution, at least indirectly, has something to say about privacy. If you watch police dramas, you will undoubtedly have seen police searching the houses, cars, or offices of criminal suspects either with or without a warrant. Whether or not these shows are legally accurate, it is true that we have reasonable expectations of privacy in our own personal spaces consistent with the Fourth Amendment of the Constitution, which states: "The right of the people to be secure in their persons, houses, papers, and effects, against unreasonable searches and seizures, shall not be violated, and no Warrants shall issue, but upon probable cause, supported by Oath or affirmation, and particularly describing the place to be searched, and the persons or things to be seized."

While the language is old-fashioned, the Fourth Amendment is important in today's privacy context. It is really the backbone of what little privacy protection we have that derives from our Constitution. The Fourth Amendment does not specifically use the word *privacy*, and it was obviously drafted long before the advent of digital technology. However, it does say that people should be protected from unreasonable government searches of their homes, and in relation to their personal affairs. On this basis, courts have developed the idea of a person's *reasonable expectations of privacy* as the yardstick for determining whether the Fourth Amendment has been violated in any given situation.

The most significant challenges for the Fourth Amendment over the years have come from developments in technology. This makes logical sense when you realize that a "reasonable" expectation of privacy will change as technological advances allow more subtle invasions of private spaces. For example, in the early part of the twentieth century, no one would have reasonably expected that police would be able to use thermal imaging devices to figure out whether a person was growing marijuana in their home. The new technology and its potential to invade a suspect's privacy were the subject of the landmark 2001 Supreme Court decision in *Kyllo v. United States*.

In that case, the Court considered the police's use of thermal imaging to determine that the main heat in the suspect's house was concentrated on the lower levels, supporting their case that he was growing marijuana and using heat lamps situated in the lower levels to cultivate the plants. Heat typically rises, so the usual pattern would be for higher heat readings to be taken in upper levels of a house. The Court held that this use of the technology was a "search" for Fourth Amendment purposes and thus a warrant was required. Without a warrant, the search infringed the occupant's reasonable expectations of privacy.

Even nontechnological police activities can raise concerns about privacy in the home. In 2013, in the case of *Florida v. Jardines*, the Supreme Court held that police had violated a suspect's Fourth Amendment rights when they brought a drug-sniffing dog to the front door of his house without first obtaining a warrant. The reasonable expectation of privacy does not give anyone absolute immunity from a police search, but rather requires police to obtain a warrant, which, in turn, necessitates the police to explain their suspicions to a judge with reasonable specificity and in good faith.

The main applications of Fourth Amendment law in relation to reasonable expectations of privacy have to do with police investigations, because that was what the Fourth Amendment was developed for: to prevent unreasonable searches and seizures by the government. This is the only place in the Constitution that even obliquely hints at privacy in the form of a constitutional right, which is why so much of our law about privacy in the home—and privacy generally—is based on the concept of "reasonable expectations" of privacy. Interestingly, the protections of the Fourth Amendment have been extended to cover other privacy situations outside of police searches—for example, searches in government workplaces. If you are a government employee, the Fourth Amendment protects you from unreasonable workplace searches, because your employer is a government actor. Workplace privacy issues are taken up in more detail in chapter 3. And, of course, new technology raises concerns about mass government surveillance, which are discussed in more detail in chapter 11.

OVERVIEW ON PRIVACY IN THE HOME

The law about privacy in the home is largely a matter of state-based tort law, which tends to be disharmonized in practice. More importantly, companies selling digital products and services that encroach on our privacy usually require us to contractually waive any privacy we might otherwise expect. We will look at some of those contracts in more detail in chapter 4. The Constitution occasionally touches on privacy, where government action is implicated. Having read through this chapter, you might be despairing of taking control over any of your privacy.

This is where public education and public action can potentially be useful and can even facilitate the development of the law over time. If more people start to read and understand these laws and associated contract terms, it will be much easier to understand when an activity, often a purchasing decision, is worth the privacy trade-off. When people understand the privacy problems, they can more meaningfully mobilize against a company to convince it to alter its policies or mobilize to lobby the government for greater privacy-protecting laws—or at least lobby a government department, like the FTC, to investigate a company, or contact a public advocacy center like the Electronic Frontier Foundation[4] or Electronic Privacy Information Center.[5]

While many people think change is impossible, bear in mind that it has happened before. Facebook has changed its privacy policies on several occasions in response to consumer outcries about its privacy practices.[6] Amazon has increased customer discounts at Whole Foods as a result of complaints that people were giving away their spending profiles for nothing.[7] The FTC has recently issued several landmark settlements on privacy-related matters.[8] In 2018, the State of California enacted its own Consumer Privacy Act as a result of concerns about protecting consumers from worrisome corporate data practices. California has brought its law much more in line with the European Union's General Data Protection Regulation, and there is increasing pressure on other states, and even the U.S. Congress, to do the same thing.[9]

In many ways, the privacy situation in America is dire but not hopeless. As we make our way through the rest of this book, we will emphasize where changes have been made in the past, or where they may be possible or likely in the future, in order to provide a more comprehensive picture about where privacy practices and regulations in the United States may ultimately be heading.

PRIVACY TIPS AND TRICKS

If you are concerned about protecting privacy in your home or in other private places, here are some steps you can take to educate yourself, both about your rights and about potential infringements or limitations on those rights:

+ If you are concerned about intrusive telephone calls or spam emails, you can register your phone number on the federal "do not call" registry (see www.donotcall.gov), and some states have implemented similar "do not spam" registries, although anti-spam legislation at the federal and state levels has not been terribly effective in practice.

+ When deciding to purchase a device for the home like an Alexa or Nest Cam, do your homework and read consumer reviews. In particular, read each company's privacy policy and compare policies across companies, and don't forget to consider any additional privacy issues that may arise if you buy add-on products or services for those devices. Read those contracts too!

+ In particular, check contract terms about where disputes must be litigated and whether arbitration is required. You likely won't be able to change any of these terms, but you can compare them between companies.

+ Set up Google alerts for privacy stories related to any devices you purchase or any particular privacy concerns you have about privacy in your home or other personal spaces. Good sources of information include the websites of the Electronic Frontier Foundation (https://eff.org) and the Electronic Privacy Information Center (https://epic.org).

CHAPTER THREE

Our Data at Work

- + Privacy rights in the workplace
- + Employment contracts—restrictions on privacy
- + Government employees and workplace privacy
- + American vs. foreign workplace privacy rights
- + Enhanced measures to protect privacy at work
- + Privacy in business devices
- + Electronic Communications Privacy Act
- + Protecting medical and genetic information in the workplace
- + Fair Credit Reporting Act
- + Employee privacy on social media

Does anyone still remember the furor that erupted in 2017 when Wisconsin corporation Three Square Market launched a program to implant microchips in employees' hands? The implants were intended to increase efficiency by operating in place of the keycards that provide access to anything from locked doors to vending machines. The program drew media attention because of its potential to track employees and encroach on their privacy. The company responded that the device was only intended to be used for convenience in place of a swipe card, and not as a tracking device, and was not GPS enabled at the time, although that functionality remained possible in the future.[1]

Nevertheless, a number of state lawmakers in the intervening years have enacted legislation to prevent employers from requiring employees to be microchipped as a condition of employment. How effective are these laws in practice? Likely, not very. For one thing, employers can still exert various kinds of pressure on employees to agree to an implanted chip—for example, making them feel they're not "part of the team" if they don't agree. Addition-

ally, a large portion of the American workforce comprises **at-will** employees—
employees who can be terminated for any reason at any time (**without cause**,
in legalspeak). Employers can simply make it clear that an employee who does
not agree to a chip may be terminated. A law that bans *requiring* a chip will not
prevent employees *consenting* to a chip that is technically voluntary.[2]

Despite the initial outcry against employee microchipping, the issue has
not attracted much media coverage in the ensuing years. Is that because
employees really are no longer worried about their privacy at work? Or is it
because there is no point in complaining, given that nothing can be done to
prevent these privacy incursions? Or might it be that microchips only raise
the same concerns that employees already faced over privacy at work? Since
the dawn of the digital age, it has been common for employers to use technology to monitor employees. The chips may simply be a new iteration of what
was already being done with surveillance cameras, email monitoring, keystroke monitoring, keycard monitoring, and biometric security measures.

This chapter examines data privacy at work, with an emphasis on the
important roles that workplace privacy policies and employee consent play
in the workplace privacy matrix. It also touches on the extent to which government employees in the United States arguably have greater privacy protections due to extensions of constitutional "due process" guarantees to
those employees. Finally, it compares the situation in the United States with
the privacy laws in other countries—notably the European Union and the
countries that have signed the European Convention on Human Rights—
where employee privacy is protected not only as a legal and constitutional
right, but also as an aspect of the fundamental human right to privacy.

As with privacy law generally, the United States has no general law about
privacy in the workplace, so legal developments here have been piecemeal.
The laws that impact employee privacy are a combination of state laws and
some federal laws that touch on the workplace incidentally.

Of course, the United States has laws and constitutional principles that
address discrimination in the workplace, including the Americans with Disabilities Act, which prohibits disability discrimination, and the Civil Rights
Act, which prevents discrimination on the basis of "race, color, religion, sex, or
national origin." Incursions into privacy may result in employment discrimination—for example, Facebook was implicated in discriminatory employment

practices when its personal data algorithms were used to target job ads to people or communities that do not include, say, women or people of color.[3]

As noted in the introduction to this book, some legal scholars have suggested that we do not need robust privacy laws if we have laws that prohibit the results of manipulation of personal information (like workplace or housing discrimination). While this book suggests that it is worth considering privacy as a separate legal issue, it is important to keep in mind that where particular harms result from unfair manipulations of personal information, other laws may help redress those harms. We will mention those laws in appropriate chapters but will keep the focus on privacy law.

GOVERNMENT EMPLOYERS AND EMPLOYEES

An interesting feature of American privacy law is that the due process protections of the constitution extend to government employees in their work lives. The idea behind due process is that citizens will not be subject to unreasonable searches, seizures, or other government actions impinging on basic constitutional rights (like life, liberty, or property) without notice and a fair hearing. This is a major oversimplification of the concept, but it explains why government employers are required to comply with the constitutional guarantee not to interfere with an employee's person, property, or workspace without a reasonable basis and, in certain situations, without a warrant.

The Supreme Court has weighed in on government employees' expectations of privacy in the workplace in several cases, leaving few clear rules on when and how the government can conduct workplace searches. The upshot, again somewhat simplified, is that as long as the workplace monitoring is for acceptable purposes, like investigating misconduct, and the measures taken by the employer are not excessively intrusive and are reasonably related to the purpose of the search, a warrant will not be required. Courts prefer to address these issues on a case-by-case basis, so while government employees arguably have "more" privacy rights than private employees, the significance of that protection varies from case to case and may not make much difference in practice in many circumstances.

Our Data at Work

THE ROLE OF CONSENT

As noted in the introduction and in chapter 1, one of the big stumbling blocks for legal attempts to protect employee privacy is consent. An employer can generally require an employee to consent to various stipulations as conditions of employment and, provided that there is no major unconscionability in obtaining the consent, the employee's agreement is usually legally valid.

Anyone who has ever signed an employment contract, or at least anyone who has ever *read* what they have signed, will probably have noticed a privacy policy somewhere in the voluminous piles of documents the employer provided. That policy will probably include reassuring wording about how seriously the employer takes your privacy, and it will probably also require consent to at least some form of workplace monitoring.

There is nothing illegal about requiring employees to consent to workplace monitoring, which can include monitoring of websites accessed from work computers, email, telephone and other forms of communication, video surveillance of workspaces, monitoring of keycard access, and the like. It is also important to note that there may be very good reasons for various forms of employee monitoring, including the following:

+ Monitoring productivity and making business decisions to increase efficiency and safety in the workplace
+ Ensuring compliance by employees with relevant laws, policies, and procedures (e.g., maintaining a harassment-free workplace)
+ Safeguarding sensitive personal data, like social security numbers, financial reporting information, and employee health information
+ Monitoring customer satisfaction
+ Monitoring devices connected to business networks for security purposes
+ Protecting trade secrets and confidential information belonging to the employer

Many of these issues can be double-edged swords. One person's "safety and security" in the workplace can be another's "unreasonable intrusion into private communications," and those are difficult trade-offs. For example, many workplaces that employ drivers utilize cameras in vehicles to

THE UPSIDE OF EMPLOYEE MONITORING

When we think about employers monitoring us, we may think of Big Brother and quickly assume that all monitoring is bad or nefarious. However, as already noted, there are lots of reasons, helpful to the business, to monitor employees. Monitoring may even be helpful to the employees themselves. In a 2014 *New York Times* article, "Unblinking Eyes Track Employees," journalist Steve Lohr outlined a number of benefits to employees, including situations where monitoring led to promotions for the highest-performing workers, improved conditions (like increased social breaks) for workers in group settings, and more directed and effective employee training programs to assist with career development.

monitor things like location and speed of driving. These cameras can be very helpful in keeping track of people and goods and providing data to insurance companies in case of an accident. However, drivers of these vehicles may feel that their every move is being monitored and that they have no privacy.

For employees in office settings, similar balances may have to be addressed. There are many ways to monitor office workers, and some may be more intrusive than others. Safety cameras in isolated areas of the office, such as parking structures, may seem less objectionable than cameras mounted in cube farms that pick up everything an employee may do at her desk. Even secure workspaces that require employees to go through scanners on the way in to the office can cause embarrassment and annoyance if, say, contents of bags and pockets must be emptied out to enter buildings. Many employers also remotely monitor actions employees take on work devices— by keeping logs of what is viewed on a computer monitor, for example. The extra safety, security, and productivity are trade-offs for a loss of privacy.

For employees who are particularly concerned about privacy, it is a good idea to keep all personal communications on nonwork devices if possible, although in the age of "bring your own devices" to work and increasing use of employer-provided devices at home and on the road, this can be a tall order.

If an employee voluntarily consents to monitoring by the employer in the workplace, that consent is usually legally valid and enforceable. In this context, giving consent voluntarily simply means that the employer has not used deceit or fraud to obtain agreement. If an employee, or prospective employee, feels pressured into giving consent, either by fear of not getting the job or promotion or by being made to feel that the workplace culture expects it, that consent is still valid. The types of behavior that would invalidate an employee's consent have to be particularly egregious to be legally invalid—for example, outright lying to the employee.

One nondigital case from some years ago demonstrates just how powerful consent can be in the workplace context, even in a situation where the employee did not fully understand what she was consenting to. This is not a case of employee monitoring, but of employee consent to share very private and personal aspects of her body as part of her job.

In the 1997 California case of *Feminist Women's Health Center v. Jenkins*, a health worker's employment was terminated because she refused to disrobe in front of other women and demonstrate a cervical self-examination, which included inserting a speculum into her own vagina. She claimed that her termination infringed her constitutional right to privacy under California's state constitution. While the court agreed that she had a right to privacy under the constitution, the initial consent that she signed when hired provided a valid defense to the employer. The court held that, in line with the employer's stated objectives of demystifying women's health issues and encouraging full and frank discussion of those issues, the cervical self-examination was a reasonable condition of employment, and that the employee had consented to it when she signed her initial employment contract.

The employee argued that she had not understood that the requirement to fulfill the "cervical self-examination" aspect of her job meant she had to disrobe and use the speculum in front of other women. However, the court sided with the health center and accepted its evidence that this was a reasonable requirement of the job.

Most privacy cases related to digital technology are not so dramatic in terms of employee consent to privacy intrusions. Most contemporary privacy policies are written in relatively general, albeit expansive, terms. The concerns raised often have to do with monitoring of personal communications in the workplace, monitoring of health information and financial information that may impact job performance, and even monitoring of social media activities—an issue we will pick up in more detail in chapter 4.

HOW DO YOU KNOW IF YOU'VE CONSENTED TO EMPLOYEE MONITORING?

Usually your consent to employee monitoring will appear somewhere in your initial employment contract. However, consent statements often appear in more obscure places and can be much harder to find—for example, where an employer asks you to sign a contract of employment that refers to a bundle of policies and procedures that you may have to go online to view. To take a random example (you can find many others online), the Nutrien group of companies,which operates in several North American locations, posts its employee privacy policy online. In terms of consent to use of personal information by the company, the policy states:

> Privacy laws do not generally require Nutrien to obtain your consent for the collection, use or disclosure of personal information for the purpose of establishing, managing or terminating your employment relationship. . . . To the extent that your consent is required, we will assume, unless you advise us otherwise, that you have consented to Nutrien collecting, using and disclosing your personal information for the purposes stated above (including any other purposes stated or reasonably implied at the time such personal information was provided to us).[4]

Generally speaking, and except with respect to certain situations and certain kinds of information (like some financial information and health information), it is correct that for at-will employees in particular, no consent is usually necessary for monitoring, collection, or use of personal information. Legally speaking, it is also typically the case that the kind of consent contemplated here will be binding and enforceable. Provided that notice is given of the privacy policy at the time of employment, the fact that the actual privacy terms appear outside the document the employee signs is not necessarily a problem legally. Unless the terms of the notice were somehow concealed from the employee, or were particularly arduous or grievously unfair, a court will typically enforce them.

Each employer's policies and practices will differ in terms of the uses for which it monitors, collects, or shares information about employees. In the Nutrien example, "purposes stated above" in the notice clause include

+ determining eligibility for employment and assessing qualifications for a particular job or task,
+ administering pay and benefits,
+ processing workers' compensation and insurance claims,
+ establishing training and development requirements,
+ conducting performance reviews,
+ gathering evidence for disciplinary actions,
+ establishing emergency contacts, and
+ ensuring security of the company's proprietary information.[5]

Some of these purposes obviously also include the need to share information with third-party insurers and other service providers, like benefits providers and those who provide payroll services. Statements of consent to sharing information with third parties are usually valid, again if they are made available to employees when signing up for initial employment.

Most employee privacy policies also allow the employer to make unilateral changes to the policy, again provided that adequate notice is given to the employee. Nutrien's policy includes the following language:

> Nutrien may from time to time make changes to this Privacy Policy to reflect changes in its legal or regulatory obligations or in the manner in which we deal with your personal information. We will communicate any revised version of this Privacy Policy. Any changes to this Privacy Policy will be effective from the time they are communicated, provided that any change that relates to why we collect, use or disclose your personal information will not apply to you, where your consent is required to such collection, use or disclosure, until we have obtained your consent to such change. This Privacy Policy was last reviewed as of the Effective Date set forth below.[6]

Note that the intention here is that the employer will be able to change its policy by simply giving notice to employees, except in situations where a particular law requires consent. In those cases, the updates will not be effective until the employer obtains specific consent from affected employees. In the sections that follow, we will look at some situations where specific consent may be required.

FEDERAL LAWS IMPACTING EMPLOYEE PRIVACY

As we already know, the United States has no federal law that covers employee privacy generally. However, there are a handful of laws that touch on employee privacy, including the Electronic Communications Privacy Act of 1986, the Health Insurance Portability and Accountability Act of 1996, the Genetic Information Nondiscrimination Act of 2008, the Employee Polygraph Protection Act of 1988, and the Fair Credit Reporting Act of 1970. Civil rights legislation and constitutional provisions also inform and impact how employees' personal information may be used by an employer, but that is a step farther down the line from the initial monitoring, collection, and use of information, which are the main concerns of this chapter.

Several states have also enacted laws that impact employee privacy, including the laws mentioned at the beginning of this chapter about prohibiting mandatory microchipping of employees. Several states are also now experimenting with general data protection legislation, like the European Union model, that would extend to employee privacy. The California Consumer Privacy Act of 2018 is an example of this approach. While the title of the Act references "consumer privacy," the law itself is broad enough to extend to employee data in many respects.

Some states are even enacting laws that protect the privacy of biometric data, like data collected via facial recognition software or thumbprint scanners, such as the Illinois Biometric Information Privacy Act (discussed in the introduction to this book). These laws would also extend to protect employee data unless that data was specifically excluded from the scope of the law. Because creating a list of state laws would be a moving target due to the piecemeal and speedy developments in this area, and because the scope of the law is so varied, the rest of this chapter focuses on federal laws that impact employee privacy, rather than state laws.

Electronic Communications Privacy Act
The Electronic Communications Privacy Act (ECPA) was initially enacted in 1986 and has been updated many times since then. Its original purpose was

to regulate government monitoring of private communications by requiring warrants for certain investigations and preventing information obtained through illegal wiretaps and the like from being used in court proceedings.

Technically, the ECPA has two main parts: the Wiretap Act and the Stored Communications Act. The first applies to intercepting communications as they are taking place, and the second applies to monitoring communications "at rest"—for example, where emails are stored in inboxes and received-mail folders (or on phone recording devices).

The law today extends beyond government investigations and prohibits the monitoring of electronic communications and other digital information (stored communications) over a private network without consent. Yes, that magical word again. *Consent.* If your employer has obtained your consent to monitor your digital communications and stored data as a condition of employment, they do not infringe the ECPA by monitoring you. Thus, the ECPA has a limited reach in terms of employment because companies know to obtain consent from employees upon hiring.

The ECPA does not apply to communications over a network that is available to the general public. Rather, it applies only to private communications like telephone calls or email communications. Modern social networking technology challenges this distinction—for example, it is not 100 percent clear whether communications over Facebook would be regarded as public or private under the ECPA. Private Facebook groups would probably be covered by the legislation, depending on whether or not consent was given to access the group. However, a public Facebook page, like that of a celebrity or politician, is probably not sufficiently private to attract the operation of the law.

Questions can arise under the ECPA as to how specific a consent must be for an employer to avoid liability. *Deal v. Spears* is an interesting case involving employers who monitored workplace phone calls of an employee they suspected of being involved in a burglary of their store. The phone line in question, owned by the employers (Mr. and Mrs. Spears) was used for both residential and business purposes.

The Spearses installed a recording device on their home extension to record all conversations made or received on the phone in the house and the phone in the store. They did not tell the employee they were recording her calls, and there was no other notification of the recordings. However, before they installed the recording apparatus, they had warned her not to spend so much time at work on personal calls and mentioned that they might resort to monitoring the phone line.

From the recordings, they discovered that she was having an extramarital affair with a third party, Lucas. Some of her conversations with him were sexually explicit. The conversations also brought to light her use of inappropriate language at work and her sale to Lucas of beer at cost in violation of the store's policy. However, the employers did not learn anything about the burglaries.

The employee brought an action under the ECPA for listening in on the phone calls without authorization. The employers claimed that she had consented to the monitoring and, alternatively, they tried to claim a "business use" exception that also applies under the law—where monitoring is undertaken for a legitimate business purpose or "in the ordinary course of business."

This was an unusual case in that the employee won. The court was not convinced that she had consented to monitoring. The warnings that the employers "might" monitor calls and the fact that the employee knew they had a telephone extension in their house that could be used to listen in on employee calls was not sufficient for consent. The business use exception also did not convince the court that the monitoring of the calls was lawful. For that exception to apply, the monitoring must be in the "ordinary course of business." While it is possible that monitoring of calls to investigate a burglary might occur in the ordinary course of business, the fact that the employers listened to a lot more of the recordings than was necessary to investigate the burglary took their actions outside the scope of the exception.

In a more recent case where Google was sued for monitoring Gmail services for targeted advertising purposes, Google failed to convince the court that the monitoring was for "ordinary business purposes." The court held that Google was able to easily maintain and operate the email system without reading the *contents* of customers' messages. Although this monitoring was outside the employment context, the case shows that if the company doing the monitoring does not have real consent and does not have a legitimate business purpose for monitoring, it can be successfully sued for infringement of the ECPA.

HOW INTENTIONAL DOES MONITORING HAVE TO BE TO INFRINGE THE ECPA?

In *McCann v. Iroquois Memorial Hospital*, two disgruntled hospital employees were inadvertently recorded on a Dictaphone complaining about the hospital and its management practices behind closed doors. Another employee had entered the room where the recording was made, to collect some papers, and quickly left when she realized she had intruded on a private conversation. It was unclear whether she had accidentally turned on the Dictaphone or someone else had done it, but the result was a recording of a private conversation.

Because of the uncertainty about who had made the recording, it was not clear whether the conversation was "intentionally" intercepted by the employer (the hospital). The question of intention was important because the ECPA prohibits the unauthorized interception of private communications without consent. At an early stage of the proceedings, the court was unable to say for sure that the interception/recording of the communication was intentional, so they were unable to grant summary judgment—that is, judgment at an early stage of the proceedings, before all arguments have been made. The case was settled before a final judgment was reached.

Medical and Genetic Information

Employee privacy for medical and genetic information is largely bound up in concerns about workplace discrimination on the basis of health, disability, or genetic predisposition to particular illnesses. As noted earlier in this chapter, most cases that involve concerns about these issues will be brought under antidiscrimination laws rather than privacy laws. However, privacy laws are relevant because sometimes an employer obtains health or genetic information in breach of an employee's privacy rights.

The two main federal laws that impact health and genetic information privacy are the Health Insurance Portability and Accountability Act (HIPAA) and the Genetic Information Nondiscrimination Act (GINA). HIPAA requires safeguards to be implemented by organizations that deal with personal healthcare information, including health insurance providers and health-care providers. Employers outside these industries are also required to comply with HIPAA if they self-insure, because they thereby effectively become health insurers with respect to their own employees. HIPAA is a far-reaching piece of legislation that regulates how healthcare information is dealt with by these organizations in general; it is not limited to the employment context, but covers patient records more generally. We will look at HIPAA in more detail in chapter 9.

GINA is concerned with discrimination on the basis of genetic informa-tion in the employment and health insurance contexts. It prevents employ-ers, and health insurers, from discriminating against current or prospective employees on the basis of genetic information including, importantly, predispositions toward particular illnesses or health conditions. This law also imposes obligations of confidence on employers who obtain genetic informa-tion about employees, requiring this information to be maintained separately from other employee information, and stored securely as a confidential medi-cal record. We will take a more general look at GINA in chapter 9.

HIPAA covers protected health information (PHI), which includes indi-vidually identifiable health records held or transmitted by any organization covered by the law. As noted earlier, some employers will be covered by the law, notably employers in the health sector and other employers that self-insure and effectively become health insurance providers under the law. HIPAA is aimed at the security of PHI, largely against data breaches. It imposes four key requirements on organizations covered by the legislation:

1. to ensure the confidentiality, integrity, and availability of PHI;
2. to safeguard PHI against reasonably anticipated security threats;
3. to protect against reasonably anticipated uses and disclosures; and
4. to ensure workforce compliance with the rules.

Like GINA, HIPAA guidance also supports the idea of separating health information from general employment records. While HIPAA is focused more on the integrity and security of data than GINA, both laws provide guidance to employers on protecting the confidentiality of sensitive health and genetic data. Neither law is particularly useful to a concerned employee

HEALTH INFORMATION AND ANTIDISCRIMINATION LAW

An example of how medical information can impact an antidiscrimination claim can be found in a 1998 California case, *Norman-Bloodsaw v. Lawrence Berkeley Lab*, in which a group of employees raised a variety of privacy-related claims over medical testing conducted by their employer, a research lab at the University of California. The offers for employment in the lab were conditioned on a series of pre-placement examinations, which included personal medical history as well as blood and urine tests.

The employer went on to test the blood and urine samples of some of the employees for syphilis, sickle cell trait, and pregnancy without specific consent to these tests and without notifying the employees. While there was no evidence that the test results were used in a discriminatory fashion or shared with third parties, the employees claimed that the testing itself violated privacy rights under the federal and California constitutions, the Americans with Disabilities Act of 1990 (ADA), and other federal antidiscrimination laws, notably Title VII with respect to the testing of African American employees for sickle cell trait and female employees for pregnancy. Title VII prohibits discrimination on the basis of race or gender.

The California court held that most of these privacy rights had been infringed by the lab because, even though consent to general medical testing had been given, consent to the specific tests was not sought or obtained. Constitutional due process rights were infringed as a result of the lack of specific notice and consent, and Title VII rights were also infringed. However, the ADA claims failed because of a loophole in that law that allows medical testing for any purpose with or without consent after an employment offer has been made but before the employee starts work, provided that the results of the testing are kept confidential and are not used as the basis for discrimination.

unless she can establish actual discrimination on the basis of health or genetic information. For an example of how discrimination laws can play out in relation to sensitive health information, see "Health Information and Antidiscrimination Law."

Employee Polygraph Protection Act

Not many employees will be faced with the need to submit to a polygraph (lie detector) test, but interestingly there is a federal law that covers privacy rights in this situation. Enacted in 1998, the Employee Polygraph Protection Act sets out a general prohibition on employers requiring employees or prospective employees to submit to lie detector tests, or to use results of these tests to discharge, discipline, or discriminate against an employee or prospective employee. There are some exceptions, the most obvious of which relate to national defense and security and to FBI activities. There is also a limited exception for employers who are engaging in ongoing investigations into damage to the business resulting from theft, embezzlement, misappropriation, industrial espionage, or sabotage.

For employers who are authorized to manufacture, distribute, or dispense controlled substances, there is also an exception for employees and prospective employees who have, or will have, direct access to those substances. Similar exceptions apply to employers of armored car, alarm, and security guard services and the employees and job applicants for those positions.

Fair Credit Reporting Act

We have likely all heard about how credit reports and credit ratings can be used and abused by employers, financial institutions, and others. The federal law that regulates credit reports is called, unsurprisingly, the Fair Credit Reporting Act. Its aim is to promote the accuracy, fairness, and privacy of consumer credit information compiled by credit reporting agencies like Equifax and Experian. We will talk about this law in more detail in chapter 10.

The law regulates the collection, sharing, and use of credit reports to ensure that information in the reports is accurate and, importantly for this chapter, is not used or shared for undesirable purposes. The federal law not only addresses what the three major credit reporting agencies can do with your information, but also applies to anyone who uses a consumer credit

YOUR EMPLOYER AND YOUR SOCIAL MEDIA

We will be focusing on privacy issues in the social media context in chapter 4. However, it is worth noting that cases have arisen where employers have required employees to share social media passwords both for social purposes and also to monitor their conduct outside the workplace. Theoretically, there is no law requiring you to share your social media information with an employer. However, there is often pressure to do so.

In the 2009 case of *Pietrylo v. Hillstone Restaurant Group,* before the meteoric rise of Facebook, an employer fired two employees for conduct it learned about after accessing their MySpace accounts. The employer's restaurant manager had asked another employee to provide her own username and password to a shared employee MySpace group to learn more about what the employees were sharing online.

The fired employees brought privacy-related claims against the restaurant, including claims under the ECPA (discussed elsewhere in this chapter) for knowingly accessing private electronic communications without authorization. They also sued under the intrusion into seclusion tort (see chapter 2 for a refresher). The tort claim failed because the court did not agree that the employees had a reasonable expectation of privacy in the online group. However, the ECPA claim was successful because the manager had compelled the third-party employee to provide her MySpace credentials to spy on her colleagues.

This case was unusual because it involved a private MySpace group. There is nothing generally stopping employers or prospective employers from investigating employees or prospective employees online, checking Twitter feeds and public Facebook pages. The tip for employees is to be savvy about what is posted online and who is given access to that information.

WORKPLACE PRIVACY ACROSS THE POND

As with most personal data privacy issues, the European and U.S. positions are very different. The General Data Protection Regulation (see chapter 8) applies to all European Union residents, including in the employment context. Interestingly, privacy protections in the European Convention on Human Rights (ECHR) have also been extended to the workplace.

In the case of *Bărbulescu v. Romania,* a Romanian citizen sued his government in the European Court of Human Rights with respect to his privacy rights under the ECHR, on the basis that the case he had brought against his employer in his own national court system failed to adequately protect the privacy of personal digital communications that his employers had monitored. The court upheld his claim against the government for failing to adequately balance his privacy rights against those of his employer in the local court. It is unusual for a human rights treaty to be the basis of a privacy action related to workplace privacy, but this case shows that it can happen, at least in Europe.

report for business purposes. Anyone, including an employer, who obtains a credit report in violation of the law (that is, without a permissible purpose) can be liable for infringing it.

It is permissible for employers to use credit reports to make hiring decisions, but they should not use the information for further, impermissible purposes, like unnecessary investigations into the private life of an employee or prospective employee. Of course, many employers will seek your consent to obtaining a credit report before they decide to hire you—and consent, once again, is usually a golden ticket. If you authorize an employer or prospective employer to check your credit, and they act within the scope of that authorization, they have not infringed the Fair Credit Reporting Act.

PRIVACY TIPS AND TRICKS

As this chapter has illustrated, one of the biggest issues with workplace privacy is related to *consent*. Most employers or prospective employers can

relatively easily compel employees to consent to a variety of pretty significant intrusions into their personal life and information. Because of this, the
best thing for employees, or those seeking employment, to do in order to
protect their workplace privacy is a combination of the following:

+   When you are asked to give consent to a privacy policy or for the
    release of any private information (credit information, health
    information, etc.) to an employer or prospective employer, make
    sure you read and understand what you are agreeing to, and seek an
    attorney's or union representative's advice if you are confused.

+   Make sure you follow, read, and understand post-employment
    updates to privacy policies.

+   Become as familiar as you can with the types of things employers
    cannot or should not be asking for, even with consent (e.g., poly-
    graph testing in the absence of a legally recognized reason for the
    testing).

+   Guard social networking passwords and information carefully and,
    if you do allow employers to access your social media, be careful
    about what you post, and make sure you remove the employer's
    access if you leave that employment or otherwise become uncom-
    fortable about them having access. Remember, there is no legal
    obligation to give an employer access to your social media.

Speaking of social media, now is a good time to turn to our next chapter, on
just that subject.

CHAPTER FOUR

Our Data on Social Media

+ Privacy in data shared on social media sites
+ Social media terms of service and privacy rights
+ Collection and use of personal data by social media companies
+ Privacy risks in online dating
+ Role of the Federal Trade Commission in protecting privacy

In the last weekend of May 2020, President Donald Trump signed an executive order that purported to remove some of the legal protections against legal action previously enjoyed by social media companies. The president was particularly keen to target Twitter because of their practice of "fact checking" his tweets and highlighting those that they regarded as potentially inciting societal violence in the wake of the killing of an African American man, George Floyd, at the hands of a white police officer, Derek Chauvin. Subsequently, in the wake of the 2020 election and his suspect claims of election fraud leading to the violence at the Capitol Building on January 6, 2021, Twitter and other social media companies banned Trump from posting altogether.

Both the constitutional validity and the likely practical efficacy of the initial executive order were dubious at best. However, the president's fury at the perceived power of the social media platform to sour the impact of his tweets, and his historical reliance on Twitter as a communication platform—especially in the lead-up to the 2020 presidential election, and after—underline the significant place that social media have in our lives today. The fact that the president relied on social media platforms to coordinate his rally on January 6, the violent results of which ultimately led to his second impeachment trial, emphasizes the power of social media in both the social and political contexts.

It is arguable that Trump might not have been elected president in the first place in 2016 if not for Russian interference in that election. But before we get to that, the question arises: What does privacy have to do with election hacking and general social unrest fomented on social media?

Perhaps it isn't all that obvious at first, and these may not be the most obvious examples of the problems related to privacy on social media, because they have to do with credibility, truth, and integrity rather than intrusions into individual privacy. However, like many worrisome activities, the genesis of the ability for election hackers to be effective, and for conspiracy theorists to garner real-world followers, has to do with the manipulation of information directed at particular sets of social media readers.

Trump's messages, and those of his allies, are most effective when targeted to his political base. After all, they are the ones who predominantly follow relevant Twitter feeds. Likewise with election hacking—the practice is effective only if the hackers know whom to target in order to galvanize those people to vote.

As private companies that use sophisticated data-collection algorithms and procedures to target specific individuals for advertisements, social media companies like Twitter, Facebook, and YouTube can do more than simply profit from targeting advertising to the most likely groups of purchasers. They are also implicated in the very fabric of our democracy, as recent events demonstrate.

Of course, as the internet in general and social media in particular become more sophisticated, the ability of new people and organizations to gather, aggregate, and manipulate personal data for various potentially undesirable uses—including election hacking, organizing riots, employment discrimination, and targeted marketing—become more widespread and harder to detect and correct.

Yet the very same technology enables incredibly useful innovations like citizen journalism, sharing messages of hope and well-being, and keeping in touch with distant friends and relatives. As with everything related to digital technology, it is a complicated balancing act. The regulation of these technologies is particularly challenging, given both their important beneficial social, commercial, and political uses and the importance that we, in the United States, place on free speech.

WHAT IS SOCIAL MEDIA?

Before explaining privacy risks on social media and how best to protect yourself from unwanted privacy invasions or manipulations of your personal data, it is necessary to think about what social media is and how it works. There is no technical legal definition of the term, but when we think about social media, we're usually contemplating private companies like Twitter, Facebook, Instagram, Pinterest, and YouTube: companies that are not run by the government and that enable us to share digital information in various formats, including text, audio, video, photography, and other imagery. Most of these services, being private entities, make their money not from membership fees but rather from advertising.

This is where personal information comes into the equation. If your business model depends on advertisers paying you to share their advertisements with your members, your ability to make money depends on your ability to target the information effectively to the people who are most likely to buy the products or services advertised. In recent years, the same thing has occurred with respect to targeted political messages.

This is why companies like Facebook are constantly in the news about their information-collecting practices. If social media companies can collect nuanced information about their members, in order to know which members are more likely to purchase which products or vote for which candidates or issues, that information becomes very relevant for their bottom line: their ability to help advertisers, whether political or commercial or both, target advertisements most effectively.

Even demographic information—information that does not identify particular individuals as potentially interested in particular products and services—can be useful and valuable. For example, if Facebook knows that its members in a certain age range or geographic location are interested in a particular kind of product or service, or likely to vote for a particular candidate, it can target advertisements effectively to those groups too.

TARGETED COMMERCIAL MARKETING: WHAT'S THE BIG DEAL?

In the early part of the new millennium, a lot of consumers were concerned about the increased sophistication of targeted marketing that digital technology enabled. More and more bulk unsolicited commercial emails (or

spam emails) became the norm, and people's inboxes were flooded with junk mail—still a problem today, as noted in chapter 2. These emails are annoying, just like bundles of unwanted paper catalogues in your mailbox or **robocalls**—automated and unsolicited telephone calls promoting a product, service, or cause (also discussed in chapter 2).

On one hand, such advertisements may simply be an annoyance. On the other hand, our peace and quiet may be disturbed or shattered. It's not just the constant intrusions into our inboxes, social media accounts, and phone lines that are problematic. The content of the messages has also become increasingly worrisome over time. Unsolicited advertisements that are truthful commercial speech are probably no more than annoying, although the volume can become overwhelming. However, the same technology that enables this widespread advertising also enables other kinds of solicitations that may be more harmful.

With the early days of email came the notorious "Nigerian email scams," created by people, purporting to be in Nigeria, who were fishing for details of bank accounts and credit information fraudulently, usually on the basis of a fictional business deal or the need to help a fictional person in another country. These scams continue today, often with greater sophistication. Many of us are aware, and suspicious, of unsolicited contacts, but a surprising number of otherwise tech-savvy people can get caught out by the scammers.[1] Members of more vulnerable groups, including the elderly and others who are not particularly tech-savvy, are often particular targets of modern-day scammers. The best way to avoid getting caught up in a scam is to be cynical and not to answer calls from unfamiliar numbers or emails from strangers.

More and more, bad actors are able to impersonate or "spoof" a person or business you actually know or deal with and pretend to be legitimately asking you for financial information like bank account details. Many of us have seen fake emails purporting to be from, say, Netflix or Hulu, saying there's a problem with our account and if we don't click on the screen and insert our bank account or credit card details, our service will be canceled (or has been canceled, pending our doing so). These scams were initially easy to spot, but increasingly—through concealing the phone number or return email address—they are harder to identify. The bottom line is that if you are not sure about an email or phone call, it is best not to respond to it and, instead, to contact the company directly through official channels to check if the message is real. It is always safest to go to the company's website directly from the browser rather than clicking a link or opening an attachment in an email. Attachments in fraudulent emails are often riddled with malware, which can allow a hacker to take control of your computer, steal your information, and/or render the device useless.

As with employment discrimination (see chapter 3), there are laws that deal with particular harms caused as a result of these scams. For example, the federal Identity Theft and Assumption Deterrence Act of 1998 provides some recourse against people who steal personal information to engage in credit card fraud, tax fraud, healthcare fraud, and so on. However, it can be notoriously difficult to locate the culprits in order to bring a legal action. Attempting to identify who sent fraudulent emails is called **cyber attribution**. Much identity theft law is really just criminal law adapted for advances in technology, which means that the government takes action on your behalf and then you can apply for "victim restitution" to seek compensation to help redress the damage.[2]

ONLINE FRAUD: THERE OUGHT TO BE A LAW!

You may have very valid concerns about spam, emails, robocalls, or fraudulent advertisements and solicitations on social media. However, there are no robust legal regulations against these activities. The problem with passing such regulation is that it is restricted by the First Amendment, so any law that regulates speech, even speech that may be fraudulent, must pass a high degree of constitutional scrutiny. This means that it is relatively easy for scammers to challenge online fraud laws on constitutional grounds.

There are federal and state laws that attempt to regulate things like spam emails and robocalls in particular and that prohibit misleading, deceptive, and fraudulent content in commercial activities, but these laws are limited in their scope because of First Amendment concerns. Additionally, it is very difficult for private individuals to bring meaningful legal action against companies and people who engage in fraudulent and deceptive conduct online, because of the cost of such action (not to mention the difficulties of identifying and locating the people engaging in the problematic conduct).

Spam email and robocalls implicate personal privacy when they are targeted at the most vulnerable people. For example, a phone or email scammer

EVEN FACEBOOK GETS HACKED

Even companies that deal with tremendous volumes of our personal information can get hacked. Amid general concerns about its privacy practices
that have historically dogged it in the marketplace, Facebook admitted in
2018 that an attack on its computer network had exposed the personal
information of around fifty million users. The hackers exploited a security
weakness in Facebook's system, allowing them not only to harvest customer data but also to impersonate customer accounts and, by posing as
those customers, trick other users into sharing personal information. Iron-
ically, some of the weak points in Facebook's security were the result of
updates intended to enhance consumer privacy. The lesson is to never
assume that your information is secure, once you have shared it with an
online service provider.

may identify a vulnerable person's email address or phone number and use it
to take advantage. Some of this personal identifying information may be
found online. Often, it is available from services we sign up for online. If you
sign up for an app or other online service, and you provide your phone number
or email as part of the sign-up requirements, that information becomes more
vulnerable to theft via hacking of that service provider's storage systems.
Additionally, some companies you sign up with will sell your information to
third parties, enabling further dissemination of your personal information—
allowing bona fide advertisers to target you, as well as scammers.

SOCIAL MEDIA TERMS OF SERVICE AND PRIVACY POLICIES

One reason we have little legal protection with respect to our personal data on
social media, besides the lack of effective and comprehensive privacy-
protecting laws, is that, as private entities, social media companies are free to
impose their own terms of service (or TOS) on their members. These are the
contracts you enter with the social media platform when you set up your
account. Most of these contracts include detailed privacy policies, either
within the TOS or referred to in the TOS and presented on a separate webpage.

These policies have become more detailed as concerns about digital privacy have increased in recent decades, and they often talk about things like respect for members' and third parties' personal information and the need to obtain consent to post private information about other people.

For example, at the time of this writing, Facebook's "Community Standards," which are incorporated into its TOS, state:

> Privacy and the protection of personal information are fundamentally important values for Facebook. We work hard to keep your account secure and safeguard your personal information in order to protect you from potential physical or financial harm. You should not post personal or confidential information about others without first getting their consent. We also provide people ways to report imagery that they believe to be in violation of their privacy rights.[3]

This clause says that it protects members' privacy and personal information and also requires members to obtain consent before posting confidential or personal information about other people who may or may not also be Facebook members. There are also provisions in the Community Standards about not posting in a way that would bully or harass others.[4]

These kinds of terms are not unusual in social networking contracts, and they are generally legally enforceable, which is the good news. The bad news is that, in order to enforce them, a person actually needs to know that their privacy was infringed, how it was infringed, and what the policy says. Even if you are a member of the network, you likely have not bothered to read or understand the terms, and if you are not a member, but your private information is misused (without consent) by a member, you may never even know about it.

Assuming that you do know about the terms of service and that your privacy or reputation has been damaged, you will also need to have the resources to threaten, or bring, a legal action against the social network for breach of its TOS. If you are a member of the network, you can sue, or threaten to sue, for breach of contract—that is, breach of the TOS. If you are *not* a member, you will have to convince the social network provider to take action against the member who misused your information. Alternatively, you could try to sue that person under a privacy tort if you could find one that applied to your situation. See chapter 2 for a refresher on privacy tort law.

FACIAL RECOGNITION TECHNOLOGY AND SOCIAL NETWORKS

In February 2021, Facebook agreed to pay $650 million to settle a class action lawsuit regarding the company's facial recognition technology. The plaintiffs in the case claimed that Facebook had violated the Illinois Biometric Information Privacy Act (BIPA) by using technology that enabled them to identify and "tag" members' faces in photographs, allowing Facebook to suggest connections between users and to more effectively target advertisements to them on the basis of what their friends did or liked.

Illinois enacted BIPA in 2008 to regulate the collection, use, safeguarding, and storage of biometric information. Given the unique nature of biometric data and fundamental privacy concerns, including markers that are unique to particular individuals, specific protections were thought to be necessary for biometric information. BIPA regulates how private entities, including social media companies, can collect, retain, disclose, and destroy biometric information (e.g., facial images and thumbprints). The law also sets out procedures for obtaining consent before collecting biometric information in many situations.

Facebook allegedly violated BIPA by collecting, using, and storing biometric identifiers without obtaining a written release and without establishing a compliant retention schedule when it launched a feature called Tag Suggestions in 2010. With Tag Suggestions enabled, Facebook could use its facial-recognition technology to detect the identities of a user's friends in his or her uploaded photos. When a photo is uploaded, the technology scans the photo and extracts geometric data points. The technology then compares the face to others in Facebook's database. If there is a match, Facebook suggests tagging the person in the photo for the reasons noted above. Although the case was ultimately settled privately, a judicial award could have been in the billions, since the law mandates a $5,000 fine per privacy violation.

Some social networks also provide in-house means of dealing with privacy-related complaints. The excerpt from Facebook's Community Standards quoted above notes that Facebook provides people "ways to report imagery that they believe to be in violation of their privacy rights." This sounds good in theory, but the Standards are very vague about the ways you can report the problem and what Facebook will actually do about a complaint. A large concern about in-house regulation of these kinds of complaints is that the complaint mechanisms are often not particularly transparent, and it is very difficult for anyone to know how effective they are in practice.

ONLINE NETWORKS SHARING YOUR INFORMATION

The terms of service of most online entities typically allow them to share at least some of your personal information with third-party advertisers and with others. After all, this is a common business model. If the service does not charge its users fees, then it must rely on money from advertisers. These services most effectively profit by providing information to advertisers, and other third parties, that maximizes the effectiveness of ads and other kinds of outreach to users. The more sophisticated the information provided about the users, the more advertisers and others will pay for that information. For example, Nike will pay more money to advertise on a social network that targets its ads to the users most likely to buy its products: those interested in physical fitness.

Most of the time, social networks and other online businesses use their TOS to ensure that you provide consent to certain uses of your personal information, including sale of that information to third parties (see chapter 7 for more information about how this works in practice). If you want to know what your contract with any of those services allows the service provider to do with your information, you (unfortunately) need to read its TOS. And remember that many of these companies will reserve the right to change the terms unilaterally without your consent, and sometimes without even giving you notice.

Be aware that in the privacy regulation world, notice and consent are two different things. *Notice* just means that the company must tell you that they have taken some action or changed some contract terms. *Consent* refers to situations where you must affirmatively agree to an action or change in contract terms. Remember the example in chapter 3 about the workplace privacy policy that could be changed unilaterally with notice except where an applicable law additionally required consent.

Some companies avoid the need to obtain consent by creating business models whereby they can profit from your personal information without technically *sharing* it with any other company. Facebook is an example of this business model. Its TOS state clearly that it *does not sell members' information to third-party advertisers.* Instead, Facebook gathers data on members and uses the data to target advertisements *on behalf of the advertisers.* Facebook is the one doing the actual targeted advertising on behalf of other companies, without technically sharing the information with those companies. Facebook's TOS, at the time of this writing, prominently state:

> We don't charge you to use Facebook or the other products and services covered by these Terms. Instead, businesses and organizations pay us to show you ads for their products and services. By using our Products, you agree that we can show you ads that we think will be relevant to you and your interests. We use your personal data to help determine which ads to show you.
>
> *We don't sell your personal data to advertisers, and we don't share information that directly identifies you (such as your name, email address or other contact information) with advertisers unless you give us specific permission* [emphasis added]. Instead, advertisers can tell us things like the kind of audience they want to see their ads, and we show those ads to people who may be interested. We provide advertisers with reports about the performance of their ads that help them understand how people are interacting with their content.[5]

The fact that Facebook does not actually sell your information to other companies does not mean that those companies cannot reconstruct much of the information themselves, based on who expresses interest in their products or services as a result of Facebook advertising. If Facebook places a particular company's **click-through advertisement** (an ad you click on to find out more about the advertised products or services) on your Facebook page, and you click-through the ad and make a purchase from the company—sharing, say, your postal address for shipping—that company can construct its own database of Facebook members interested in its services. Facebook

ELECTION INTERFERENCE—THE CAMBRIDGE ANALYTICA SCANDAL

Cambridge Analytica is a political data-analysis firm that provides consumer data profiles to its clients so that they can create targeted advertising based on psychographic factors, which are factors that drive consumer behavior. In 2013, Cambridge Analytica gathered the data of more than eighty-seven million Facebook users through use of a third-party app called "thisisyourdigitallife," which asked users to complete a survey that was meant to be for academic use. The 270,000 people who downloaded the app not only turned over their own personal data, but that of their friends, without their knowledge or consent. President Trump and Ted Cruz used this data for targeted advertising during their 2016 presidential campaigns and it was also used for the Brexit "Leave" campaign.

Facebook offers a variety of privacy settings so that users can customize what information others can see about them. These privacy settings were subverted for users who were friends of someone who took the "thisisyourdigitallife" survey. Facebook employees were suspicious of Cambridge Analytica's practices as early as September 2015, but the company did not take action until March 2018. Facebook admitted to the mishandling of data in congressional testimony and was fined a record $5 billion by the Federal Trade Commission, the largest privacy-related fine ever imposed at that time. The fine was related to an earlier settlement for charges that the company had violated a 2012 FTC order about consumer privacy. This chapter includes a look at the FTC's role in relation to consumer privacy.

has not technically sold your information to them, but they end up with the information anyway.

ENFORCING ONLINE TERMS OF SERVICE:
LIMITS OF CONTRACT AND TORT LAW

Even when a company breaches its terms of service by failing to live up to the representations it makes about privacy, the law often does not provide much in the way of recourse for people concerned about misuse of their personal data. Apart from the difficulties in finding out that the information has been misused, and how, it can be prohibitively expensive to sue, or even to hire a lawyer to threaten to sue, a large company with its own team of lawyers.

Class actions are a possibility here. Sometimes. Those are situations where a group of people with the same complaint against a company join forces to sue. The problem with online companies' TOS, as we saw in chapter 2, is that they often contain provisions not only preventing class actions, but also requiring disputes to be arbitrated rather than litigated. **Arbitration** is a private, behind-closed-doors, way of resolving a legal dispute, and, because it is private, the arbitrators must be paid—which can, in certain situations, make this option more expensive than litigation. Additionally, as explained in chapter 2, the TOS usually state where arbitration or litigation may take place—usually in a city and/or state that is convenient to the company and not necessarily to its customers.

Even if you get past these hurdles and manage to get yourself into court with your privacy-related complaint, a significant bar to success is that it is almost impossible to prove, to the satisfaction of a court, that you have suffered any concrete damages in most situations (for a refresher on why that is, look back at chapter 2). In contract law, where you are suing on the contractual terms of service, the usual amount of legal damages is based on the difference between what you contracted for and what you actually received under the contract. If your private data is misused, say, by being shared with an advertiser or other third party, what is your contractual loss? It cannot be the value of the information to the advertiser, because that has nothing to do with the value you are receiving under your original contract with the online social network.

For example, if I join the hypothetical social network FriendLink and agree to standard TOS that say it won't share my personal data with third-party advertisers, what happens if it sells my information to Ads-R-Us for a profit? If I manage to sue FriendLink under contract law for breaching its TOS, a court will look at the difference between what I contracted for and what I received from FriendLink. I received everything I contracted for. FriendLink just made a tidy profit from my personal data. I didn't lose anything under the contract in a monetary sense. I may have lost control over my data, but it's not the kind of damage that contract law typically compensates—and this is where more tort law comes in. You may want to jump back to chapter 2 for a reminder on the limitations of tort law in a situation like this.

The only privacy tort likely to come close to dealing with this kind of situation is the **misappropriation tort**: the one about unauthorized commercial uses of another person's name or likeness. While selling your information is a commercial activity involving your personal data, it tends not to be the kind of unauthorized commercial use this tort deals with. The misappropriation tort is really about presenting your name or likeness publicly in a way that suggests you endorsed a particular product or service. It is not about private sales of your personal information. It is possible, in the future, that courts may interpret the tort more broadly, but that has not happened so far.

ENFORCING ONLINE TERMS OF SERVICE: THE ROLE OF THE FTC

One avenue of legal recourse for those concerned that social media, and other online companies, are infringing their terms of service with respect to privacy, is the role increasingly played by the Federal Trade Commission (FTC) in this area. As explained in chapter 1, the United States, unlike many other countries, does not have a central federal government department that monitors privacy concerns. This role is shared among different government entities in different sectors of the economy. We will take a closer look at the health privacy regulators in chapter 9, and banking and financial privacy regulators in chapter 10. These different sectors are regulated under different laws, and so the government departments that oversee those sectors tend to be the ones charged with monitoring and enforcement of those laws as they relate to privacy.

In the absence of a general privacy regulation, the FTC has stepped up to monitor the way companies comply with their own privacy policies under its powers to regulate misleading and deceptive commercial practices. Section 5(a) of the Federal Trade Commission Act, the statute that establishes the FTC, prohibits "unfair methods of competition in or affecting commerce, and unfair or deceptive acts or practices in or affecting commerce" within the United States. The FTC is granted the power to regulate these unfair or deceptive practices.

In recent years, the FTC, increasingly concerned about the impact of misuse of personal data by American companies, has focused on investigating, and engaging in settlement actions, against companies that infringe their own terms of service, especially those related to consumer privacy. The FTC has taken the position that a company's failing to adhere to its own stated privacy policy is an unfair or deceptive commercial act. When the FTC takes action against a company, it does so in its own name, as a government agency, so that the people whose data has been misused are not out of pocket and are not parties themselves to any legal proceedings.

FTC action has its upsides and its downsides. It is obviously useful for the American consumer public to have a government authority looking to protect their privacy. However, there is no obligation for the FTC to act on any particular complaint. The FTC is limited by its own budget and enforcement priorities and cannot act on every single concern. The fact that you complain to the FTC about a misuse of your personal information by a company that has apparently infringed its own privacy policies is no guarantee of government action.

On the upside, the FTC does not have to prove any particular financial loss or damage on behalf of any affected consumers. It can impose fines, which may be distributed to affected consumers, but it does not have to establish that consumers suffered specific monetary damage. FTC settlements can also require companies to engage in remedial action—for example, requiring them to undergo regular privacy audits conducted by third-party experts for specified periods, and/or to change their privacy practices to avoid the behavior the FTC was concerned about.

In the historic 2019 YouTube/Google settlement with the FTC, which related to infringements of the **Children's Online Privacy Protection Act (COPPA**—see chapter 5), not only did YouTube and Google have to pay a $170 million fine, it was also required to develop, implement, and maintain a system to help YouTube channel owners clearly identify child-directed content aimed at children under thirteen to ensure that YouTube complied with COPPA. YouTube was also required to institute a system to notify channel owners that child-directed content is subject to COPPA, and to provide annual training about COPPA compliance for all employees who dealt with YouTube channel owners.[6]

In many cases, these additional requirements in FTC settlements are likely to have a much greater long-term impact in protecting individual privacy than even hefty fines, which, for some large social media and other online companies—like Google, Facebook, and YouTube—may only be a drop in the bucket.

FINDING LOVE ONLINE: THE PRIVACY RISKS

While most of this chapter has focused on general social media networks like Facebook, YouTube, and Twitter, there are also plenty of networks devoted to finding love online. Dating apps and services may, in fact, know more about users than any other social media application. For example, the dating website eHarmony previously required users to fill out 149 questions in order to create a profile. Although eHarmony no longer requires the questionnaire, it and other dating services still collect a vast amount of personal information about their users, all the better to find their perfect match based on sophisticated matchmaking algorithms. These networks collect everything from a user's name and occupation to private photos and sexual preferences. The information is often made available to both advertisers and spurned ex-partners.

In addition to the information you provide the dating service directly, if you use the app on your smartphone, it may well be collecting data from the phone, including access to contacts, locations, photos, and wireless network connections. Some of these apps even track how you behave on the service, including whom you swipe left or right on, how long you spend looking through a profile, and the types of people that attract you. When you stop using the app, it may update your profile to indicate that you are likely in a relationship.

All this data can be used for targeted advertising. Dating networks are typically not solely reliant on advertising revenue, because they also tend to charge money for membership. Most will initially offer some level of free access to allow you to try out the service and will later offer a subscription including additional features.

In 2019, Facebook entered the online dating game with its Facebook Dating services, which are free for its members. While it does not share the dating information with a user's general account, it does track location data, which can be used for targeted advertising.

THE DOWNSIDE OF DATING DATA

Outside of concerns about targeted advertising on dating services, it is important to recognize that the companies you share your dating preferences and histories with will tend to retain all this data even after you are finished with the service. Match Group, a company that owns many popular dating apps—including Match, Tinder, Plenty of Fish, and OkCupid—reserves the right to share your data between apps. Although Match Group claims it does not sell personal user data, there remains the possibility that one of the companies could be sold, leaving user data at risk to also be sold or at least be subject to different privacy policies.

This is actually a risk for any company that gathers large amounts of personal data from consumers, an issue we will take up in more detail in chapter 7. When a company is sold, particularly if the sale is in bankruptcy, its customer database may be one of its most valuable assets. The FTC has been involved in privacy settlements involving sales of customer databases in the bankruptcy context, in an attempt to protect the privacy of the customer information.[7]

Like Facebook and other social media services, online dating services have also faced their fair share of data breaches and, considering how much sensitive personal information they may have stored, these breaches can be of particular concern to those seeking love online.[8]

REAL–LIFE RELATIONSHIPS GONE BAD: REVENGE PORN

Whether you find love online or in real life, a very real problem that has arisen in the digital age is **revenge porn**—when an angry ex-lover shares explicit material online without your consent. This material is often in the form of digital imagery like pictures and video. The practical problem here—other than the initial recording of the material, which may or may not be consensual—is the speed and volume of dissemination online. It is virtually impossible to stem the tide of information gone viral.

A rural wife and mother, Ruth King, was the victim of such an attack—which she described as the "gift that keeps on giving" precisely because,

REAL-WORLD RISKS OF ONLINE DATING

One of the particular concerns that arise about sharing too much personal data online through dating apps (or other social networks) is the damage ill-wishers might do to you in the real world by accessing your identifying information online. We talked briefly about doxing attacks in chapter 2: the ability to aggregate personal data about an individual from different places and publish it online in a way that might harm the person by holding them up to scorn or ridicule—or worse. Unfortunately, the ability to use social media information to locate people in the physical world can lead to stalking and harassment both online and in physical space. Sometimes the line between the two is difficult to see. Cyberstalking may result in a person experiencing emotional trauma in the real world, even if no physical harm ensues. We will address some specific examples of these problems in chapter 5. It is important to note at the outset, though, that these harms are very difficult to address in practice.

There are state laws about cyberstalking and cyberharassment, but many may be unconstitutional on First Amendment grounds. There are federal criminal laws that prohibit using telecommunication services to harass victims, but the enforcement of these laws relies on prosecutors having the resources and the inclination to bring an action in a particular case. The bottom line is that an ounce of prevention can be worth a pound of cure online, so it is often better to reveal less about yourself, even if you are desperate and dateless, than to give away information that may be used to harm you.

once the harmful material is out there, it is pretty much impossible to control.[9] An ex-partner had posted explicit videos of her online and, by the time she found out about it, the videos had been shared between all her colleagues at work, including her father, who also worked with her. Not only was it impossible—practically, technologically, and legally—to delete all the images from the websites where they were shared, but other people "piled on" by inserting nasty comments about what they would do to her if they ever met her. The continual onslaught of comments from strangers and friends, both online and in real life, led King to contemplate suicide.[10]

This situation occurred in the United Kingdom, but we face much the same issue in the United States, arguably on a broader scale because of our comparative lack of privacy protective regulations compared with those in the United Kingdom and the European Union. See chapter 8 for a more detailed comparison of the laws. One of the problems we face in the United States that is reflected in other countries is the lack of reliable data on the scope and scale of these kinds of online attacks, because many victims fear reporting them.[11] While there is no federal law in the United States preventing revenge porn, a number of states have experimented with such laws in recent years.[12] Their effectiveness in practice has yet to be seen.

PRIVACY TIPS AND TRICKS

Because our use of social media and the information that we share about ourselves and others can then be disseminated more broadly outside the networks we use, this is an area where an abundance of caution is important. Many people think the risks of engaging in social media are not worth the benefits and decide not to participate at all. If you do participate in social media, here are some tips and tricks worth considering:

+ Even if you carefully read the terms of service and/or privacy policies of social media companies, do not assume that those companies are adhering to their policies. (Even if the company adheres to its policies, it may suffer a data breach—we will discuss the risks of those in chapter 7.)

+ Do not believe everything you read on social media, especially as it relates to current affairs and politics. Even if a social media company states that it is fact checking content, there is no guarantee they are doing so effectively or comprehensively.

+ Change your social media passwords regularly and follow the instructions the services provide about how to make your passwords more robust.

+ If possible, use **multifactor authentication**. This means that when you log in, you have to confirm that you are who you say you are with the use of an email address, phone number, or other information outside the service you're logging on to. Facebook offers a two-factor authentication service, but you must opt in to enable it.[13]

+ Review your privacy settings on social media platforms and be wary of providing information via surveys and other forms and questionnaires presented online.

+ Do not assume that you are only sharing your information with selected friends and family, no matter how you have set your privacy preferences. The social media companies themselves can access that information—and hackers can, too. Think carefully about what you post about yourself and others before you share information online.

CHAPTER FIVE

Our Children's Data

+ Children's Online Privacy Protection Act
+ Role of the Federal Trade Commission in protecting children's privacy
+ American protection of children's data vs. foreign regulations
+ Practical and technological tips for protecting children's digital data
+ Cyberbullying and harassment

In May 2020, a coalition of twenty children's and consumer advocacy groups lodged a complaint with the Federal Trade Commission (FTC) against popular video-sharing app TikTok, a company that later faced media attention over concerns about the Chinese government using it to spy on American citizens. The May 2020 complaint stated that TikTok had not complied with an earlier FTC order in relation to children's privacy, notably that TikTok had failed to adequately protect children's personal information and had enabled children to set up accounts as adults, all in contravention of provisions of the Children's Online Privacy Protection Act (COPPA).

The COVID-19 pandemic had already significantly increased the amount of time children were spending online before the complaint was lodged. Concerns about protection of children's information were rife. However, even before the pandemic, the FTC had been very active in protecting children's privacy. In 2019 alone, the FTC imposed record fines against TikTok, YouTube/Google, and Facebook for failing to comply with COPPA.

In this chapter, we will talk more about COPPA and other laws aimed at protecting children's privacy, and the significant difficulties in both creating and enforcing children's privacy laws in the face of First Amendment concerns and tech companies ignoring the laws. Children's privacy also raises social and political issues about whose job it is to protect children online. In the early years of the personal computing revolution and the nascent internet, Congress was pressured to act, but many of its initiatives were criticized for being unconstitutional restraints on speech and/or for interfering in decisions that parents should be expected to make about what children can and cannot do online. These challenges were exacerbated by the increasing amount of time children were spending online and the limited ability of parents and caregivers to monitor their children's activities.

We will take a brief look at the pressure initially brought to bear on Congress to create laws addressing children's privacy—a little jaunt back to the mid-1990s—and what became of many of those laws when challenged on constitutional grounds. We will then turn to COPPA and the practical limitations inherent in relying on that law to protect children's privacy, given its limited scope and the difficulties in enforcing it. We will also touch on the risks and harms that children and young adults face as a result of undesirable online conduct such as cyberbullying, and the lack of effective legal protections for addressing those harms.

PROTECTING CHILDREN ONLINE: THE DAWN OF THE INTERNET AGE

In the early days of the internet, much ink was spilled over how to keep children safe from harmful material, with an emphasis on obscene and pornographic content. Concerns were also raised about children's privacy, and also eventually about cyberbullying and other harmful conduct.

From the mid-1990s to the beginning of the new millennium, Congress enacted various laws to protect children from harmful online conduct. Many of these laws—such as the Child Online Protection Act (COPA; not to be confused with COPPA), the Child Pornography Prevention Act, and broad sections of the Communications Decency Act—were struck down by the Supreme Court as being unconstitutional on First Amendment (free speech) grounds. Congress could not find a way to ensure that adults could access protected speech while still preventing minors from coming into contact with, say, pornographic material.

The Supreme Court considered the state of filtering technology available in the 1990s, which was not very sophisticated. Parents and online services were encouraged to investigate and implement filtering technologies to the extent possible. In fact, section 230 of the Communications Decency Act (CDA), the section that the Trump administration complained about in 2020, was originally enacted to protect "good Samaritan" blocking of potentially harmful online content. Prior to the enactment of that law, a company that held itself out as blocking harmful content, but failed to do so effectively, could be sued for failing to live up to its promises. Section 230 enabled companies to do their best to filter content without being penalized if their filtering was imperfect.

In 2000, Congress enacted the Children's Internet Protection Act in the wake of the failure of earlier laws to protect children's privacy. The Supreme Court held that, unlike some of the earlier laws, this one was constitutionally valid. It differed from the previous laws in that it simply tied government funding for libraries to a condition that those libraries must employ filtering technologies and procedures to protect children from harmful material. Instead of banning harmful online content outright, like earlier failed laws, it simply required libraries that took advantage of a widespread government funding program to put filtering mechanisms in place. A number of states also enacted their own laws requiring libraries, particularly public libraries and those at educational institutions, to filter material accessible to children. Many of these state laws were challenged on constitutional grounds, but some remain in force today.

Outside of the law, many libraries, especially those that cater to children, have taken their own initiatives to put filters and other measures in place to protect children from harmful or inappropriate material, much as they do in their decisions to acquire certain books or other services for their collections. We will look at the decisions of schools and libraries to protect children from harmful material in a little more detail in chapter 6.

Despite Congress and the Supreme Court going back and forth about the constitutionality of many early laws aimed at protecting children online, COPPA was passed and remains in force today. It is currently the main federal child-protective law in this area. By the 1990s, lawmakers were already aware of the ability of private companies to collect spending profiles and other personal information for targeted marketing and other purposes. Go back to some of the earlier chapters (notably the introduction and chapters 1 and 4) for a reminder of these concerns.

CYBERBULLYING

While laws that limit the collection and use of information about young people are a useful step in preventing online harm, legal regulations focused on data collection and use are not a panacea. A big concern once digital technology had become more widespread, around the dawn of the new millennium, involved use and dissemination of personal/private information to bully and harass others.

In the early decades of the twenty-first century we saw a tremendous upsurge in cyberbullying and harassment, often with horrific results. The suicide of teenager Megan Meier in 2006 as a result of a MySpace cyberbullying campaign was an example that garnered significant media attention, as was the 2010 suicide of Rutgers University student Tyler Clementi, who was outed when his roommate recorded and shared video of Clementi kissing another man.

One problem for legally redressing these harms is the lack of effective, and constitutionally valid, laws aimed directly at cyberbullying and harassment, despite repeated calls for such laws. While the people involved in the bullying/harassment in both the Meier and Clementi cases were prosecuted under existing criminal laws, those laws were largely either federal laws about unauthorized uses of computer systems (in the Meier case) and state laws about invasion of privacy (in the Clementi case).

Prosecutors resort to these laws because the United States has no comprehensive federal laws on cyberbullying or cyberharassment, largely for the reasons described at the beginning of this chapter: such laws would likely be characterized as unconstitutional government restrictions on free speech under the First Amendment. At the time of this writing, a proposal is before Congress to tie cyberbullying legislation to government funding, like the approach taken in the Children's Internet Protection Act (discussed in this chapter). This approach is more likely to be perceived as constitutionally valid.

As more and more children became active online, many people, and ultimately Congress, became concerned about what all of this would mean for the aggregation and use of children's personal information for targeted marketing and other activities. Not only could data aggregation and use of information about children be helpful in health and educational settings, but they also had the potential to lead to serious harms—for example, cyber-bullying and child pornography. There are laws about stalking and bullying, and the horrible specter of pedophilia and other crimes involving children, at both the state and federal levels. However, one of the easiest ways to address these problems is to significantly limit the amount of information that bad actors can obtain about children in the first place.

CHILDREN'S ONLINE PRIVACY PROTECTION ACT

Unlike the failed laws targeted at restricting speech—such as the Child Online Protection Act and the Child Pornography Prevention Act—COPPA requires companies to put procedures in place to keep children's data secure and to keep parents and guardians informed of what information is being gathered about children and the purposes for which it may be used. The law came into operation in 2000 and required the FTC to create regulations for online companies to follow in order to protect children's privacy. These regulations are known as the "COPPA Rule." The FTC itself oversees compliance with the rule, which applies to information about children under thirteen years old.

The FTC's website includes FAQs and additional information, including periodic press releases about the COPPA Rule and any updates made to it, along with other issues impacting children's privacy. As noted in previous chapters, in the absence of a general government department focused on data privacy, the FTC has taken on much of this burden.

The FTC website also summarizes the main goals of COPPA, which were initially, and largely still are, to put parents and guardians in greater control of information collected about their children online. Any companies (inter-net services, apps, social media, etc.) that direct services to children under the age of thirteen and collect, use, or disclose personal information about those children have to comply with strict notice and verifiable consent practices.

Several problems with this approach became immediately obvious and continue to hamper the effectiveness of the law. One challenge is that even with notice and consent procedures in place, many parents and guardians simply agree to whatever privacy terms are presented by an online service without reading them. We have already noted in earlier chapters that it is physically impossible for an individual to read all the online terms of service presented to them in the course of their, and their children's, lives.

Additionally, many online service providers—to avoid the risk of accidentally infringing the law and/or the expense of putting all the requisite notice-and-consent procedures in place—simply phrase their terms of service to prohibit anyone younger than thirteen from using their services. By requiring anyone signing up for a service to state that they are thirteen or older, most of these companies—including Facebook—have been able to sidestep the operation of the law altogether. If someone lied and said they were older than twelve when signing up, the company could say it did the best it could to avoid targeting its services to children. After all, we currently have no foolproof methods to verify the age of someone interacting with others online.

Besides the concern over children lying about their age, parents and guardians are often themselves complicit in setting up accounts for children, effectively flouting the age limits imposed by the terms of service.[1] If a child wants to be online with all their friends, how many parents will prevent them from signing up?

Another major problem with COPPA's effectiveness has been resistance to the idea that Congress should be the arbiter of children's online privacy. Many people feel that parents can take care of their children's privacy without laws in place, and arguably more effectively than Congress can. Even people who think a legal approach is useful may find COPPA too unwieldy to understand or worry about.

A lot of people simply misunderstand the focus and limits of COPPA. The law is actually much more limited in operation than many believe. It simply gives parents and guardians additional control and information about online service providers' practices in relation to collection, use, or disclosure of information about children. It does nothing to stop children from accessing specific websites, viewing any particular type of information online, or becoming victims of harmful conduct. It only gives parents additional information about, and the ability to consent (or not) to, particular uses of their children's data.

Under COPPA, personal information includes name, address, and online contact information; screen name, username, or other online identifier; telephone number; social security number; photo, video, or audio files containing the child's image and/or voice; geolocation information; or other information about the child or parents that a company collects and may combine with other identifying information.

The FTC's COPPA Rule requires companies that host content targeted at children to

+ prominently post a clear and comprehensive privacy policy on their websites describing how they deal with personal information collected from children;

+ provide notice to parents that information about children is being collected and obtain verifiable consent from those parents;

+ give parents the choice of allowing internal use of the child's information but prohibiting the company from sharing it with third parties;

+ allow parents to access their child's information to check for accuracy and request deletions;

+ provide parents the ability to prevent further collection or use of their children's information;

+ maintain confidentiality, security, and integrity of information collected from children; and

+ retain the information no longer than required (for the purposes for which it was initially collected) and promptly delete it after that, using reasonable measures to prevent later unauthorized access or use.[2]

THE VERDICT ON COPPA

Despite Congress's best intentions, COPPA has been widely regarded as a bit of a flop. It does not actually achieve a lot more than most parents and

WHAT IS VERIFIABLE PARENTAL CONSENT UNDER COPPA?

While COPPA itself does not explain precisely how an online company or service should obtain verifiable parental consent, the FTC has suggested that acceptable methods for obtaining consent include having the parent(s) do as follows:

(a) sign and return a consent form;

(b) use a credit or debit card or other online payment system that provides notification to the parent/guardian account-holder;

(c) call a toll-free number or video conference call staffed by trained personnel;

(d) provide a copy of a government-issued ID;

(e) answer a series of knowledge-based questions that only the parent or guardian should know the answers to; or

(f) use facial recognition technology to verify a picture of the parents' photo ID. (We talk more about facial recognition technology—artificial intelligence that can identify images of people's faces—in chapters 4, 7, and 11.)

guardians could manage on their own. It has been a mixed bag in terms of incentivizing companies to take greater care about children's privacy, as well. Many online service providers, as we have already seen, simply restrict access to people who are thirteen or older. Those who do accept children as users often ignore the regulations or fail to ensure adequate compliance.

Even when the FTC does pursue companies for failure to comply with COPPA, the best it can do is impose fines (which may or may not be significant, depending on the context) and monitor companies to ensure greater compliance with the law going forward—all of which takes up time and government resources. For large companies like YouTube and Google, fines are often a mere drop in the bucket. And for smaller companies, fines may prove prohibitive and may put some service providers effectively out of business, or out of the business of providing innovative services for children. So the

CHILDREN AND REVENGE PORN

We mentioned revenge porn in chapter 4, and another of the more worrying online developments is a related issue: the number of minors sharing sexually explicit content about each other online. Because of the increased availability of digital cameras in devices that children commonly take to school and into social situations, it is easier than ever for this conduct to occur, and for resulting images and videos to be shared widely outside of the victim's control. There are many examples of this, including reports of how legal mechanisms are brought into play to combat this behavior. For example, in October 2015, two students at Ponderosa High School in El Dorado County, California, were charged as sex offenders under the California Penal Code when they secretly made a video of one of them having sex with a third student.

Even if the victim is prepared to report the issue, and the police are prepared to prosecute, digital technology still enables video content posted online to take on a life of its own. As noted in chapter 4, it is virtually impossible to stem the tide of virally shared information, or to delete all instances of the harmful content online. Social media networks are an obvious way this content can be shared and shared again, and—even outside dissemination on social media networks—high school students increasingly use shared cloud storage systems to disseminate harmful online content, like revenge porn.

law can cut both ways by making the costs of providing child-friendly services prohibitively expensive. This is a concern that has been raised in relation to recent moves in the United Kingdom to impose more rigorous guidelines for children's online privacy protection.

Parents and guardians do not seem to have derived much comfort from COPPA. Rather than working in tandem with the law and the FTC to ensure that companies directing content at children act appropriately, many parents help their children flout the regulations—and/or simply find the regulations annoying. Most parents and guardians who are seriously concerned

YOUTUBE'S FTC SETTLEMENT

In September 2019, Google and its subsidiary YouTube were ordered to pay a record fine of $170 million to settle allegations by the FTC and the New York attorney general of failure to comply with COPPA. The basis of the complaint was that YouTube hosted "child directed channels" that collected personal data from viewers under the age of thirteen, but were not set up to incorporate the notice and consent required from parents or guardians. The company earned millions of dollars by using this data to target advertisements to children.

In this case, the information was collected through the use of **cookies**: software that automatically collects information about viewers, including their viewing preferences. The settlement terms with the FTC required Google and YouTube to develop and implement a process to permit YouTube channel owners to identify child-directed content—which would, in turn, enable YouTube to comply appropriately with COPPA. YouTube was also required to provide annual training to employees who deal with YouTube channel owners about COPPA compliance. These measures, if adequately overseen by Google/YouTube and the FTC, may be more effective than the fine.

about their children's privacy online take their own precautions, like requiring their children to access online services in areas where they can easily be monitored physically (like in a living room) or virtually (as when parents "friend" their children online to keep an eye on what's happening in virtual spaces their children inhabit).

Questions also arise as to whether the cutoff age of thirteen is appropriate for protecting children. A lot problems with online bullying and harassment arise in the teenage years, as is obvious from the cases of Meier and Clementi. Recent guidelines in the United Kingdom set a higher age limit—eighteen years old—for child protective regulations. The European Union also sets a higher age limit for children's privacy protections—sixteen years old—but individual EU countries can set limits higher than that. We will discuss these UK and EU guidelines and regulations next. When comparing the needs for child protection at different ages, it is worth bearing in mind that teenagers are less likely to be effectively monitored within the home than younger children, because they are more autonomous in their movements and often carry their own networked devices.

CHILDREN'S PRIVACY OUTSIDE THE UNITED STATES

As with most privacy-related regulations, the children's privacy situation is very different in many other countries. The EU countries are an obvious example of the difference, as is the United Kingdom—which, while no longer part of the European Union, has maintained a stronger regulatory stance on data privacy than has been the case in the United States.

All EU countries, regardless of any other existing national laws, are required to comply with the strictures of the General Data Protection Regulation (GDPR), mentioned in earlier chapters and covered in greater detail in chapter 8. The GDPR requires consent to most **data processing** ("processing" includes collection, use, analysis, and disclosure of information) unless there is another reason why the processing is necessary—such as public health, national security, or compliance with a court order or other legal obligation.

The GDPR provides specific protections for children. For example, when online services are provided to a child under the age of sixteen, the consent of a parent (or other person who exercises parental responsibility) is required for the collection and processing of relevant data.[3] The GDPR also requires that explanations about information processing, especially when directed at children, should be provided in clear and concise language.[4]

Technically, because the GDPR is a comprehensive law related to data privacy throughout the European Union, EU countries do not need child-specific privacy laws, as long as they comply with the overarching provisions of the GDPR. However, some EU countries do maintain specific children's data privacy laws, in addition to the general EU framework of privacy laws safeguarding the needs of children. For the current UK approach, see "United Kingdom: 2020 Bill on Children's Privacy."

Like the European Union, Canada does not have a child-specific privacy law, but the Office of the Privacy Commissioner of Canada has created a

UNITED KINGDOM: 2020 BILL ON CHILDREN'S PRIVACY

In January 2020, the UK government announced the Age Appropriate Design Code (aka Children's Code), a set of rules intended to give minors new online rights and protections. These protections are broader than those already enshrined in national law in compliance with the GDPR before Brexit. Even though the United Kingdom is no longer an EU member, its parliament enacted the Data Protection Act in 2018 when it was a member, and that law remains in force, along with EU regulations implemented before Brexit came into effect.

The Age Appropriate Design Code is not a law, but rather sets out standards and explains how the GDPR applies in the context of children using digital services. The Code comprises fifteen standards and applies to any information services that may be accessed by children. These services may include social networks, gaming apps, and connected toy manufacturers. The Code bars these services from allowing minors to share unnecessary personal information, limits the information that can be collected from them, and prohibits online services from using their data in a detrimental manner.

Specifically, online service providers are required to enable their highest privacy settings by default if an account belongs to a minor. This includes disabling location tracking and data mining for targeted advertising purposes. Companies who violate the code can face fines of 4 percent of their annual worldwide revenue. Unlike COPPA in the United States, which only applies to children under the age of thirteen, the Age Appropriate Design Code applies to all children under the age of eighteen.

The Code also calls for "age appropriate" application of privacy controls, without giving any specifics of how to design a system that would appropriately protect privacy for different age ranges. The onus is on online service providers to assess which age groups access and use their services, and to design privacy protections appropriately for all relevant age groups. Digital content providers can choose to utilize a single privacy protection system that would cater to all groups who use the service, but, by default, this would have to be a system that caters to the most vulnerable child users.

> The tech industry lobbied, but without success, to have the rules
> relaxed for lack of specificity. As with COPPA, the temptation for businesses
> in the United Kingdom will likely be to simply ban people under eighteen
> from accessing services if the service provider does not want to incur the
> additional costs, and face the additional risks, of compliance. Ultimately,
> this result could lead to less innovation in child-friendly online spaces.

website that includes user-friendly explanations of the importance of online privacy for young people, and tips on how they can safeguard their privacy.[5] This website contains useful guidance for anyone, anywhere in the world, concerned about children's privacy, through readily accessible videos and privacy-protection checklists. It also contains useful resources for parents and teachers. We will look at the involvement of parents, teachers, and schools in educational privacy settings in more detail in chapter 6.

PRIVACY TIPS AND TRICKS

This chapter has emphasized the limits of legal regulations that protect children's privacy, compared with other approaches like greater parental and school involvement. We will focus more on the role of schools in chapter 6. Even in countries with robust privacy legislation, like the GDPR in the European Union, there is a need for children to be savvy and for parents/guardians to remain vigilant to protect both the privacy of children's personal data and the uses to which it may be put.

Here are some particular tips and tricks for addressing privacy concerns related to children:

+ Parents and guardians can take advantage of specific children's
  social media applications (e.g., Facebook's Messenger Kids app) that
  allow children to chat online but only with friends whom their
  parents have pre-approved.[6] Even if parents/guardians do rely on
  these kinds of services, it is still worth monitoring what kids are
  doing online, to the extent possible.

+ Regardless of which online services children use, parents and guardians should at least skim through privacy information provided by those services and note any particular concerns. Parents or guardians with questions or concerns should follow up directly with those service providers and/or—if the concern is significant—contact the FTC. There is no guarantee that the FTC will investigate any particular concern or complaint, but it is worth going on record, if possible, in case later problems arise.

+ Where possible, try to keep children's use of devices in "public" areas of the house (like living rooms and kitchens) and/or monitor what children are doing in more private spaces like bedrooms. Checking in periodically may ease many parents' minds.

+ Open lines of communication with children about their online activities so they don't feel the need to keep their interactions hidden from parents and caregivers. Make it clear in those communications what some of the potential dangers of online interactions can be.

+ If it's not overly intrusive, "friend" or "follow" your children online. Use an alias if it is less embarrassing to your child.

+ Use online resources to help educate yourself and your child about dangers inherent in online interactions, including useful resources from other countries, like the Office of the Privacy Commissioner of Canada, on safe online practices.

+ In terms of concerns about bullying and harassment in particular, several pro bono organizations, including the Megan Meier Foundation[7] and the Tyler Clementi Foundation,[8] provide useful resource guides about monitoring, preventing, and reporting online bullying and harassment.

CHAPTER SIX

Our Data at School

+ Privacy rights in student records
+ Student vs. parent/guardian access to data
+ Family Educational Rights and Privacy Act
+ Protection of Pupil Rights Amendment
+ Privacy of educational records in public health/welfare emergencies
+ Remote schooling/COVID-19—new data security concerns
+ Individuals with Disabilities Education Act
+ Data privacy and student safety—bullying, harassment, and stalking
+ Student profiling

During widespread shelter-in-place orders during the COVID-19 pandemic, Google offered deals to a number of governments and school systems to provide free Chromebooks and software to students forced to study at home. While many lauded these initiatives, the privacy devil was in the technology details, as some parents and teachers soon discovered. Google found itself defending several class action lawsuits, including one under an Illinois law that prevents unauthorized use of facial recognition software and another in New Mexico for mining students' Gmail accounts for targeted advertising purposes (for a refresher on how targeted advertising works online, see chapter 4). The New Mexico litigation was brought by the state's attorney general and raised claims under both the Children's Online Privacy Protection Act (COPPA, discussed in chapter 5) and state unfair competition laws.

As we have already noted, new digital technologies often create the need to rethink the balance between the benefits of technological innovation and the related losses of personal privacy and autonomy. Particularly when new technologies are offered for "free," privacy is usually implicated. This is because "free" does not actually mean no strings attached. We typically pay for the technology by giving away personal information, including information on how we use the technology and often significantly more than that.

The Illinois class action against Google involved claims that the Chromebooks were set up to require students to use cameras and microphones to access necessary systems, thus creating facial and vocal digital footprints for the students' online activities. The New Mexico case involved Google mining information in emails to collate students' interests and other demographic information.

Trading off privacy for technological convenience (or even technological necessity in situations like COVID-19) is nothing new. However, as noted in chapter 5, particular issues are raised by the unauthorized collection and use of information about children as a vulnerable population. Children are vulnerable to harassment and bullying as well as to other, less overt harms, like targeted marketing directed to them or their parents. Additionally, information collected from children can be used to track them for the rest of their lives, for purposes of marketing but also, potentially, for other, more worrisome challenges—like racial profiling, which could lead to discrimination from an early age.

Some more controversial uses of private information about children have also arisen recently in the wake of a number of school shootings, including the tragedy at the Marjory Stoneman Douglas High School in Parkland, Florida, in 2018. The Florida legislature subsequently enacted a law requiring the compilation of a database to identify potentially dangerous students and, while that aspect of the law has been challenged, the Florida governor, Ron DeSantis, implemented an executive order in late 2019 to much the same effect. An executive order is a directive implemented by a member of the executive government, like the president, a state governor, or a director of a particular government department. It is not a law enacted by a legislature that everyone in the jurisdiction has to comply with, but rather usually a directive to one or more government officers or departments to act in compliance with the order.

While the aims behind these moves are laudatory—protecting children and their teachers—concerns about personal privacy and autonomy abound, as well as concerns about questionable records following young people for the rest of their lives, depending on how rigorously the information is vetted when it is compiled and the procedures in place, if any, to rectify inaccurate or incomplete records.

This chapter builds on chapter 5 by looking at our children's privacy at school, and at the particular laws outside of those already discussed (COPPA, etc.) that impose obligations on educational institutions and third-party software/hardware providers to protect student data. It also considers the extent to which privacy laws in the United States protect college students and graduate students. The main federal law protecting student privacy, the **Family Educational Rights and Privacy Act (FERPA)**, applies to both K–12 students and college/university students. We will also touch on the Protection of Pupil Rights Amendment and make reference to some laws about protecting health information, which will be taken up in greater detail in chapter 9.

It is also worth noting here, for completeness, that the Children's Internet Protection Act applies to school and university libraries that accept government funding under the federal E-rate program, as it does to any other libraries that obtain such funding. As discussed in chapter 5, this is the law that requires libraries receiving certain government funding to put internet safety protocols in place, including filtering technology where necessary.

PRIVACY AT SCHOOL: KEY DIGITAL CONCERNS

Although some of our privacy-protective laws were enacted prior to the dawn of the digital age, they take on a heightened significance today as sophisticated digital technology enables the large-scale data collection, aggregation, and uses discussed earlier in this book. With respect to students in particular, these data uses have both upsides and downsides.

Student Data Collection: The Good with the Bad

The ability to collate information about individual and collective student performance in different geographic areas and across different demographics has the power to transform education in terms of making decisions on how and where best to deploy often scarce resources. Additionally, on a case-by-case basis, the ability to track how individual students are doing in particular courses and to use technology to help them improve in problem

PRIVACY AT (REMOTE) SCHOOL: A RECIPE FOR DIGITAL DISASTER

As students returned to largely "virtual" school in the fall semester of 2020, in the throes of the COVID-19 pandemic, many children were required to spend a significant amount of time in front of screens, learning via Zoom and other interactive digital software. On September 4, 2020, the *Washington Post* published a story by Heather Kelly about the dangers of too much screen time during the pandemic, noting the case of a nine-year-old child in San Francisco who was required to spend at least six and a half hours a day in front of a screen. As noted elsewhere in this chapter, many of the digital services implemented by schools and universities for the purposes of virtual teaching during the pandemic were not fully vetted in relation to privacy.

Six and a half hours in front of a screen could translate to six and a half hours of data collection on even our youngest children. Equally worrying is the fact that, while much of this data collection probably fails to comply with laws like FERPA, the Department of Education is years behind in handling privacy complaints. By 2018, a report by the Office of the Inspector General, published on the Department of Education's Student Privacy Policy Office webpage, noted that the department had racked up a "years-long backlog of unresolved cases . . . without any mechanism for effectively tracking the number or status of the complaints received." It is difficult to imagine the challenges posed by the recent slew of likely breaches of FERPA. It seems more than likely that many of these complaints will never be addressed. They will certainly not be addressed in time to give much comfort to those affected.

areas can be an incredibly powerful educational tool. Student data can be used to track individual class or task participation and attendance, and to support academic growth between the classroom and the home setting, while developing more targeted educational plans for individual students.

However, the downsides of these practices are also significant. We have already talked about targeted advertising and discrimination, as well as the potential for bullying and harassment as a result of the collection and use of personally identifying information. In the school setting, there is also the worry that students will lose their autonomy through a sense of being "watched" in all their educational activities. This could stifle personal development and creativity, and make students less inclined to participate freely in class and related activities.

While many of these concerns may be greater for younger student populations, some remain applicable in college and graduate school. The college years are often when students experiment and "find themselves." They may feel stifled in their willingness to try new things—new courses, new projects—if they feel that their failures are being tracked along with their successes, or that their data is being used to encourage them to pursue particular directions in their studies.

As schools, colleges, and universities increasingly rely on third-party technology companies to provide devices, software, and services to students, the administrators must be vigilant to ensure not only that those third-party companies have appropriate privacy safeguards and policies in place, but also that they are abiding by their own policies and any relevant laws. Speaking of relevant laws, this is a good time to start thinking about the most significant law that impacts student privacy rights: FERPA.

FAMILY EDUCATIONAL RIGHTS AND PRIVACY ACT

The Family Educational Rights and Privacy Act of 1974 applies to student privacy across the board, from kindergarten to graduate school. This law is particularly important given the lack of a comprehensive federal privacy law in the United States. Outside of sector-specific laws like FERPA, there is no comprehensive legal mandate to protect the privacy of Americans generally, or American students in particular. As we noted in chapter 5, many European countries do not have, or need, child-specific privacy laws because children are automatically covered under the more comprehensive General Data Protection Regulation and its predecessor law, the Data Protection Directive of 1995. We considered the ways in which these general regulations apply specifically to children in chapter 5, and we'll take a broader look at the European position on privacy in chapter 8.

FERPA guarantees that parents have access to their children's educational records. However, once a child reaches the age of eighteen or attends

IDEA: INDIVIDUALS WITH DISABILITIES EDUCATION ACT

While FERPA applies to student records, including health records, in general, the Individuals with Disabilities Education Act (IDEA) provides additional, and higher, standards of confidentiality for students with disabilities who are covered under that law. IDEA provides for a "free appropriate public education," which may include special educational and other services, for children with disabilities. Information about students' disabilities and special education plans implemented under the law are subject to higher confidentiality requirements on top of those required under FERPA, so theoretically, at least, any school or school district putting policies and procedures in place to protect student privacy should be particularly mindful of appropriate safeguards for information about students covered under IDEA.

an institution of postsecondary education prior to that age, FERPA's guarantees are transferred directly to the student. That is why the parents of a college student have no automatic right to ask for the student's college records, even if they are the ones footing the bill for the tuition. A parent needs authority from the child to access postsecondary school records.

More importantly for the purposes of our discussion, FERPA limits the parties to whom schools can disclose student information (i.e., **educational records**) without specific consent. The term *educational records* is broadly defined under FERPA to include any information directly related to an individual student, including health and immunization records, as well as records of special services provided to the student under legislation requiring disability accommodations.

FERPA applies to any educational institution that receives funding from the U.S. Department of Education. This is a large number of educational institutions, because many private schools also receive some government funding—therefore, even if you or your child attends a private school, that school may be subject to FERPA.

Can a School Share Student Information with Third Parties?

Since the dawn of the digital age, it has become increasingly common for schools to contract with third-party service providers for a variety of functions that may be cheaper, or may be provided more effectively, when outsourced: food services, computing services, various educational software packages, and so on. When those third parties will be handling student information, FERPA requires an agreement to be in place that protects that information and requires consent either from the school or from the parents for that information to be shared with, and used by, those third parties.

The default rule is that consent to the data sharing must be obtained from the parent or guardian (or student in the case of postsecondary education). However, there are two exceptions that allow a school to share information without specific consent under certain circumstances: the **directory exception** and the **school official exception**.

DIRECTORY EXCEPTION

The directory exception has very limited application in the third-party vendor situation, largely because this exception is limited to what the law describes as "directory information"—that is, information like a student's name, grade level, phone number, and address. It covers the kind of information often included in class lists or lists of sports teams or other extracurricular activities. To comply with the directory exception, the school must publicly provide a general notice of the categories of information it intends to share, and the parents (or students in postsecondary education) must be given the opportunity to opt out of sharing.

For a school trying to set up, say, a payment system with a third-party cafeteria vendor, the fact that financial information and student food preferences may not be considered "directory information" will usually render the directory exception pretty useless. Additionally, the fact that every relevant parent or student must be given the ability to opt out of the data sharing under that exception would make its use administratively unwieldy. In these situations, schools more typically rely on the school official exception, rather than the directory exception.

FERPA allows a school to disclose personal student information to a third-party service provider if the provider in question meets the criteria set out in the statute. Among other things, the provider must

+ perform an institutional service or function that the school itself would otherwise provide through its own employees,

+ be under the school's direct control to the extent that it uses and maintains records about students, and

+ use the records only for authorized purposes.

The provider is not permitted to share student records with any other parties without specific authorization from the school or school district. It must also provide access to student records, on request, to the school or any eligible parent or student.

There are additional requirements and exceptions under FERPA, but the basic scheme of the law is that schools, colleges, and universities can share information about students when necessary to provide a function or service the school itself would otherwise directly provide (i.e., outsourcing), provided that it imposes requisite controls on the use of that information and maintains direct supervision of how the information is used.

Educational institutions can also contract all sorts of services to third-party providers of educational, food, and financial services *with* the consent of parents/guardians or postsecondary students. However, it is often much easier administratively to utilize one of the FERPA exceptions than to obtain specific authorization from every affected student or their parents.

Third-Party Service Providers and COVID-19
The COVID-19 pandemic caused many educational services to suddenly move online, and some of the technologies used by schools to provide instruction, resources, and other services in a pinch were not fully compliant with FERPA. The increased reliance on these technologies has caused some concern about student records and data privacy. Additionally, in cases where third-party service providers retain the right to unilaterally change their terms of service (as we discussed with respect to online TOS generally

THE "HEALTH OR SAFETY" EXCEPTIONS IN FERPA

Not only did the COVID-19 pandemic raise concerns about insufficient protocols protecting student records, it also brought into sharp relief the use of the "health or safety" exceptions in FERPA. These exceptions enable schools to share student information in connection with a health emergency, when the information may be needed by law enforcement officials, public health officials, trained medical personnel, or parents. Information sharing is allowed if knowledge of the information is necessary to protect the health or safety of the student(s) in question, or to protect others.

The emergency exception lasts for the duration of the emergency—which in the case of COVID-19 could be several years—but generally is restricted to disclosure of information that is necessary to protect the student's (or others') health or safety. It is not a blanket ability to disclose any information about the student.

A COVID-19 FAQ document released by the Department of Education in March 2020 made it clear that *media* would *not* be an appropriate party for an educational institution to release student information to, under the health or safety emergency provisions of FERPA: "While the media may have a role in alerting the community of an outbreak, they are not 'appropriate parties' under FERPA's health and safety emergency exception because they generally do not have a role in protecting individual students or other individuals at the educational agency or institution."

in chapter 4), educational institutions have to be careful that any changes in those terms continue to comply with FERPA requirements.

Another issue of some concern, particularly in light of how much information has been gathered by third-party online service providers in the wake of COVID-19, is how those services might use that information in the future. Under FERPA, if a school is relying on the school official exception, the student information can only be used for the purposes for which it was originally shared—that is, for performing functions the school itself would have otherwise performed. The third party is not legally permitted to, say,

PPRA: PROTECTION OF PUPIL RIGHTS AMENDMENT

While FERPA is the main federal law dealing with student privacy, another federal law, the Protection of Pupil Rights Amendment of 1978 (PPRA) specifically regulates surveys, evaluations, and other analyses funded by the Department of Education that are administered to elementary and secondary school students. The law requires parents to provide written consent before any student participates in an Education Department–funded survey that could reveal personal information about things like political or religious beliefs, antisocial behavior, or family income.

Parents can give children permission to participate in such a survey, analysis, or evaluation, or to opt out of sharing any such information with the school or any third-party provider engaged by the school. The PPRA also prohibits the collection of information from students for marketing purposes except for developing, evaluating, or providing educational products or services to students or educational institutions.

create targeted marketing profiles and advertising campaigns based on the relevant information, because that would be outside the scope of the legal authorization. Likewise, a third party could not legally sell the information to anyone else for targeted marketing or associated purposes. The extent to which unauthorized information sharing has actually occurred during COVID—particularly given the large amount of personal information that has now been shared with Google, Zoom, WebEx, Microsoft, Slack, and other providers—remains to be seen.

Data Privacy and Student Safety

The provisions of FERPA related to health and safety emergencies notwithstanding, there have been many notable school-related situations in recent decades where FERPA did not come into play, largely because information that could have identified or prevented a health or safety problem is not the kind of information usually kept in student records. Think about the horrific reports of school shootings, or the bullying and harassment that results in student suicides.

For example, none of the information in anyone's student records could likely have been used to prevent the suicides of Megan Meier and Tyler Clementi, the victims of online bullying and harassment discussed in chapter 5. Nor was either victim's student information used by the bully. In Meier's case, Lori Drew, the mother of a classmate, set up a fake MySpace profile to bully Meier, using information about Meier available from other students and from social media. In Clementi's case, the information used to bully him was video gathered by his roommate in their dormitory, and nothing in the latter student's records would likely provide evidence of a potential problem. Thus, since no information from student records was implicated in either case, FERPA did not come into play.

FERPA, then, does not provide answers to these kinds of problems. In many ways, these are not problems of student data privacy law at all, but rather are related to general social norms about confidentiality, personal space, and appropriate/ethical conduct. Additionally, it was clear in the Meier case that Lori Drew, who set up the fake MySpace profile, had breached MySpace's terms of service by creating a false online persona to "befriend" and ultimately to bully Meier. Legal issues related to terms of service are really contract issues rather than privacy law issues. They are contract issues about privacy, but the legal remedies come from contract law.

To the extent that schools can do anything about these situations, their resources are perhaps best spent developing anti-bullying policies and appropriate social media usage policies, as well as educating students about these policies and enforcing "zero tolerance" measures against bullying and harassment. Schools may be limited in their effective "jurisdiction" over things happening at school and at school functions, but at least having conversations about acceptable conduct, and imposing consequences (detentions, suspensions, etc.) for infringing school guidelines, goes some way toward developing a sense of appropriate behavior among students. As should already be apparent from previous chapters, law is not always the answer to privacy concerns.

Many schools, colleges, and universities have dedicated personnel for confidentially reporting these kinds of problems, as well as for officially taking action against bullying, harassment, stalking, and other kinds of inappropriate conduct on campus, including in dormitories and communal areas.

Profiling Potentially Dangerous Students: The Pros and Cons

When harmful conduct involving students moves from bullying and harassment toward actual physical violence directed at others, additional data privacy issues can arise—for example, where schools or governments attempt to collate information on students likely to engage in harmful activities. In the wake of the mass shooting at Stoneman Douglas High School, the Florida legislature and governor's office have attempted to operationalize a comprehensive database of students who are perceived as potentially dangerous. The idea is to identify and monitor those students, particularly in relation to any attempts to purchase firearms and/or engage in violent behavior.

An official statewide database was rolled out by the Florida Department of Education in August 2019. This system allows school administrations and police to enter information about students who they believe have the potential to pose a danger to their school communities. Relevant information includes a student's history with law enforcement and discipline as well as any social media posts that contain threat indicators, and information about whether the student was ever involuntarily committed to a mental health facility under Florida law. A press release from the education department stated that the database would not be used to profile or label students as potential threats, but rather to evaluate the seriousness of already reported or identified threats.[1] Privacy advocacy groups quickly raised concerns about student privacy, related to what information would be collected and how it would be used. Particular concerns have been raised that victims of bullying might be identified as potential threats for future violence (based on the idea of retribution for the bullying). The worry is that these victims may be less likely to report bullying if the result could be their inclusion in a threat assessment database.[2]

Additionally, if bullying is based on race, religion, disability, or sexual orientation, children could be tracked on the basis of characteristics that are federally protected under antidiscrimination laws.[3] While information about protected classes is not expressly included in the Florida database at present, the fact that someone was bullied may be based on those characteristics, and

DOWNSIDES OF THREAT ASSESSMENT DATABASES

On February 28, 2020, the *Orlando Sentinel* published an article by Grace Toohey noting that a five-year-old preschooler had been added to Seminole County's threat assessment database for threatening a classmate, and that his information could be included in the database for up to twenty-five years.

The county sheriff was reported as saying that the information in the threat assessment database was not linked to student records or criminal records, which may or may not give comfort to students or parents concerned about monitoring and profiling. It may also be the case that certain groups are more likely to be included in these databases—if, for example, perceptions of violence in the classroom are evaluated disproportionately between white students and students of color.

Another problem with these databases is how threats are assessed in terms of who makes the decision to include a student in a database, and on what basis. In the case reported in February 2020, the school administration made the assessment of potential dangerousness and arranged for the student's inclusion in the database, even though the school staff involved were reported as agreeing that the threat was not credible.

may inadvertently put people in federally protected classes at higher risk of privacy incursions.

Threat assessment databases, while generally well intentioned, raise significant concerns about personal liberty and privacy, revolving around the collection and use of students' personal information without their (or their parents') consent. It remains to be seen how effective any of these databases are in preventing school shootings or other kinds of violence. In the meantime, however, they may create a Big Brother shadow over schools. Database information may also be misused, depending on any regulatory controls ultimately adopted. Because these databases are largely a matter of disharmonized state laws and executive orders, it is unlikely that a comprehensive and clearly thought-out set of appropriate data-use principles will emerge any time in the near future to redress dangerous conduct at school.

PRIVACY TIPS AND TRICKS

While this chapter has ended on a somewhat bleak note, at least there are student rights under federal laws in relation to a large amount of private information. The press coverage over the more worrying recent developments in the area of data collection and potential profiling has helped students and parents stay informed about worrying practices.

The main takeaways from this chapter are about knowing your rights under the various statutes and understanding how to follow up on concerns. In particular, and depending on what you may be concerned about, you can always consider the following:

+ Seek clarification from educational institutions about what information they are gathering and in what contexts, as well as with whom they are sharing it. There should be a dedicated legal or compliance office in every educational institution who can answer specific questions. Bear in mind that in the case of postsecondary students, only the students themselves are legally entitled to information about their records, but parents and guardians can seek information about students in kindergarten through twelfth grade under FERPA.

+ When engaging online, students should be careful about what information they share with friends and classmates and should report to parents (who can also report directly to social networks) concerns about suspicious behavior. Many popular social networks' terms of service do not allow the use of false identities or bullying/harassing behavior.

+ Parents and students should be aware that they have the right to opt out of having personally identifying information (directory information) included in class lists and other lists (for extracurricular activities, etc.). If a student's details are inadvertently included in such a list, you can ask for them to be removed.

+ As a matter of etiquette and good online citizenship, it is a wise practice not to share personally identifying details about classmates or their families online without their consent, including on social networks. Many social networks require consent under their terms of service.

+   If your school provides digital devices, you are entitled to report concerns to them about mandatory use of cameras and voiceprint software and ask for clarification of what information is being gathered from email and other services provided on the devices.

+   When you are not using your device's camera, you can place a piece of dark tape over it so that it cannot record you. This holds true for both school-provided and other devices. If you have a camera connected to your desktop, disconnect it when you are not using it.

While we are thinking about data collection by third-party online service providers, let us turn, in the next chapter, to a consideration of precisely how digital entities gather information about you, what they use it for, and the specific risks involved, including data breaches and the insecurity of your information in other people's hands.

CHAPTER SEVEN

Our Data in the Digital Marketplace

+ Corporate collection and aggregation of personal data
+ Data breach risks and responsibilities
+ Notice obligations for compromised data
+ Repairing data profiles after a data breach
+ Data brokers
+ Identity theft and fraud
+ Video Privacy Protection Act
+ Computer Fraud and Abuse Act

In July 2017, Equifax, one of the three major credit reporting agencies in the United States, reported a massive data breach that involved the data of around 150 million people. At the time, this was one of the largest data breaches ever reported globally. The incident compromised personal data including Social Security numbers, birth dates, addresses, driver's licenses, and, in a smaller number of cases, credit card data. The breach garnered a tremendous amount of media attention, revolving around questions like when the breach had occurred, when it had been discovered, whether it should have been discovered or reported sooner, and, importantly, what steps Equifax should be required to take to remedy the breach, including notifying affected individuals and offering free credit reporting and monitoring for a period of time.

Because of the voluminous amounts of data collected and aggregated by businesses and governments around the world in the digital age, concerns about data breaches like this one have grown exponentially in recent years, with the media regularly reporting on the most significant failures of data security.[1] Data breaches can harm the reputations of corporations that may be regarded as not having taken sufficient care of our data, and/or as failing to act expeditiously and effectively to remedy a problem.

The sad truth is that breaches can be very difficult to detect, even for those carefully monitoring their systems—and, when detected, they can be very hard to remedy in terms of protecting those whose data may have been exposed. While the technological security protocols can be enhanced, this is, in some ways, the same as shutting the barn door after the horse has bolted. It will help prevent future harms but will not claw back the data that was exposed in the initial breach.

After data has been exposed, attempts to protect affected individuals will, by necessity, be piecemeal: monitoring credit reports, tax records, and the like to detect any attempts at identify theft, including credit fraud, tax fraud, and health fraud. The companies at fault may be prepared to cover costs and even undertake some of this monitoring, but affected individuals may not trust those companies to do so effectively and may end up bearing the brunt of the monitoring and associated costs themselves. Additionally, anyone who is the victim of identity theft or credit fraud may have a very challenging time repairing their credit and obtaining legal compensation for the resulting harms.

This chapter looks at the life cycle of data aggregation from initial collection to potential system breaches, and ends by discussing what avenues are available to those whose data may have been exposed in a breach. It also discusses the responsibility of a breached entity to notify and assist those whose data may have been compromised.

HOW DO COMPANIES COLLECT ALL THAT DATA?

In previous chapters, we've looked at one of the most common and obvious ways that companies and others collect information about you: by seeking your *consent*. This is usually obtained when you sign up for a particular platform, app, or service. One of the conditions of accessing a service like Facebook, YouTube, or Amazon is that you consent to their terms of service (TOS), which include their privacy policies. If the TOS allow the company to compile or share your information for particular purposes, the agreement to the TOS is a contractually binding agreement (see chapter 4 for a refresher on how that works).

Our Data in the Digital Marketplace

There are other ways that companies can collect information about you, based on your online habits. These may or may not be subject to contractual agreement, depending on the circumstances. For example, some companies use "cookies" to collect data about you. **Cookies** come in many shapes and forms (and we're not talking about delicious baked goods here). However, a general definition is that cookies are pieces of software code that can be automatically downloaded onto your computer to track your movements from website to website.

A company may download a cookie onto your computer consistently with TOS (under which you agree to the use of cookies) or may do so without your attention or notice, depending on the circumstances. In some cases, you can click a button when you sign up for a service, refusing the use of cookies—you have likely seen these when you access new webpages or services. In other cases, you can set your computer not to accept cookies by default, which is generally a good idea if you are concerned about your online activities being tracked.

If you have contractually consented to the use of cookies or other data collection practices, you may not have any legal rights to complain about them later. As long as the contract is presented fairly—terms being clearly available to you whether you read them or not—a court will generally enforce them.

This section explains some technological data-protection practices that likely are not illegal with contractual consent and may not be legally problematic even without your specific consent. We also look here at how companies use the information they collect about you outside of the standard targeted advertising paradigms already discussed in previous chapters.

Besides software code, like cookies, there are other unexpected avenues that can be used by those who manufacture digital devices to track our online movements. Even when we do not have our cameras or microphones switched on, they may be automatically recording what we do, so it is a good idea to unplug these devices and/or cover cameras, at least with strips of plastic or tape, when not in use.

As we move away from using desktops and laptop computers for our digital needs, and move to more mobile devices, the opportunities for tracking have evolved, too. Touchscreen devices of all kinds, including smartphones and tablets, can be used to track what we do online simply by recording the

THE STRANGE CASE OF VIDEO RENTAL RECORDS

One area that has historically caused confusion about consumer privacy is the records of videos we have watched. The confusion is largely the result of a rather dated federal law that was enacted in 1988 in the wake of annoyance caused to Robert Bork, a nominee to the U.S. Supreme Court, when his video rental history was publicly disclosed. Even though the rental history was unremarkable, it was embarrassing to Bork, who had been quoted as saying that Americans had only those privacy rights granted to them specifically under law. (There was no law protecting the privacy in video rental histories at the time.)

The Video Privacy Protection Act (VPPA), enacted in the wake of this episode, was drafted in the days of brick-and-mortar video libraries. Does anyone remember those? The law has struggled to keep pace with new technologies involving digital content streaming services for movies, TV shows, and video games. The federal law prohibits a "video tape service provider" from publicly disclosing personally identifying information about a customer.

The challenges arise from the statutory definitions of *video tape service provider, consumer,* and *personally identifying information.* For example, under the VPPA, a consumer is defined as a person who rents, purchases, or subscribes to goods or services from a video content provider. Many of us who consume video content from the internet or various apps don't actually rent or purchase it, or even subscribe to the service in question. A lot of free content is available on Facebook, YouTube, and elsewhere without a customer relationship ever developing in the legal/VPPA sense. Additionally, the law's prohibition on disclosing personal information *publicly* has proved challenging for courts, given that many apps share video streaming information among themselves, but it is not yet clear to what extent that is regarded as public sharing under the law.

SOFTWARE FOR TRACKING YOUR DATA

There are many different ways a company can track you online, including by accessing your computer camera or microphone when you may not know they are recording you. Louise Matsakis, in a 2019 article in *Wired*, helpfully summarized some of the more common software that can track your movements online, including traditional cookies (described elsewhere in this chapter); **fingerprinters**, which collect information about your devices, like your IP address, screen resolution, and the type of computer you use; **identity trackers** that hide on your login pages and collect your email addresses; and **session replay scripts**, which record everything you do on a website, including what products and ads you clicked on and sometimes even the password you used.

Like most technology, the software code in itself isn't objectively "good" or "bad." The concern is more with the uses made of it. For example, Matsakis notes that some trackers can be very useful, explaining that session cookies are often used to keep you logged into websites, and, in particular, to remember what is in your shopping cart while you are moving around online, even if you close your browser window and reopen it.

touches on the screens. This is similar to, but an evolution of, **keystroke monitoring technology**, which still exists to monitor the keys you type on full-size keyboards.

We also wear a lot of devices that track information these days (fitness monitors, heart-rate monitors, etc.). It may be worth checking the terms of service for any such devices you use regularly to see whether, and to what extent, they may be reporting your data back to the manufacturer or anyone else. Increasingly, our vehicles monitor our data, as described in chapter 1. We also talked in that chapter about how many of our in-home devices, like Echoes, Alexas, and Nests, record what is happening in our homes. Our cell phones regularly ping towers for service, and the service providers thereby create records of our movements through cell site location information (discussed in a little more detail in chapter 11).

Many online companies use **application programming interfaces (APIs)** to provide simple interconnected services to users. For example, if a mobile app developer wants to allow users to log in to the app through Facebook or Google, they can employ an API, which is another piece of software code that can be used to link up two services that you use. In fact, APIs were at the heart of the Cambridge Analytica scandal discussed in chapter 4 because the data about individual voters was collected via an API that allowed Cambridge Analytica personnel to link their survey instrument directly to Facebook's users.[2] APIs have also raised concerns in the context of the Video Privacy Protection Act (see "The Strange Case of Video Rental Records"). Where online streaming services use APIs to link your video-watching preferences with, say, your social networks, concerns have been raised about potential infringements of this law.

Of course, not all tracking or monitoring is objectively "bad," and the goods or evils of tracking are often in the eye of the beholder. Many of us appreciate it when, say, Amazon or Audible keeps track of our purchases so that we can reorder items without having to find them again, and be notified of other books, movies, games, or clothes we might like. Of course, these practices help the online retailers, too, by making it easier for us to continue purchasing their wares.

As with all technology, software code cannot really be good or evil, and intelligent minds differ on the evils of various uses. The bottom line is really to understand, to the extent necessary, what is being done with your data, and how you can address any particular concerns you might have.

WHAT DO THEY DO WITH ALL THAT DATA?

We have talked a lot in previous chapters about targeted marketing as one of the biggest reasons companies collect personal data, particularly online service providers that do not charge members a fee for their services, like Facebook and YouTube. We have also noted that sometimes our information can be accessed by hackers and, in worrying situations, can potentially be obtained by foreign governments. In 2019 and 2020, along with concerns about not complying with American laws on children's privacy, the popular video-sharing app TikTok was criticized for opening the way for the Chinese government to obtain personal information about its users in America and other countries.[3]

It is relatively easy to be mindful of the information we share online, and we have looked at strategies for doing this in previous chapters, notably in chapter 4, where we discussed the typical terms of service and privacy policies of online service providers like Facebook, YouTube, Twitter, Pinterest, and Amazon. We are probably a little less mindful of the fact that the questions we type into search engines like Google can be stored and utilized by data aggregators in a variety of contexts, and that the mobile devices we carry with us often provide location tracking services, which are able to provide our demographic information to businesses and governments. For example, the amount of traffic in particular shopping areas can provide useful data about promising venues for new brick-and-mortar businesses.

The bottom line is that most of us never have a clear picture of how far and wide our data is being shared. Technology commentator Louise Matsakis put it this way:

> Consider what happens when someone sends a vial of saliva to 23andme. The person knows they're sharing their DNA with a genomics company, but they may not realize it will be resold to pharmaceutical firms. Many apps use your location to serve up custom advertisements, but they don't necessarily make it clear that a hedge fund may also buy that location data to analyze which retail stores you frequent. Anyone who has witnessed the same shoe advertisement follow them around the web knows they're being tracked, but fewer people likely understand that companies may be recording not just their clicks but also the exact movements of their mouse.[4]

Matsakis here makes a distinction between companies that you are actually dealing with—the companies providing particular services in exchange for your data—and companies that gather your data without providing anything to you. This second group consists largely of **data brokers**: firms that gather information both from publicly available sources and from companies with whom you have consensually shared your information.

Data brokers can aggregate sophisticated profiles on a large range of individuals, including spending habits, locations frequented, medical records, browser history, social media connections, motor vehicle information (which is often available from government registries), and more. Information gathered by these entities may contain errors or outdated elements,

THE DARK SIDE OF DATA BROKERS

Legal classification and regulation of data aggregators has proved problematic in recent years. In chapter 10, we will look at the extent to which these entities can be meaningfully regulated under fair credit reporting laws when they deal with personal financial information. Data brokers have also been involved in serious criminal conduct. For example, in the early days of digital data aggregation, a company called Docusearch was implicated in the murder of a young woman, Amy Boyer, outside her place of work in 1999. A man who was obsessed with her, Liam Youens, had stalked Boyer, partly using records about her provided by Docusearch, before fatally shooting her and then shooting himself.

Court files in the Youens case revealed that Docusearch did more than simply aggregate digital data that was available online. In order to gather more information about people to include in its database, it also engaged in a practice called **pretexting**: pretending to be a person in authority, entitled to particular information, in order to trick someone into handing it over. In the Youens case, Docusearch had received a seventy-five-dollar fee for hiring a woman who used a pretexting ruse to obtain Boyer's work address. That was how Youens learned where Boyer worked, which was where he shot and killed her.

Boyer's mother sued Docusearch for its part in the murder. The case itself revolved around claims in criminal negligence and tort law, and the results were a mixed bag. The Supreme Court of New Hampshire held that Docusearch did have a legal duty to "exercise reasonable care in disclosing a third person's personal information to a client." In terms of Docusearch's data aggregation practices, at least in relation to pretexting, the court noted that under the New Hampshire consumer protection law, "an investigator who obtains a person's work address by means of pretextual phone calling, and then sells the information, may be liable for damages."

However, these holdings are limited because they rely on a person actually having the wherewithal and willingness to bring a case in court, as well as presenting facts similar to those in this particular case. The court's decision does not prevent the aggregation of data in the first place by a service like Docusearch, although it does call into question certain of its information-gathering practices.

but there are no general legal rights to access, check, or correct this information—assuming, of course, that you can even find out who has the information in the first place. This situation (lack of access or ability to correct information) is significantly different from the position in the European Union, which we will consider in chapter 8.

Data brokers profit from selling personal information to those who can monetize it effectively in areas like marketing, retail, tenant screening, customer management, insurance risk assessment and mitigation, and many others.[5] Some data brokers even assist law enforcement in tracking down criminal suspects.[6] We will consider ways in which governments access and use personal information in more detail in chapter 11.

Some states have attempted to regulate data brokers, at least so that individuals can have a greater sense of who is collecting what information about them, and potentially also have a chance to correct or delete it. In 2019, the legislature in Vermont enacted a law requiring all data brokers to register on a government database and provide information about how they collect data about Vermont residents. California's Consumer Privacy Act also theoretically gives Californian residents the ability to opt out of data collection more generally. However, these laws are notoriously difficult to enforce. In Vermont, many data brokers have simply failed to register, and, for those who did register, there was much confusion about how to redress the multitude of erroneous data on individuals included in their databases.[7]

A particularly problematic aspect of widespread data collection by these aggregators and by others who have access to volumes of personal data, often from public sources, is the ability of stalkers and other bad actors to obtain sufficient information about individuals to pose serious threats in the virtual world, and sometimes even in real space. A number of data brokers market themselves as being like phone books: they sell personally identifying information, including location information and contact details, to those prepared to pay for it.

Occasionally these companies will run afoul of a specific law, like the **Fair Credit Reporting Act (FCRA**, discussed in more detail in chapter 10), but only if they fall within the narrow ambit of the law in question. For example, in 2012, data broker Spokeo settled a complaint with the Federal Trade Com-

Our Data in the Digital Marketplace

mission (FTC) for $800,000 when aspects of its "person lookup" function were found to violate the FCRA.

Spokeo had marketed itself as a provider of information to companies for the purposes of employment background checks, but, because it dealt with consumer credit information regulated under the FCRA, and had failed to comply with the legal protections extended under the Act, it had violated the law. The FTC held Spokeo accountable for failing to make sure that the information sold would be used solely for purposes permitted under the law, failing to ensure the accuracy of the information, and failing to tells its users they had an obligation to notify employment applicants about the use of the information if an adverse employment decision were made on the basis of the information.

The Spokeo settlement was groundbreaking in the sense that it was the first time an online information service company was held to the standards of a credit reporting agency under the FCRA. However, online "person lookup" services that do not deal with credit information will not face the same problems. This is why online lookup services can be very dangerous if they provide personally identifying information to abusers and stalkers.[8] Many doxing attacks (see chapter 2) are enabled by the ready access to personally identifying information through these sources.

DATA BREACHES

This chapter began with an example of a large-scale data breach, which is unfortunately part and parcel of the risk that comes with the voluminous aggregations of data by brokers and others. The Equifax data breach involved a credit reporting agency, and we will discuss the role and regulation of those agencies in more detail in chapter 10. However, any entity that maintains a large amount of data can be hacked. There is no perfect encryption methodology. Each advance in encryption technology is simply another challenge for hackers, for better or worse.

So, what is a data breach and what can you do if your information is compromised? In simple terms, a data breach is an incident that involves unauthorized access to, or use of, data that is supposed to be secure. Big Data, machine learning, and artificial intelligence provide the context in which massive data breaches can occur, often affecting thousands, millions, or even billions of individuals.

GOOD THINGS ALSO COME OF DATA AGGREGATION

While this chapter has painted a rather bleak picture of data aggregation, the news is not all bad. As noted at the beginning of this book, data aggregation, machine learning, and artificial intelligence can be used for many socially beneficial purposes. For example, social media posts have been studied to learn more about social and cultural issues, because researchers have found that people tend to be more honest on sites like Facebook and Google than they are on traditional survey instruments. In his book *Everybody Lies: Big Data, New Data, and What the Internet Can Tell Us about Who We Really Are,* Seth Stephens-Davidowitz has noted that while 20 percent of people admit, in traditional surveys, that they watch porn, an analysis of Google searches demonstrates that the term *porn* is searched more often than *weather.*

Current moves in artificial intelligence and machine learning also enable systems themselves to identify things like hate speech, which allows online services like Facebook and Twitter to more easily tag speech that may be offensive or problematic in these and other respects. Of course, the algorithms are only as good as the data they're programmed with, and Google's "hate speech" detecting software has been criticized for being racially biased. By learning to identify words and phrases that have negative connotations or that are offensive in many contexts, including the n-word, Google's algorithm has flagged a lot of nonharmful speech, largely within African American communities.

Facebook has enhanced the algorithms it uses to identify and remove hate speech from its platform. However, as with Google, the system is not perfect. Although, in 2020, more posts than ever were removed by the software, it is unclear how many of those posts truly were hate speech. Moreover, a research study cited in *Wired* magazine on May 12, 2020, showed that Facebook's algorithms appeared to be more robust in removing racial and ethnic slurs than, say, misogynistic speech.

The **Computer Fraud and Abuse Act (CFAA)** of 1986 is a federal law that prohibits breaking into a computer system without authorization or in a manner that exceeds authorization (it was used to prosecute Lori Drew in the Megan Meier case, discussed in chapters 5 and 6). The CFAA has been amended a number of times and has raised consternation in terms of the harsh penalties it has imposed on those whose conduct is not particularly harmful or dangerous.

A highwater mark for the overcriminalization, or at least overpenalization, of those engaged in hacking as a matter of academic interest, and/or as part of internet activism, was the suicide of researcher Aaron Swartz following his arrest for infringing the CFAA in 2011. His crime was hacking into an academic database to download academic articles without paying for them. He faced up to thirty-five years in prison and up to $1 million in fines. His suicide led to the introduction of "Aaron's Law" before Congress in 2013—a bill intended to mitigate the harshness of the penalties that could be imposed for this kind of conduct by amending the CFAA. While the bill was never enacted, the fate of Aaron Swartz still informs discussions about the impact of the CFAA today.

The hackers who attempt to break into these massive databases may be motivated by financial gain: the possibility of stealing the data and selling it or using it for identity theft, fraud, and other nefarious purposes. However, some breaches are carried out purely for the challenge. In the early days of the internet, hackers were often computer science researchers or software enthusiasts who engaged in these activities to test the robustness of various systems. Some of these people were ultimately hired in-house to test systems for weaknesses.

While data breaches can be very harmful to individuals, particularly those who end up as victims of fraud and identity theft, it is often very difficult for companies to know that a system has been breached until after the fact and, even then, it can be challenging to identify the extent of the

THE IDENTITY THEFT ACT

Identity theft and **identity fraud** refer to crimes revolving around the theft of personal data in a manner that involves fraud or deceit, usually for economic gain—for example, setting up a bank account or filing a tax return for a refund in someone else's name. The terms are not limited to the digital world. You can commit identity theft by rummaging through a person's garbage and stealing old tax records or bank statements. This is why it is important to dispose of sensitive documents securely. Identity theft can even be done by listening to a person giving out credit card information over a telephone.

There are a number of state laws that criminalize these activities, but in 1998 a federal law was passed: the Identity Theft Act. Because there is no central government department focused on protecting individual identity or privacy, enforcement of this law is coordinated between the FTC, the FBI, the Secret Service, and the Postal Inspection Service. Other federal crimes are often also implicated in identity theft cases, including wire fraud, credit card fraud, and computer fraud under the CFAA.

damage. There are few laws addressing standards necessary to protect individual data outside some of the sector-specific laws discussed in other chapters of this book (e.g., chapter 6 on educational privacy, and chapters 9 and 10 on health and financial privacy). In many ways, the biggest incentive for companies to avoid data breaches is the fear of negative publicity if a breach comes to light. Of course, this creates a disincentive to report suspicions of data breaches.

In terms of legal recourse for individuals affected by a data breach, as we already know, there is no central government agency dealing with privacy concerns. The FBI does have the power to investigate and prosecute identity theft, to the extent its resources permit. And the FTC can take action against companies that fail to live up to their privacy policies. As we will see in chapter 10, the FTC also has the power to enforce the FCRA. When credit reports are compromised in a data breach, the FTC can also impose fines and settlements requiring companies to enhance their security measures and often to provide free credit reporting to affected individuals.

DATA BREACH NOTIFICATION

Many state laws and some federal laws require companies that have experienced a data breach to notify one or more government departments, as well as the individuals whose information may have been compromised. For example, under the Health Information Portability and Accountability Act (HIPAA, discussed in more detail in chapter 9), where a data breach involves health or medical information, any entity covered by the law must notify the affected individuals and the secretary of health and human services, and, if the breach affects more than five hundred people in a particular state, must also provide notice to prominent media outlets in the state.

The most dangerous breaches, and the ones that have risen exponentially in recent decades, involve health and financial information. Laws related to compilation and protection of this information are explained in more detail in chapters 9 and 10.

WHAT DO I DO IF MY DATA IS COMPROMISED?

Unfortunately, when your information is compromised in a data breach, even if you are notified of the breach by the entity that lost control of your data, a lot of the grunt work of monitoring and protecting your information will be your responsibility. Even when companies offer a period of free credit monitoring, it is wise to take your own precautions as well, which should certainly include changing passwords and PINs on your various accounts and services. You should also carefully monitor your bank and credit card statements for any irregularities, irrespective of other measures you may take, like credit freezes and credit alerts (discussed below, and in more detail in chapter 10).

Unfortunately, nothing you do will provide absolute protection against identity theft or fraud. However, knowing what possibilities are available may give you some comfort. Hopefully, the compromised business will offer some financial help with attempts to monitor and/or repair damaged credit. Whether the business ponies up to help or not, all consumers can check their credit reports for any signs of identity theft or fraud under the FCRA, which enables you to obtain a free credit report from each of the three major American credit agencies—Equifax, TransUnion, and Experian—once every twelve months to ensure that all information is accurate and up-to-date. And, yes, it is ironic that one of these very agencies suffered its own major breach in 2017—not a great endorsement of the security of our sensitive financial information.

You can also place a **credit freeze** on your credit reports at any time, which restricts access to any of your credit information under the FCRA. A freeze makes it much more difficult for anyone to attempt to open any new accounts in your name, because opening new accounts typically requires a bank or financial institution to check your credit report. However, if you want to open a new account yourself, you have to remove the freeze first. A credit freeze does not stop an identity thief from hacking into an existing account, but only makes it more difficult to open new accounts. A credit freeze, importantly, does not affect your credit rating (more on that in chapter 10). To implement a credit freeze, you must contact all three credit agencies individually, but it may be worth it for the peace of mind.

It is also possible to place a **fraud alert** on your credit reports. Unlike a freeze, you can implement a fraud alert by notifying any one of the three major credit reporting agencies (and then it must notify the other two). Fraud alerts last for only ninety days and must be renewed if there is a continuing concern about credit fraud. With a fraud alert in place, it may take longer for some lenders to approve new lines of credit, which can be problematic for anyone who requires instant lines of credit periodically, say, for business purposes.

Other actions you can take to protect your credit, and credit information, include filing taxes early to get the jump on anyone who may be attempting tax fraud in your name. The FTC also maintains an online service to help affected individuals report problems related to credit fraud or identity theft and create a tailored plan for addressing the problem. It provides comprehensive resources and step-by-step guides for addressing identity theft and fraud (see https://www.identitytheft.gov).

PRIVACY TIPS AND TRICKS

We've looked at lots of significant threats to personal data in this chapter and discussed the limited recourse that individuals may have in the event of, say, a large-scale data breach. However, there are some things you can, and probably should, do to minimize the chances of too much of your data being exposed to the risk of a breach. Many of these strategies focus on ways of limiting initial data collection because, once the data is out there, you cannot turn back the clock to prevent its misuse. Here are some concrete ideas worth considering:

+ Disable cookies in your computer settings where possible and don't "accept" cookies when a website asks you to do so. If the website won't work properly without accepting cookies, try to temporarily accept the cookies just for that single website and/or for the single session in which you are using the website—you can generally do this from the "settings" menu in your internet browser.

+ If your computer has a camera and microphone, place tape or some other cover over them when not in use, to prevent external parties from using them to monitor you when you're unaware of it. Some companies now sell stylish adhesive and clip-on plastic covers for laptop cameras and microphones.

+ Likewise, if you have a stand-alone camera and microphone that you attach to your computer, unplug it and put it in a box or drawer when not in use.

+ Carefully check the contract terms on data collection and use provided by the main websites and apps you use, and for any devices you purchase.

+ Take care to protect records of sensitive information. Do not throw bank statements, tax records, receipts, or similar documents in the trash, but dispose of them securely. There is no law stopping people from going through your garbage, and you don't want them to find your bank statements there.

+ Do not quote credit numbers over the phone in public places.

+ Protect your PINs and other sensitive numbers, codes, and passwords, especially when in public (e.g., using an ATM or public computer). Do not keep them written down where other people might see them—and if people stand behind you in line at the ATM, make sure they cannot see you typing your PIN.

Our Data in the Digital Marketplace

+ This should go without saying, but not enough of us probably do it regularly: *always* check your credit card statements (at least once a month, when the statement is issued) for any discrepancies. Even a small discrepancy may be a sign of a data leak.

+ Make sure you have activated any fraud alerts that your financial institutions and credit card providers may offer you.

+ If you are concerned that you may have been the subject of a data breach (or if you want to avoid the possibility), consider activating credit freezes and fraud alerts through the credit reporting agencies as discussed in this chapter.

+ Use robust passwords and PINs and change them periodically, especially after a data breach that may have compromised your personal information.

+ If you receive an email, text, or phone call (or other form of communication) seeking personal information about you or a close friend or family member, take all available steps to verify the identity of the person contacting you. Ask for verification or credentials and for a callback number or website where you can check their bona fides. Check with a lawyer or privacy expert before you divulge personal information if you are unsure of the identity or authority of the person seeking the information.

CHAPTER EIGHT

Our Data across the Pond

- + Data protection regulations in Europe
- + History of privacy in Europe
- + The "right to be forgotten"
- + Comparison of the United States and Europe in terms of data collection, access, and use
- + Impact of European regulations on American consumers and businesses
- + European Convention on Human Rights
- + International Covenant on Civil and Political Rights
- + Foreign Intelligence Surveillance Act

In July 2020, the Court of Justice of the European Union (CJEU), the court that interprets EU laws, held that the existing EU-U.S. Privacy Shield was invalid because it failed to adequately comply with EU privacy rights. The Privacy Shield Framework had been finalized in 2016, as a successor to the earlier EU-U.S. Safe Harbor program, as a way for American businesses engaged in commerce with the European Union to ensure safe and secure data flows under EU law.

The application of the Safe Harbor, and later the Privacy Shield Framework, to airlines was especially important in the wake of the 9/11 terrorist attacks. Some international commerce requires the sharing of personal information about customers, employees, or others. Without a general framework in place, each individual company dealing with EU residents' data would need to individually comply with European privacy laws. With the Privacy Shield Framework in place, companies could simply follow preset standards and self-certify compliance.

A program like the Privacy Shield is especially helpful to smaller organizations that can save significant resources by simply complying with the requirements of the framework, rather than having to use their own resources to develop individual policies and procedures to comply with both U.S. and EU law. The Privacy Shield allowed companies to self-certify that they were complying with privacy protection requirements that met the standards under EU law. Over five thousand companies had joined the program by the time it was struck down.

The CJEU held that a number of American surveillance laws were in conflict with EU residents' privacy rights, noting that U.S. laws allowed for surveillance of individual data in ways that were not necessary and proportional to the purposes of the data collection. An important tenet of EU privacy law is that data collection is limited to the purposes for which the data is collected, and that no entities (government or private) can collect data more broadly without individual consent. The court also found that remedies for breaching data-protective laws in the United States were inadequate to meet EU standards. This should come as no surprise to anyone who has read the preceding chapters.

The case originally arose when an Austrian citizen, Maximilian Schrems, complained that Facebook Ireland was sharing his personal data with the American government under U.S. law, in contravention of EU privacy protections. The particular American laws in question were Section 702 of the **Foreign Intelligence Surveillance Act (FISA)** and a 1981 executive order on foreign intelligence gathering for national security purposes. The case had made its way through the European courts for a number of years before the final decision on the Privacy Shield in 2020. That decision took immediate effect, with no grace period for companies to retool their policies and practices to provide stronger protections for EU residents' data.

In the wake of the decision, companies that had contractual privacy terms in place that sufficiently protect the data of EU residents could rely on those terms to avoid infringing European regulations. However, companies that had not developed their own detailed privacy policies because they relied on the shorthand self-certification under the Privacy Shield would have to go to the immediate cost and effort of developing those protections.

The problem for American companies, and for those whose data is collected by them, is that American companies are required to comply with U.S. surveillance laws—the ones that proved problematic in the eyes of the CJEU. So, simply ensuring that contractual provisions are in place to comply with European laws will not necessarily provide the level of privacy protection required under those laws. It's a Catch-22: American entities that gather data from European residents (customers, suppliers, employees, etc.) are damned if they do and damned if they don't. They can have all the privacy policies in place they want, but if the U.S. intelligence laws require them to hand over information to the government, they could infringe European laws in the process.

While a detailed discussion of the uneasy relationship on data privacy between the United States and Europe is beyond the scope of this book, it is important to look at why and how the European laws on individual data privacy differ so significantly from those in the United States. These fundamental differences in approach create challenges for entities that engage in cross-border commerce and other interactions involving European residents. Many American customers of online service providers, for example, saw swift and detailed changes in data privacy policies in the wake of the 2020 CJEU decision.

WHY SHOULD WE WORRY ABOUT EUROPEAN PRIVACY LAW?

If it is not yet obvious, privacy regulation is a very nation-specific issue. Even within a nation, laws may vary widely: as we've already seen, various states in America have stronger privacy laws than exist at the federal level. Think about California's Consumer Privacy Act, for example. That law actually has more in common with European law than with U.S. federal law.

But why should Americans care about European law? For one thing, European law can impact how American businesses operate with respect to data privacy, as illustrated in the opening example in this chapter. For another, the countries of the European Union, and in some respects Europe more generally, are widely regarded as the leaders in data privacy protection laws. The laws of those countries are increasingly held up as the global standard in a digitally connected world.

American lawmakers, as well as those in many other countries, increasingly look to Europe for guidance as to the most effective approaches for protecting individual privacy. Of course, this is not to say that the European position is perfect, or that it will suit every country, but it has been developed over many decades, and has received significant press coverage as it evolves to meet the needs of the digital age. For those reasons, it is worth spending a little time thinking about how European countries have addressed data protection, notably in the digital age. If this isn't something you are particularly interested in, feel free to skip this chapter. However, considering the position on privacy in other countries (in particular, European countries) can be a useful exercise in thinking about different frameworks for data protection generally, and possible future avenues American lawmakers might take.

A BRIEF HISTORY OF EUROPEAN DATA PROTECTION REGULATION

The focus on data protection throughout Europe can be traced back to World War II, during which the German government, in particular, targeted certain groups for horrific treatment, including genocide. After the war, when discussions of reparations, redressing of war crimes, and human rights violations took center stage at the international level, much thought was given to the potentially devastating results of the collection of personal data about individuals and groups that could be used to target those groups. We see similar issues arising in the United States today in relation to issues like racial profiling in the criminal justice context.

In many ways, modern-day privacy regulations throughout Europe derive from the **United Nations Declaration of Human Rights**, adopted in 1948. Many of its key provisions were restated in the 1976 **International Covenant on Civil and Political Rights (ICCPR)**. Article 12 of the Declaration specifically enshrines a right to privacy: "No one shall be subjected to arbitrary interference with his privacy, family, home or correspondence, nor to attacks upon his honour [sic] and reputation. Everyone has the right to the protection of the law against such interference or attacks."

Although the United States signed the Declaration of Human Rights, its provisions have never been implemented into national law in the United States. Because the Supreme Court has expressly held that rights set out in the Declaration do not apply in the absence of an implementing law, the Declaration largely stands for ideals the government has supported, without giving them any particular teeth in a legal sense.

By contrast, not only have European countries individually adopted privacy rights into their own domestic laws, but the 1953 **European Convention on Human Rights (ECHR)** also specifically adopts a right to privacy in very similar terms to those set out in the UN Declaration. Article 8 of the ECHR states:

1. Everyone has the right to respect for his private and family life, his home and his correspondence.

2. There shall be no interference by a public authority with the exercise of this right except such as is in accordance with the law and is necessary in a democratic society in the interests of national security, public safety or the economic well-being of the country, for the prevention of disorder or crime, for the protection of health or morals, or for the protection of the rights and freedoms of others.

Unlike the United States, the European countries accept privacy as a basic human right, and balance it against the other values set out in Article 8(2) of the ECHR: protection of public safety and security, health, and other freedoms. That sets a very different stage for privacy protection in European countries than is the case in the United States. It is against this backdrop— privacy as a basic human right—that more detailed data privacy laws have developed and become harmonized under the rubric of the European Union.

Like the ICCPR, the ECHR generally does not automatically become effective as national law without most European countries implementing its provisions into their own national laws. However, as noted above, many European countries had already enacted privacy protections in the years after World War II. Additionally, EU member countries are required to strengthen those laws to comply with the realities of the digital world by virtue of the General Data Protection Regulation.

GENERAL DATA PROTECTION REGULATION

While many European countries historically had, and continue to have, their own national data privacy laws, the advent of the European Union (initially the European Economic Community, or EEC) led to much greater harmonization of those laws. The idea behind the EEC, later subsumed into the European Union, was to create a single, harmonized internal market between member countries, doing away with taxes and tariffs across national borders and ultimately adopting a single currency, the Euro. With the harmonized trading area came the realization that data protection should be accepted as an important aspect of the process, because trade involves cross-border data exchanges.

In 1995, the European Union's Data Protection Directive was implemented: the first attempt at a broadly harmonized regulation to protect data privacy across EU countries. The Directive was superseded by the General Data Protection Regulation (GDPR) in 2016, which came into effect in 2018. The idea behind the GDPR was to update and streamline the operation of the Directive, especially with respect to digital-age developments, and to give EU countries less discretion over implementation. The Regulation also imposes more significant penalties for those who gather or disseminate personal data in contravention of its provisions.

Key features of the GDPR include the focus on a "consent" model of information exchanges, and transparency with respect to collection and processing of an individual's data. The GDPR prohibits collection and processing of most categories of personal information without specific consent from the individuals in question. Greater protections are extended to particularly sensitive categories of data, such as information about an individual's race and ethnic origin, religious or philosophical beliefs, political opinions, trade union memberships, biometric data, genetic data, health information, and information related to one's sex life, gender identity, and/or sexual orientation.

The GDPR also limits data processing to legitimate reasons, as well as prohibiting the collection of data—particularly sensitive data—outside the original purposes for collecting it. The Regulation applies to any entity that collects data, including large and small companies and government departments. For better or worse, it creates a one-size-fits-all model, unlike the situation in the United States.

The GDPR also provides significant rights to individuals with respect to their personal information after it has been collected. An entire chapter

ONE-SIZE-FITS-ALL ISN'T GOOD NEWS FOR EVERYONE

A 2020 report by the European Commission evaluating the GDPR noted the challenges reported by smaller companies in complying with many of its provisions. Small and medium-sized companies often do not have the resources that larger companies enjoy to employ data protection personnel and to develop technological and other systems for protecting customer, employee, and others' data in compliance with the GDPR. The European Commission noted that it would not be appropriate to give smaller entities more leeway in complying with the law, because the size of the company does not correlate to the risks inherent in processing of individual data. Small companies may sometimes, in fact, present greater risks to customers, employees, and others exactly because they cannot spare the resources to ensure adequate data protection.

The European Commission recommended that the solution is an expanded role for local/national data protection agencies that can provide practical tools to help smaller entities comply with the GDPR—like training courses, templates for processing contracts and personal records, and hotlines for consultation. The Commission noted that the European Union has funded a number of these initiatives, and there is a hope that these national/local approaches will be relatively harmonized as they become more widespread to prevent barriers to, and inconsistencies in, cross-border commerce and other activities.

(chap. 3) of the Regulation is devoted to individual rights with respect to data after it has been collected. Under these provisions, any entity that gathers personal data is required to do so—and to make records available—in a transparent, concise, and easy-to-understand manner. Entities that collect data have the obligation to inform individuals about what data is being collected and why, as well as whom the data might be shared with and how long it will be stored. They must also inform individuals about how to access, check, and rectify mistakes in data collected (including completing incomplete information), and where and how to lodge complaints.

Our Data across the Pond

Where personal information is being processed through artificial intelligence or machine learning, individuals also have the right to obtain "meaningful information about the logic involved, as well as the significance and envisaged consequences of such processing."[1] Companies operating under the GDPR are required to have dedicated "data protection officers" in place to monitor compliance with the regulations and to oversee complaints about data collection, use, and processing.

Individuals are also given specific rights under the GDPR to inspect and rectify records about them, as well as to obtain information about how data is being collected and used. If data is to be shared outside the European Union, individuals are also entitled to be informed about the safeguards that will be put in place to maintain the security of the relevant information. This is one reason that the failure of the EU-U.S. Privacy Shield has been problematic. Now, each company must individually make sure it complies with this requirement, rather than being able to rely on a standardized self-certification process.

The "Right to Be Forgotten"

One interesting feature of the GDPR, which originally arose under the prior Data Protection Directive, has become known as the **right to be forgotten**. This phrase is really a misnomer, because the right set out in the Directive, and now enshrined in Article 17 of the GDPR, is actually a right to have outdated, inaccurate, harmful, or misleading information erased or suppressed. It is not a right to delete all records about an individual. Under Article 17, a person can seek erasure of data only on the following grounds:

+ The information is no longer necessary in light of the purposes for which it was originally collected.

+ The individual has withdrawn consent to processing of the data (where there are no other grounds, like national security, justifying the use of the data).

+ The individual objects to the data processing in the absence of overriding legitimate reasons for processing (like health, national security, public interest, etc.).

+ The information has been unlawfully processed.

Our Data across the Pond

While some American laws allow individuals to inspect and correct information about themselves (e.g., the Fair Credit Reporting Act, discussed in chapter 10), few, if any, provide a right to erasure of information like the European Union's right to be forgotten. Because this right was such a novel concept when first introduced, it caused a lot of consternation for American companies operating in Europe. In particular, social media networks and other platforms that rely on user-generated content were heavily impacted.

Google was one of the most high-profile companies to be sued under the right to be forgotten in the days of the Data Protection Directive. Throughout Europe, many people had complained in national courts about Google search results prioritizing old and embarrassing information about them. Many of those complaining argued that, under the right to be forgotten, Google should be required to adjust its search algorithm to effectively "forget" this information—in other words, suppress it from search results.

A landmark case hit the CJEU in 2014, involving a Spanish national, Mario Costeja González, who complained that Google search results on his name prioritized a link to a newspaper listing of a bankruptcy sale from more than ten years earlier. The prioritizing of this listing on the first page of the Google search results (in Spain) was embarrassing to him personally and professionally, so he brought an action, originally in the Spanish courts, to have both the newspaper's website and Google remove the listing from online access. Both Google's American head office and its Spanish subsidiary (Google Spain) were parties to the action.

Google argued that an internet search engine should not be considered a "data processor" under EU law, and so the company should not face any legal liability. The CJEU disagreed: the court held that Google was indeed processing individual data as defined by the Directive, which was still in force at the time. The same reasoning applies under similar provisions in the GDPR today. The decision in the *González* case opened the door for many online platforms that handle personal data to potentially be held liable for violations of EU data privacy laws.

Companies like Google, Facebook, Wikipedia, and YouTube all process large volumes of personal information and have argued that they have very little control over what information is accessible through their services. Google, in particular, as a search engine merely indexes, largely through

WHY IS GOOGLE A "DATA PROCESSOR" UNDER EU LAW?

It may seem odd to think of Google (or Facebook or Wikipedia) as a "data processor," and it is beyond the scope of this chapter to go into the detailed definitions of the specialized terms used in the Data Protection Directive and GDPR—terms like *data, data processor,* and *data controller.* However, it is worth noting that the Directive and the GDPR define these terms fairly broadly, and those broad definitions have been supported by CJEU decisions.

In an early case under the Data Protection Directive in 2003, the *Bodil Lindqvist* case (no. C-101/01), for example, the European Court of Justice (as the CJEU used to be known) was asked to consider whether a church employee in Sweden had infringed the provisions of local law complying with the Directive. The employee had posted the names and telephone numbers of parishioners preparing for confirmation on a church website, along with the occasional piece of personal information related to work, hobbies, and the like, often in a humorous way. The parishioners objected to the availability of this information, and ultimately the court was asked to decide whether the Directive had been infringed.

The court considered the Directive's definitions of *personal data* and *processing* of data and concluded that the church employee had infringed the law. Personal data includes any information "relating to an identified or identifiable natural person" both under the Directive and the later GDPR. Information including names, telephone numbers, jobs, and hobbies clearly fell under that definition.

"Data processing" includes any operation or set of operations performed on personal data, whether by automatic means or not. The court held that loading the information into a computer page accessible to people connected to the internet *did* amount to processing for these purposes. This early holding perhaps clarifies why a company like Google, Facebook, or Wikipedia can be regarded as an entity that processes personal data under the Data Protection Directive and the GDPR.

HOW DO SEARCH ENGINES AND SOCIAL MEDIA COMPLY WITH THE
RIGHT TO BE FORGOTTEN?

Google and other online entities, in the wake of the *González* decision,
implemented systems that enable individuals to complain about information appearing on their platforms, usually by filling out an online form. Personnel at the relevant company then consider the complaint and decide
whether or not to suppress the information in question from search results
or other webpages.

   If you want to see what the complaint forms look like, it is easy enough
to do a quick search online. Google, for example, uses a specific complaint
form for each of its online services, so an individual may have to fill out a
number of forms if the concern is about information that appears on a
variety of platforms. The Google Search Engine privacy form, at least at the
time of this writing, asks for the individual's geographic location, name,
and contact details, as well as links to the specific URLs that contain the
information in question. Then there is a box in which to explain the nature
of the complaint: why the person thinks Google should remove the link to
the URLs. The form itself does not say precisely how Google processes
requests or if/when the person complaining will hear back from Google.
There is also no clear process of appeal or complaint: Google has sole discretion as to whether or not to remove particular material, although failing
to do so may, of course, subject Google to legal liability under European
privacy law.

software algorithms, information on the internet. Social media platforms
like Facebook, and user-generated information services like Wikipedia,
have argued that they are in much the same situation. Requiring them to
monitor everything posted on their platforms for potential violations of data
privacy law would impose a tremendous financial burden.

   Leaders of those companies have also complained that the costs of
implementing personnel to process and respond to requests to remove particular information are exorbitant and unreasonable, and an unfair burden

to place on them. Moreover, commentators have suggested that to give social media companies and search engines the power to decide what information is and is not made available to the public is to misplace the power of censorship in those entities.[2] This concern definitely arose in a different context when President Trump was permanently banned from Twitter in early January 2021 for infringing its terms of service. He claimed, in response, that the social media companies had too much censorship power, without the responsibilities of traditional media organizations.

Geographic Scope of the GDPR

The 2014 CJEU decision, and subsequent implementation of the GDPR, raised the question of whether the right to be forgotten applies only to search engines in EU countries or may have broader reach, outside those countries, to apply to information about EU residents and citizens accessed elsewhere in the world. In the wake of the 2014 decision, nothing was stopping people in the European Union from using proxy servers to trick systems into believing they were situated outside Europe, thereby accessing "erased" information. A 2019 decision of the CJEU clarified that the GDPR applies only inside the European Union, maintaining the existing position that internet users can access very different search results depending on the jurisdiction in which they perform a search (or the proxy server they use).[3]

WHAT CAN AMERICA LEARN FROM THE EUROPEAN DATA PROTECTION EXPERIENCE?

This brief survey of European attitudes toward and approaches to protecting personal information brings the clear differences from the U.S. experience into sharp relief. Many applaud the European approach as being revolutionary in keeping personal data protection at the forefront of digital legal developments, and ensuring a more appropriate balance between privacy and other interests (like free speech and national security) than had occurred in other parts of the world. Others criticize the European Union for overregulating and imposing unnecessary obstacles on businesses and others, particularly those trying to innovate online.

Some American states have attempted to take a leaf from the European book—for example, California's Consumer Protection Act is the first truly

AN AMERICAN "PRIVACY BILL OF RIGHTS"?

Given all the movement in Europe toward protecting personal privacy in the digital age, it is unsurprising that discussions have also taken place in the United States about a more comprehensive federal approach to personal privacy for the twenty-first century. Nothing comprehensive at the federal level has yet been implemented, although there have been lots of suggestions made and bills introduced into Congress.

Advocates of the idea of more comprehensive privacy protection in the United States often use the names "Consumer Privacy Bill of Rights" and "Internet Bill of Rights" to refer to the various bills that have been proposed over the years. These proposals contemplate issues like data security (businesses protecting personal information in their systems), transparency (businesses being more up-front about letting consumers know what data they hold and share), access (limitations on how much businesses can share personal information), consent (the idea of individuals being required to opt in and affirmatively consent to collection, use, and sharing of personal data), and accountability (government enforcement of these initiatives).

In 2015, the Obama administration put forward a Consumer Privacy Bill of Rights to create an American law along similar lines to the GDPR in Europe. The bill included provisions for opting out if personal data is used unreasonably; limiting information use to the purposes for which it was initially provided; deletion or de-identification of data; security measures for personal data; and the development of a code of conduct for handling personal data in some industries.

Many industries objected to this approach, noting the time and resources that would have to be devoted to complying with it, and the potential for stifling competition or innovation. It will be interesting to see if future federal administrations have the time or the inclination to revive this initiative and, if so, what form it might take.

comprehensive U.S. privacy law. Many other states have either shied away from broad privacy protections, choosing instead to take little action or to limit action to areas of particular concern, like Illinois's Biometric Information Privacy Act (discussed in chapter 4). This law is indeed revolutionary, but it only protects biometric information like fingerprints, DNA, and faceprints.

Historically, the United States has approached privacy on a piecemeal, sectoral basis, at least at the federal level. The U.S. Congress, for example, has been comparatively reluctant to enact comprehensive privacy-protecting laws. The key areas of sectoral information protection have been in health and financial services, and these are the subjects of the following chapters. However, in recent years, as public concerns about election interference and health data privacy (especially in regard to contact tracing) have taken center stage, Congress has become more focused on considering far-reaching data protection measures. Interestingly, some federal moves seem to be mirroring actions already taken at the state level. In August 2020, for example, a bill was introduced in Congress for a national biometric information privacy law, modeled on the Illinois statute.[4] In some ways, it appears that state laws are becoming the testing ground for possible federal developments.

PRIVACY TIPS AND TRICKS

Unlike the preceding ones, this chapter has not really provided a basis for any privacy protection tips or tricks. Of course, if you are in an EU country or another jurisdiction with privacy protections stronger than those in the United States, you may be able to avail yourself of laws and business procedures that protect your personal information there. However, companies like Google, Facebook, and Wikipedia are not required to extend the same privacy protections to American residents. This is one reason why a search results page on Google can look completely different from its U.S. counterpart when you type in a particular person's name as a search term. If that person has made a "right to be forgotten" request in Europe, the European internet searcher will likely see significantly less, or less damaging, information about the person than the internet searcher in the United States.

Of course, those of us in the United States can engage in **search engine optimization (SEO)** technologies to sanitize our search results, and we may even hire **reputation protection experts** to ensure that those searching for us online in the United States do not find damaging or embarrassing information about us prioritized in search results. SEO involves techniques for ensuring that certain information is prioritized in search results—for example, use of particular meta-tags and keywords when setting up a website. Businesses use SEO to try to have their webpages prioritized over those of their competitors in search results. SEO can also be used to make sure that "positive" information about you is prioritized over "negative" information.

For those without the technological expertise to engage in these practices on their own behalf, a whole industry has developed to help—for a fee, of course. All you have to do is Google "reputation defender services" and you will find a whole list of companies that will help you protect or sanitize your online reputation. One of the earliest players in this space is Reputation Defender (https://www.reputationdefender.com), which touts itself as having "pioneered" the "online reputation management space." You can take a look at their website to get an idea of the services they provide.

The development, and success, of such businesses should serve as another reminder that even where a legal right may not be available to protect aspects of your privacy online, there are often technological solutions that do not rely on establishing a legal right to protection of your reputation. The law is only one avenue for those concerned about protecting their privacy online. Hopefully, this book is highlighting that, even when there are few or no legal protections available, there are often practical steps you can take to protect your information from prying digital eyes.

CHAPTER NINE

Our Data and Our Health

+ Federal health and genetic information privacy laws
+ Health information data breaches
+ COVID-19 and public health emergency challenges for privacy
+ Commercial DNA registries and privacy concerns
+ Digital and robotic healthcare devices and consumer privacy
+ Federal healthcare privacy regulators
+ Employer-provided health insurance and privacy of medical records

In 2011, the health system of the University of California, Los Angeles, was fined almost a million dollars and agreed to implement a corrective action plan to settle complaints that its employees had improperly accessed and disclosed the health records of a number of celebrities, including Tom Cruise and Britney Spears. The State of California had also fined the hospital system for similar employee conduct in relation to private health records pertaining to Michael Jackson (both before and after his death). Health information about celebrities is obviously valuable in the celebrity gossip market. By contrast, we may ask whether we should have similar concerns about our own personal health information, given that members of the tabloid press are not likely to be particularly interested in whether any of *us* have a broken leg or a difficult pregnancy, or in any other medical condition that we may prefer to keep private.

But do we wonder, or care, who outside our own hospital network can legally access our health and genetic information and what they are legally permitted to do with it? Health information is one of those areas where the American sectoral approach to data privacy at the federal level comes to the fore. As noted in previous chapters, the United States does not have a comprehensive federal law to protect our data privacy, but there are some laws aimed at protecting specific aspects of our personal information. These areas include health, genetic, and financial information. (We have previously considered the extent to which federal law attempts to protect information about children and students in chapters 5 and 6.)

One disadvantage of the American sectoral approach to the protection of particularly sensitive health and financial information is that the focus on key players in the industry (e.g., hospitals and medical insurance companies in the case of health information) limits the reach of the protections. As new technologies hit the market, like health and fitness applications marketed by private companies, the laws fail to extend to data collected and aggregated through those devices. By contrast, a comprehensive privacy law, like the General Data Protection Regulation (GDPR) in the European Union, automatically extends to most new technological developments that enable increased data collation and use.

In the United States, the major law related to health information is the **Health Insurance Portability and Accountability Act** of 1996 (**HIPAA**), which has been amended several times since the 1990s to take account of new developments in technology for health information sharing, including the advent of electronic health records. Alongside HIPAA, some other laws protect particular aspects of health and related information. One example is the **Genetic Information Nondiscrimination Act** of 2008 (**GINA**), which is more of an antidiscrimination law than a privacy law. This statute limits uses of genetic information to discriminate against individuals, particularly in the context of employment decisions (hiring, firing, promotion, etc.).

In the employment context, other laws do attempt to prevent discrimination on grounds that may be connected to health information—including some of the laws mentioned in chapter 4. However, these laws deal with actual discrimination rather than infringements of personal privacy in the abstract. As discussed in this book's introduction, a number of scholars and lawmakers argue that it is more effective to target laws at prohibiting things like discrimination that cause specific harm, rather than focusing on more abstract encroachments, or privacy in and of itself. That may be a significant reason why American lawmakers have not been particularly willing to create a more comprehensive data privacy law at the federal level, despite experiments at the state level like California's Consumer Privacy Act.

This chapter will introduce HIPAA and its privacy requirements in relation to medical records, including the limitations of this law in protecting privacy. Because the law is fairly complex, the discussion is somewhat simplified but should serve the purposes of those seeking to better understand their rights under the law in relation to privacy. We will also discuss recent technological developments in healthcare devices (Fitbits, genetic testing, home healthcare robots, etc.) as well as the current piecemeal regulation of these devices with respect to consumer privacy. The chapter concludes with a survey of the laws on privacy rights in relation to genetic information and the impact of GINA and other legal developments in that context.

AN INTRODUCTION TO HIPAA AND PHI

Everyone has probably heard of HIPAA, and most people know it has something to do with the privacy of our health information. However, it is a fairly complex law that has been updated a number of times, largely to take account of digital developments. Outside of signing HIPAA privacy notices at the doctor's office, most of us probably do not think much about what the law does for us, and what our rights are in relation to our health information.

The fact that most of us have signed those HIPAA consent forms at the doctor's office should immediately demonstrate that, like most American legal approaches to privacy, HIPAA relies on a "notice and consent" model to allow players in the health industry to share information. If you refuse to grant consent to information sharing, you may not receive treatment in many American medical facilities.

But what are you actually consenting to, and why?

Concerned about the threat to individual privacy posed by widespread sharing of health information in the 1990s, Congress created four administrative standards or rules for use of this kind of information under HIPAA: the Privacy Rule, the Security Rule, the Breach Notification Rule, and the Transactions Rule.

The Privacy Rule requires appropriate safeguards for using and disclosing **personal health information (PHI)** as well as giving individuals the right to access and check the accuracy of their PHI. The Security Rule requires entities that collect and store PHI to implement appropriate safeguards to protect the information. The Breach Notification Rule requires actions to be taken in case of a data breach, including notifying relevant government departments. The Transactions Rule imposes safeguards in relation to digital information exchanges, such as health insurance claims and payments.

The **Department of Health and Human Services (DHHS)** has the main administrative responsibilities over HIPAA, and the website of the DHHS's Office for Civil Rights provides up-to-date information on individual health privacy rights, explained in simple terms, including simple procedures for anyone who wants to file a HIPAA complaint for misuse of PHI (see https:// www.hhs.gov/hipaa/index.html). This information is provided in multiple languages for increased accessibility.

The two HIPAA rules that are probably of most relevance to individuals concerned about the privacy of their health and medical records are the Privacy Rule and the Breach Notification Rule, because those are the rules that give particular rights to individuals both to check their health records and to learn whether their data may have been breached. In terms of who can access your information without specific consent, HIPAA generally limits information sharing to those who are directly involved in your medical care, such as healthcare providers and health insurance companies. But HIPAA's coverage in this regard is more limited than many people would expect.

The health entities or **covered entities** that have to comply with HIPAA include health insurance plans, healthcare clearinghouses (independent third-party companies that process health information), and most health-care providers (hospitals and medical offices). "Business associates" of these kinds of companies are also covered—they are defined as service providers to covered entities. Business associates include those who provide things like payment services, claims processing, data analysis, billing, e-prescription gateways, legal services, actuarial or accounting services, financial services, and benefits management. A subcontractor of a business associate is typically also a business associate under HIPAA.

Entities that may have access to your health information, likely because you have provided it to them, and that are *not* covered by HIPAA include life insurers, employers (for the most part—see "Employers and HIPAA"), most schools and school districts, most state agencies (e.g., child protective services), most law enforcement agencies, and municipal offices. Direct-to-consumer businesses like genetic sequencing companies (e.g., 23andMe),

WHAT EXACTLY IS PERSONAL HEALTH INFORMATION?

The law defines PHI as **individually identifiable health information** that is stored or transmitted in any medium, and **electronic PHI (or ePHI)** as PHI that is maintained or transmitted electronically. Under the law, individually identifiable health information includes information that is created or received by a healthcare provider, health insurance plan, employer, public health authority, life insurance provider, school or university, or healthcare clearinghouse and that relates to issues including (a) a past, present, or future physical or mental health condition, including genetic information; (b) the provision of healthcare to an individual; or (c) the past, present, or future payment for healthcare.

To come under the definition of PHI or ePHI, the information must be of a kind that identifies or could reasonably be used to identify a particular individual. As with other categories of personal information protected under federal laws in the United States, general demographic information that has been anonymized will typically not meet the definition of PHI or ePHI.

PHI usually comprises a combination of (a) information your doctors, nurses, and other healthcare providers include in your medical record; (b) conversations your doctor may have about your care or treatment with nurses and others; (c) information about you in your health insurer's computer system; (d) billing information about you at your clinic or doctor's office; and (e) other information compiled by a covered entity or business associate that individually identifies you.

weight loss services, gyms, and providers of devices (e.g., Fitbits) are not covered by HIPAA and are not bound by its requirements to protect confidential health information.

Who Is Permitted to Share Your Information under HIPAA?

HIPAA closely regulates the uses and disclosures that can be made of PHI, which is good news for health information privacy advocates, but the downside is that the law applies only to covered entities. Many companies that

EMPLOYERS AND HIPAA

Generally speaking, employers are not covered entities or business associates under HIPAA even if they sponsor an employee health plan. The plans that employers sponsor typically *are* covered entities, although there are some exceptions. An employer's self-funded group health plan that does not rely on a third-party administrator and has fewer than fifty employees is not a covered entity under HIPAA and does not have to comply with the HIPAA rules. While your healthcare provider and health insurance provider may be limited in what information they can share with your employer, the opposite is not necessarily true. Your employer may be able to share some of your personally identifying information with a health insurance provider, depending on your contract with your employer.

share health information, including private DNA registries like 23andMe and Ancestry.com, are not regulated by HIPAA.

Under HIPAA, in the absence of specific consent to use or share information, covered entities can make only the following uses or disclosures of PHI:

+ Disclosures to an individual about their own health information
+ Uses or disclosures of information for treatment, payment, or healthcare operations
+ Uses or disclosures that may be required by law (e.g., in the case of court proceedings)
+ Some disclosures for public purposes, such as reporting victims of abuse, neglect, or domestic violence; some research purposes; and other governmental purposes
+ Use of de-identified information for research or public health purposes
+ Use of de-identified demographic information for certain fundraising activities

HIPAA and the Coronavirus Pandemic

During the COVID-19 pandemic, the Office for Civil Rights at the DHHS released clarification of the kinds of disclosures of PHI that are likely to occur in the prevention and treatment of the virus and that are permissible under HIPAA. In particular, a covered entity can share information about an individual's infection with or exposure to the virus with law enforcement, paramedics, other first responders and state public health authorities in various circumstances. For example, disclosure of information about COVID-19 exposure may be made when the information is needed to provide treatment (e.g., by medical transport personnel), when a state law requires reporting of confirmed cases (e.g., for admission to a hospital), to notify a public health authority (e.g., the Centers for Disease Control and Prevention, or CDC), and to state, tribal, local, and territorial public health departments who need the information to prevent or control the spread of the disease.

In April 2020, the Office for Civil Rights also announced that it will not impose penalties for violations of certain aspects of the HIPAA Privacy Rule for good-faith uses and disclosures of PHI by a covered entity for public health and health oversight activities during the coronavirus public health emergency. Examples of good-faith uses include those made to the CDC or a state public health authority in order to prevent or control the spread of COVID-19, and to the Centers for Medicare and Medicaid Services or similar state health oversight agencies in order to provide assistance to the healthcare system as it responds to the pandemic.

Prohibited Disclosures of Health Information

Some uses and disclosures of your PHI are always prohibited under HIPAA, including any use or disclosure of genetic information for underwriting purposes and most sales of PHI for commercial profit. Disclosures of information for employment-related actions or decisions are typically also not permitted unless specific consent has been obtained by the individual in question. Genetic information is specially protected by GINA, which prohibits using genetic information to make determinations about eligibility for health benefits, to compute premium or contribution amounts under a health plan, or to discriminate in the provision of health insurance coverage on the basis of a preexisting condition.

EMPLOYERS AND COVID

While HIPAA does restrict uses and disclosures of information that would include information about individuals' contact with the COVID-19 virus, it is again important to remember the limitations on those who are covered by HIPAA. For example, employers who learn that particular employees have been exposed to the virus or tested positive for the virus are usually not constrained by HIPAA. Employers may not be entitled to obtain PHI related to coronavirus exposure from employees' doctors or insurance companies without consent, but if an employer otherwise knows of an infected or exposed employee (through, say, self-reporting by the employee), the employer is not prohibited from sharing the information with other employees under HIPAA. Other privacy laws may come into play—as may antidiscrimination laws, if an employer discriminated against an employee because of exposure to the virus—but HIPAA generally has no role to play here. Additionally, if the employer breaches any employment or other contracts in sharing such information, it may face contractual liability.

HIPAA also includes what is known as a "minimum necessary standard" for disclosures of any health information even when permitted, which is similar to the stance taken toward personal information generally under the GDPR (see chapter 8). The rule is that when a covered entity or business associate discloses information for a permissible purpose, it must disclose the *minimum amount of information necessary* to accomplish the intended purpose, unless the individual in question has authorized the disclosure of more information or the disclosure is required by law.

Your Rights under HIPAA
Your rights under HIPAA in relation to your PHI are also similar to the rights that EU residents receive over their personal information generally (see chapter 8). These include the right to review your health records; the right to correct inaccuracies in your health records; the right to receive a notice telling you how your PHI will be used/shared; the right to obtain a report on

Our Data and Our Health

how or why particular information was shared; and the right to file a complaint with a healthcare provider or insurer, or with the relevant government authority (i.e., DHHS).

HIPAA Privacy Rule

HIPAA's Privacy Rule is probably the most important part of HIPAA for those of us concerned with our health information privacy. Under the Privacy Rule, we have the right to obtain our medical records (both hard copy and electronic records), ensure that our PHI has been recorded correctly, and find out who else may have seen our PHI. If an error is found in a health record, the healthcare provider is required to remedy it. If the healthcare provider disagrees about whether the record is correct, the disagreement must be noted in the file.

All entities covered by HIPAA must provide individuals with notices of privacy practices—these are the forms given to you when you first make an appointment with a new medical professional. It's always best to read them and try to understand them. Additionally, the Privacy Rule requires covered entities to appoint a designated privacy officer in-house to develop and implement PHI policies and procedures and to train their workforce in those policies and procedures. That person may be a starting point within the organization if you have a privacy complaint.

The first notice you sign should include details about how your PHI may be used, the rights you have to check your PHI and correct it, and the duties owed to you to protect and maintain the accuracy of your PHI. The notice should clearly describe the nature of any information collection, use, or sharing, including uses of the information necessary for your healthcare and any additional uses that may be contemplated.

The form you sign is required to be written in plain English and to clearly explain

+ the types of uses/disclosures of your personal information the entity is authorized to make under the law without your specific consent (e.g., uses for treatment or payment);
+ any other circumstances in which the entity may be allowed or required to disclose your PHI without specific consent (e.g., legal purposes);

+ any legal prohibitions or limitations on uses of your PHI; and

+ any uses or disclosures of PHI that require your authorization, including an explanation of how to revoke your authorization of such uses.

It must also set out your rights with respect to PHI and explain how to exercise them. These include the rights to restrict particular uses of your PHI; to receive communications about your PHI; to inspect, copy, and correct PHI; to learn who has seen your PHI; and to obtain a paper copy of your PHI, even if you initially agreed to electronic notices.

Finally, the notice must explain the entity's obligations with respect to your information, including its duties to maintain the privacy and security of the information, to explain its privacy practices regarding PHI, to notify individuals if their PHI has been breached (see next section), and to describe how any changes in its privacy policy will be communicated. The notice should also explain how privacy complaints will be handled, with details of whom to contact and how to lodge a complaint.

Covered entities and business associates that share PHI are required to have contracts in place to ensure the confidentiality and security of all information covered under HIPAA.

Health Information Data Breaches

HIPAA includes provisions about data breaches that, like other American privacy laws, typically focus on giving affected individuals notice of the breach, along with notifying the relevant authorities. In the case of HIPAA, the authorities are typically the DHHS, alongside state health authorities.

HIPAA allows penalties to be imposed for health information data breaches and also requires detailed notices to individuals affected. A HIPAA data breach notice must be written in plain English and include a description of the nature of the breach, including the date it occurred and the date it was discovered; a description of the types of information involved in the breach; details of steps individuals should take to protect themselves; details of what the breached company is doing to investigate and to lessen harm to individuals, along with how it intends to protect against further breaches; and contact information for individuals who wish to seek further details.

HEALTHCARE ROBOTS AND YOUR PERSONAL DATA

One significant limitation of America's sectoral approach to data privacy in the medical area is the recent increased use of "healthcare robots." Often used in the care of the elderly and children (largely for therapeutic purposes, to provide assistance and comfort), healthcare robots are particularly useful for those diagnosed with autism, diabetes, or cancer. They are often designed to look like animals—typically cute and cuddly animals to make their use more comforting.

One example is Paro, a fluffy robot—in the shape of a seal and about the size of a human baby—that can be stroked or held and can recognize touch, tone of voice, temperature, and posture. It can respond to these stimuli and mimic the sounds of a baby harp seal. It can recognize its name, greetings, and praise and can learn how its user prefers it to react to various words and conditions. This robot is typically used to assist and interact with dementia patients. For another example, Hasbro has developed "Joy for All Companion Pets" to look, sound, and feel like real pets (cats and dogs) for companionship. There are also more directly useful or functional robots like the Care-O-bot 3, a German invention, which helps seniors live independently by fetching items and providing communication services and streaming entertainment services.

Under current U.S. law, these devices are not regulated by HIPAA or any other health-specific laws, even though they may collect data that is very useful in the care and treatment of the user—including daily routine, sleep cycles, medicines taken, dietary intake, and so on. Most of these robots are purchased directly from manufacturers or through retailers that are generally not covered entities under HIPAA.

The FTC may have a role to play in ensuring that contractual privacy promises made by manufacturers of these devices are honored. The Food and Drug Administration (FDA) also has a role in the premarket approval of medical devices, and so, to the extent that these robots are classified as medical devices, the FDA may vet them for compliance with its cybersecurity guidelines, but these guidelines do not have the force of law.

Covered entities are required to notify prominent media outlets in cases of breaches of PHI involving more than five hundred residents of a particular state or jurisdiction. This media notification should contain the same information outlined above. Generally, for a breach involving more than five hundred individuals' data, the organization breached must immediately notify the DHHS, although smaller breaches are only required to be reported annually.

The Federal Trade Commission's Health Breach Notification Rule
Alongside the HIPAA data breach notification requirements, the Federal Trade Commission (FTC) has implemented a rule that requires some organizations that handle PHI to notify it of data breaches. The FTC's Health Breach Notification Rule is applied to various vendors of health records and third-party service providers that handle health information and that do not come within the narrow definitions of covered entities and business associates under HIPAA.

The FTC rule operates similarly to HIPAA on data breach notification. A breached entity must report the breach to the individuals affected, to the media in some circumstances, and to the relevant government authority (in this case the FTC, rather than DHHS). The effectiveness of the FTC's rule has been rather limited. As of 2020, the FTC had never launched an enforcement action in relation to a health data breach and had received notice of only two major health data breaches.

The lack of notification and enforcement under this rule is largely due to the fact that its original intention was to cover electronic health records, which were initially not well covered under HIPAA, prior to the later revisions of that law. The FTC's rule was really a gap-filler in many ways and has never covered information uploaded directly by individuals into their own private health devices and services (Fitbits, weight loss programs, calorie trackers, direct-to-consumer genetic testing, etc.). In 2020, the FTC sought public comment on the scope of the rule in particular, including whether it should be extended to cover more types of health information. As of this writing, the review of the rule is ongoing. For more information about data breaches in general, and health information data breaches in particular, see chapter 7.

Our Data and Our Health

Surveys have suggested that many Americans do not take advantage of devices that might help them improve or maintain their health because of concerns about data breaches and the lack of robust regulation of medical and healthcare devices like wearable fitness trackers. For example, survey findings described in an article from January 2020 suggest that only 38 percent of Americans believe that appropriate safeguards exist to protect their personal health data, and 60 percent of those surveyed said they did not use telemedicine or wearable fitness trackers because of those fears (see https://www.healthcareitnews.com/news/data-privacy-concerns-hamper-adoption-use-personal-medical-devices). The telemedicine fears may or may not have been alleviated in the age of COVID, when many healthcare providers moved their services online. The need to engage in more medical practices remotely, using digital technology, is likely to have a significant impact both on healthcare privacy and on how individuals feel about healthcare privacy.

In March 2020, the Office for Civil Rights at the DHHS announced that it would exercise significant discretion in enforcement of HIPAA-covered entities providing telemedicine during the pandemic, allowing them to use popular video applications like Zoom without necessarily breaching HIPAA's Security Rule. At the time of this writing, the extent to which private health information has become insecure as a result of these developments remains to be seen.

GENETIC INFORMATION NONDISCRIMINATION ACT

Unlike general personal health records, which are the province of HIPAA, genetic health records are a more recent innovation and come from more recent research on the makeup of the human genome. Because of advances in genetic testing, genetic data has become significant in diagnosis and treatment of many diseases known to have a genetic component, including Alzheimer's, some cancers, and some mental illnesses, including schizophrenia.

Genetic data can be obtained from cell samples of hair, skin, saliva, blood, and other bodily products. Because genetic information is unique to each individual (except identical twins, triplets, etc.), it cannot be effectively de-identified, so it raises more significant privacy and confidentiality problems than many other kinds of health information.

To the extent that genetic data is included in the kinds of health records protected under HIPAA, the HIPAA Privacy Rule extends to that information. In 2008, Congress also enacted GINA, which is not actually a data protection law at all but rather an antidiscrimination law focused on genetic information. GINA prohibits discrimination in employment decisions (hiring, firing, promotions, etc.) based on genetic information. It also prohibits employers from asking for, or purchasing, genetic information about employees and job applicants. Additionally, it prohibits retaliation against those who complain about misuse of genetic information, as well as prohibiting harassment in the workplace on the basis of genetic information. The law applies only to employers who have more than fifteen employees.

Because access to genetic information is a necessary precursor to discrimination based on such information, GINA also regulates the privacy of this information to some extent. Genetic information protected under the law includes information about an individual's genetic tests or those of a family member, family medical history, previous requests for or receipt of genetic services by an individual or family member, and genetic information about a fetus carried by an individual or family member.

The only circumstances where an employer or prospective employer can request, require, or access genetic information under GINA are

+ where the information is acquired accidentally;
+ where the information is voluntarily provided by an employee to a health or genetic service (e.g., employee wellness program) offered by the employer;
+ where the information is necessary under the Family and Medical Leave Act or other laws or employer policies that require documentation to support a leave request;
+ where the information is obtained from a commercially or publicly available source (e.g., a magazine or webpage);

- + where the information is part of a genetic monitoring program that is either required by law or provided on a voluntary basis; or
- + by employers who conduct DNA testing for law enforcement purposes (e.g., for a forensic lab or human-remains identification service).

An employer with access to an individual's genetic information must keep the information confidential and separate from any regular medical files. The information may be disclosed only to the employee or a family member on receipt of a written request; to an occupational or health researcher conducting research that complies with certain federal regulations; if required by a court order; to government officials investigating compliance with GINA; if required to certify an FMLA or other medical leave request; or to a public health agency if the information concerns an imminent health emergency related to the spread of a contagious disease like COVID-19.

Some states have gone further than the federal laws in their protection of genetic information. For example, the California Genetic Information Non-discrimination Act (CalGINA) doesn't stop at prohibiting employment discrimination based on genetic information. It extends those protections to discrimination in housing, provision of emergency services, education, mortgage lending, and elections.

Like HIPAA, GINA is somewhat limited in its operation and applies mainly to employers, although it also covers some other organizations, such as labor organizations, employment agencies, and federal government agencies. There are no privacy or discrimination laws in the United States specifically targeted at protecting information voluntarily disclosed to direct-to-consumer businesses such as private genetic testing companies like 23andMe or genealogy websites like Ancestry.com.

CONFIDENTIALITY AND GENETIC HISTORY

A detailed consideration of the privacy implications of assisted reproduction—helping women become pregnant using donor sperm, eggs, and embryos—is well beyond the scope of this book. However, it is worth thinking briefly about the right to privacy of those who donate sperm, eggs, and embryos, and

GENETIC INFORMATION AND THE LONG-LOST FAMILY

In recent years, private DNA testing companies have provided the possibility of making family connections through genetic data registries—for example, 23andMe offers a "DNA Relatives" feature. The temptation for those who have delved into genetic testing to find out more about long-lost relatives is a great one and has led to some interesting results. In a *Wired* article in 2020, titled "There's No Such Thing as Family Secrets in the Age of 23andMe," Caitlin Harrington followed the story of the discoveries of people in various countries that they were half-siblings due to a sperm donation in 1974 by Jeff Johnson, at the time an entry-level employee at New York publishing house Farrar, Straus and Giroux. Johnson had donated sperm for the money and because he thought it would make a fun story at bars.

It wasn't until the age of private commercial DNA testing services that children born from sperm donations like this one could locate genetic parents relatively easily. In Johnson's case, his genetic offspring included Denise, the daughter of a couple struggling with infertility in Birmingham, Michigan; Colin, a scientist, also from Michigan, whose parents had not told him he was the product of artificial insemination; Amy, an actor from Los Angeles who was curious about her genetic father and set out to find him; and Ben, whose brother had received a 23andMe kit for Christmas and discovered he was not Ben's genetic sibling.

Laws have struggled to keep pace with both the parental rights and confidentiality interests of sperm donors. In Amy's case, the clinic where the donation was made could not disclose the information to her but was legally able to disclose it to her mother. Interestingly, in that case, the record about Johnson was supposed to have his identifying information (name, address, employer, etc.) but did not, so she was able to track him down through the Donor Sibling Registry, a nonprofit organization in Colorado that assists individuals conceived through sperm, egg, or embryo donations in finding genetic relatives.

The lack of clear legal regulation around private genetic companies is not necessarily a good or a bad thing, and even regulation would not help much in cases where mistakes are made, like accidentally sending information that is supposed to be kept private. However, genetic information is an area that is likely to need more regulation and oversight in coming years, both in the United States and globally.

ARTIFICIAL INSEMINATION IN THE NINETEENTH CENTURY

A lot of confidentiality questions about genetic relatives arise today in the context of massive, and growing, DNA databases run by commercial enterprises. These issues are not as new as we might think. In her 2020 *Wired* article already mentioned, Caitlin Harrington noted that the first reported donor-conceived birth occurred in 1884, when a Philadelphia doctor artificially inseminated a patient using sperm from one of his medical students. He did this without the woman's consent and eventually told her husband what he had done, but neither man told the woman herself. The medical students involved were sworn to secrecy, although one of them wrote about it later. As recounted in Harrington's article, the idea to artificially inseminate the woman came about as a result of a joke by one of the attending medical students that the only solution to the couple's infertility problem was to "call in a hired man."

---

a competing interest, the right of children born through assisted reproduction to know about their genetic relations, whether for a sense of completeness emotionally or to be informed about genetic health conditions. Legal systems around the world have struggled to balance these rights and interests, and the commercialization of DNA testing services increases the challenges for lawmakers. Additionally, even with regulations in place, mistakes can be made in revealing too much, or incorrect, information.

Another area where commercial DNA testing services impact individual privacy and raise legal concerns about the balance of privacy against other competing interests is in law enforcement. Increasingly, police departments have utilized genetic databases to help identify suspects, often in the most violent crimes.[1] The legalities of these practices have been in the news in a number of states, with various state lawmakers proposing and enacting laws around these practices.[2] Genetics, and the privacy implications of DNA testing, will be fascinating areas to watch in the future. Due process restraints on government uses of personal information are considered in chapter 11.

PRIVACY TIPS AND TRICKS

Health information privacy and genetic privacy are some of the more challenging issues in the current American legal system and globally. The sectoral approach to privacy regulation at the federal level in the United States, in particular, creates a lot of gaps and uncertainties in regard to legal privacy protections, especially with data that is not collected or stored by organizations covered under laws like HIPAA and GINA. The COVID-19 pandemic has not helped foster health information privacy, because more information has had to be shared over less secure networks as a result of moves to telemedicine in 2020. Some things you can do to keep an eye on the status of your private health and genetic information include the following:

+ If you are using healthcare devices at home like Fitbits, digital calorie counters, or other kinds of health information trackers, make sure you read and understand the terms of service provided with those devices.

+ Insist on receiving, and make sure you read and understand, any privacy notices provided by medical practitioners and health insurance providers.

+ Keep an eye on the website of the Office for Civil Rights at the DHHS, especially during the COVID-19 pandemic and other public health emergencies that may arise, about the kinds of issues they foresee in relation to private health information and the steps they may be taking (or that you can take) to mitigate concerns about privacy.

- Watch the videos on the same website to better understand your rights (*Your Health Information, Your Rights!*, available at https://www.hhs.gov/hipaa/for-individuals/guidance-materials-for-consumers/index.html).

- Ensure that you understand how to access your electronic health records, and those of your dependents, and check them routinely for accuracy.

- If you use private DNA testing services, make sure you understand the terms and conditions of use, especially in relation to privacy.

- If you donate genetic material for private purposes (such as sperm donation), make sure that you understand the contract you are entering into, especially in relation to the privacy and confidentiality of your personal information.

CHAPTER TEN

Our Data and Our Money

+ Protecting your credit information
+ Understanding your credit score
+ Avoiding identity theft
+ How consumer credit agencies work
+ Confidentiality and security of bank records
+ Privacy notices from financial institutions
+ Rights to protect your financial information
+ Banks' duties to report suspicious account activity
+ Financial data breaches

How many times have you received a notice, from your bank or credit provider, letting you know of a data breach and the possibility that your financial information was compromised? Probably so often that you don't even bother reading the notices anymore. The name for this reaction is "data breach fatigue," and it is becoming more and more common in the digital age, with the loss of data security as a result of malicious attacks and/or system errors increasing exponentially. As we know from previous chapters, data breaches can happen in any number of industries, but statistics show that the information most likely to be targeted by hackers is financial and health information, due to its value on the black market. Financial, tax, and health identity theft are the main aims of those who want to profit from consumer information. A 2020 study demonstrated that 71 percent of all data breaches are financially motivated, and that the cost of detecting and remediating data breaches has now reached almost $20 million annually in the banking industry.[1]

Other sobering statistics about data breaches in the financial services industry include the fact that over 90 percent of ATMs are vulnerable to various kinds of security attacks, more than five hundred million consumers do not realize that their digital device is infected with crypto-mining software, and over half of American banks have failed web security tests.[2] Despite these risks, it seems that many of us either don't care about the threat of a data breach involving our financial information or just feel helpless to do anything about it. Financial data breaches are among the largest contributors to the exponential problem of identity theft in the United States.

This chapter will talk mainly about the American laws that regulate privacy protections for our financial information, and the kinds of recourse we do and don't have in the case of a financial data breach. The discussion will also cover practical tips for securing and monitoring your financial information, especially with respect to concerns about identity theft. If some of the chapter feels repetitive, it is because much of the law and practice related to financial data privacy in the United States is effectively the same as for other kinds of sensitive information, like health information, children's data, and student records. So you may want to refer back to the tips and tricks at the ends of chapters 5, 6, and 9 for a refresher on best practices in protecting those categories of data.

Because of the sectoral approach to privacy protection in the United States—as compared with, say, the more comprehensive position in the European Union (see chapter 8)—there are a number of different laws that impact financial privacy as distinct from, say, health privacy or student privacy. The scheme of much of this legislation is similar: generally, the onus in the United States is on consumers to protect their own information, and the main obligation of financial institutions is to notify customers of data breaches. Additionally, most of the relevant laws enable a financial institution to obtain valid and enforceable customer consent for various uses of private financial information. If your financial institution requires you to sign a statement consenting to certain uses of your information, you may have no choice but to agree, or else seek another bank that may or may not have similar terms for opening an account or a credit line.

The main federal laws that cover financial privacy include the Fair Credit Reporting Act of 1971, the Right to Financial Privacy Act of 1978, some provisions of the Gramm-Leach-Bliley Act of 1999, and to some extent the Bank Secrecy Act of 1970 (though that law has more to do with what information a bank can collate and report to the government without a customer's consent). The **Fair Credit Reporting Act (FCRA)** is largely about what credit reporting agencies can do with information in your credit report: who it can be shared with and when you are required to be notified. The Right to Financial Privacy Act provides some level of privacy in regard to government scrutiny of personal financial information, enacted after the Supreme Court held (in 1976) that the due process provisions of the Fourth Amendment did not apply to information held by a financial institution. We will consider the impact of the Fourth Amendment on privacy more generally in chapter 11.

The Gramm-Leach-Bliley Act (often referred to as the GLB Act or GLBA) largely updated preexisting regulations to broaden and clarify the definition of a financial institution for the purposes of regulation of the financial services industry, as well as to provide clearer privacy protections for customers. One of its key innovations was the requirement that every financial institution has to provide every customer with a privacy notice annually.[3] The customer is also given the ability to opt out of certain information-sharing practices, as discussed in more detail later in this chapter. Because it is an opt-out system rather than an opt-in system, the onus is on the customer to specify whether certain financial information can or cannot be shared with third parties.

The Bank Secrecy Act is more about ensuring that financial institutions maintain sufficient customer records and report suspicious transactions in order to help the government prevent financial crime—for example, money laundering and associated underlying criminal activities, like drug dealing. While this is not a law that specifically *protects* privacy (actually, it does the opposite), it is important in a book like this to understand circumstances when a financial institution might be required to share information about financial accounts or transactions with government authorities without informing the account holder.

One wrinkle that has arisen again and again in the regulation of the financial services industry is in defining which institutions should be covered by regulations like those listed above. Initially the laws were more concerned with banks and credit card companies, but today they extend to many other organizations that provide lines of credit—for example, auto dealers that provide credit for purchasing vehicles, or casinos that provide lines of credit.

Even the definition of a consumer reporting agency has been extended over the years as more and more companies set up services that help track an individual's financial background and other personal details. While this chapter is about the finance industry generally, the laws in question cover institutions outside of regular banks and the three major credit reporting agencies.

It is important to note at the outset that, as with the earlier discussion of health privacy laws, this chapter's discussion of many of these finance-related laws is somewhat oversimplified, as our intention here is to introduce the basic everyday concerns individuals may have about financial privacy. While the laws establish regulation of different kinds of financial institutions by different bodies with varying sets of rules,[4] this chapter focuses on what we might call lowest-common-denominator practices: the minimum that individuals need to do to keep an eye on their financial records. In other words, this chapter will not make anyone into an instant expert on the complex web of financial regulatory laws in the United States.

INTRODUCTION TO THE FAIR CREDIT REPORTING ACT

Probably the one law that most Americans are familiar with in regard to the financial services industry is the FCRA, which imposes obligations on consumer reporting agencies and some other organizations with respect to uses and disclosures of personal information—largely credit scores and general creditworthiness, but other personal data as well.

Under the law, a "consumer reporting agency" is fairly broadly defined to include any person or organization that regularly assembles or evaluates consumer credit information or *other information on consumers* in order to furnish reports to third parties like financial institutions, landlords, employers, or insurance providers. The idea of a "consumer report" under the law is not limited to reports about creditworthiness but also includes character, general reputation, personal characteristics, and mode of living. Because of these broad definitions of the organizations and information regulated by the law, a number of companies outside of the major credit reporting agencies (Equifax, Experian, and TransUnion) fall under the definition of a consumer reporting agency and may be regulated under the law—for example, banks, credit unions, auto dealers with financing operations, and others that aggregate consumer information.

The FCRA imposes obligations related to notice and accuracy when information about an individual is used in particular contexts, such as for a background check for a prospective employee, a check of creditworthiness when applying for a loan, or a credit check for a potential tenant. The law limits who can access information in a credit file to those with a valid need for the information—like banks, prospective employers, or prospective landlords. Generally, when these parties want to obtain a report about you, they will seek your consent, although consent is not always necessary under the law. Most employers and prospective employers are required to seek your authorization to access your report.

Importantly, if a negative decision is made about you on the basis of a consumer report—for example, denying credit or insurance or making an adverse employment decision—you must be told about the report and given the name, address, and phone number of the agency that provided the information.

YOUR RIGHTS UNDER THE FAIR CREDIT REPORTING ACT

Other than the right to consent (or not) to certain information disclosures and to be notified of adverse decisions based on consumer reports, consumers also have a number of other rights under the law. For example, you have the legal right to inspect your file at any consumer reporting agency. Generally, you may have to pay to obtain information in your file, but the information can be provided free of charge in certain situations—for example, if an adverse decision has been made on the basis of the information, if you are the victim of identity theft, if your file contains inaccurate information due to fraud, if you are on public assistance, or if you are unemployed. You can also obtain a free credit report every twelve months from Experian, Equifax, or TransUnion. During the COVID-19 pandemic, these three credit agencies have expanded a program that provides free weekly credit monitoring.

Additionally, you always have the right to ask for your credit score, which is a numerical summary of creditworthiness based on compiled information from credit bureaus. Typically you have to pay for this information, but in some contexts (usually involving financial transactions like mortgages) the bank may provide the information free of charge.

WHO CAN BE A CONSUMER REPORTING AGENCY?

When most of us think of consumer reporting agencies (to the extent we ever think about them), our minds immediately go to the three major companies that maintain our credit reports: Equifax, Experian, and TransUnion. However, as noted in this chapter, many other entities that handle personal information can fall under the Fair Credit Reporting Act's definition of a consumer reporting agency.

In 2016, the U.S. Supreme Court heard a case—*Spokeo, Inc. v. Robins*—that considered whether online "people-finding" services can be regulated as "consumer reporting agencies" under the FCRA. The case involved a complaint that an online "people search engine" (Spokeo, Inc.) had infringed its obligations under the Act to ensure that information about individuals profiled in its reports was accurate.

Spokeo is one of the proliferation of online people-finding companies you may have come across if you've ever tried to do a reverse phone-number-lookup or find someone when you only knew small bits of information about them. Those companies generally trawl a wide array of databases to gather information about individuals, which they can then sell to a variety of customers, including prospective employers and private investigators.

The Supreme Court's role was to determine whether the complainant had established harm that a court could address. The Court simply accepted, for the purposes of its discussion, that Spokeo was a consumer reporting agency under the law. Ultimately, there has been no clear judicial decision or legal ruling on whether such people-finding companies are consumer reporting agencies or not. Spokeo itself currently asserts on its website (largely hidden in small print at the bottom of the homepage) that "Spokeo is not a consumer reporting agency as defined by the Fair Credit Reporting Act. . . . Do not use this site to make decisions about employment, tenant screening, or any purpose covered by the FCRA."

Of course, saying you are not a consumer reporting agency does not make it so, but in the absence of a clear legal ruling, the question is open for debate. Some lower courts in the United States have assumed that companies like Spokeo are consumer reporting agencies, but so far there is no definitive answer from the highest court in the land.

WHAT IS A CREDIT SCORE?

In the United States, a credit score (ranging from 300 to 850) is a tool used predominantly by lenders to decide how likely you are to repay debts. Theoretically, it helps them determine whom to offer credit, and on what terms. The score is compiled from information held by consumer reporting agencies and includes information related to your payment history on past debts. This approach can be problematic for young people without a debt history and also for immigrants who have not yet established credit in the United States.

The credit score may also reference the total amount of debt you owe (on all kinds of loans, including student loans, motor vehicle loans, credit cards, etc.). The score may also include your pattern of managing different kinds of debt, including keeping credit balances low and paying bills on time, as well as how often you apply for credit. If you apply for lots of credit cards around the same time, it can negatively affect your credit score.

Credit scores can seem mysterious because there is no right to see how your particular score has been calculated. However, to keep a bit of a handle on it, you can monitor your credit regularly and keep an eye on the factors likely to affect your credit score.

Under the FCRA, you also have the right to dispute inaccurate or incomplete information and to have the relevant consumer reporting agency or agencies correct or delete inaccurate, incomplete, or unverifiable information within thirty days of receiving notice of the problem. In particular, the law prohibits consumer reporting agencies from reporting negative information that is more than seven years old or bankruptcies that are more than ten years old.

IDENTITY THEFT

Data breaches can lead to identity theft: the crime of using someone else's identity to establish credit or other services, including often expensive healthcare services, or to submit fraudulent tax documentation for a refund.

CREDIT FREEZES VS. FRAUD ALERTS

Two important tools in the American credit reporting system for combating identity theft and fraud are **credit freezes** (sometimes called **security freezes**) and **fraud alerts**. A fraud alert is basically what it sounds like: you notify the credit reporting agencies to insert a notation on your file that requests any business seeking your credit report to confirm your identity. There are two main types of fraud alert: an extended alert and a temporary alert.

The extended fraud alert is used when you have previously been a victim of credit fraud or identity theft, and lasts for seven years unless you remove it before then. It requires documentation like a police report to be submitted in support of the request for the alert. A temporary fraud alert stays on your file for one year unless you renew it. Neither form of fraud alert affects your credit score. There is also a separate "active duty fraud alert" for members of the military who want to protect their credit while deployed.

A fraud alert enables businesses—like potential employers, insurance companies, financial institutions, car rental companies, landlords, and others—to check your credit, but they are required to confirm your identity when they do so. Criminals may be able to get around these constraints, particularly if they have established a solid identity in your name, but the fraud alert does give you some extra protection against fraudulent lines of credit being opened in your name.

Credit freezes are more stringent than fraud alerts and prevent anyone from accessing your credit history and opening a line of credit in your name unless you request the removal of the freeze first. This strategy is unwieldy for people who need to open new lines of credit periodically, say, for business purposes (cell phone accounts, rental properties, etc.), but does provide greater protection for your credit than a fraud alert. Older people who have established credit and are not likely to be seeking further credit may find freezes more useful than younger people who are still establishing credit.

Useful information about the difference between fraud alerts and credit freezes, and about how to set up either, can be found on the Federal Trade Commission's website (https://www.consumer.ftc.gov/articles /what-know-about-credit-freezes-and-fraud-alerts).

Any data breach can lead to these activities, but financial data is particularly susceptible, along with health data, because of its value in enabling these activities.

Despite the exponential increase in the prevalence of identity theft, especially in connection to health and credit, many misunderstand its significance and the difficulties of preventing or remedying it. Between 2010 and 2020, more than thirty-eight billion financial and other records have been exposed to identity theft.[5] So, even if you are not aware of it, there is a good chance that some of your personal information is floating around in cyberspace, vulnerable to fraud.

Many people misunderstand the scope of identity theft and how serious it can become, along with the time and resources involved in combating the criminal activities. As one victim, Amy Krebs, said in 2014,

> people don't really understand what identity theft is. . . . People think it's credit card identity theft—someone went to Target and bought something, so why are you all upset about this? In that case, you call your credit card company and say, this is a fraudulent charge, fill out some papers and get on with your life.
>
> That wasn't the case for me. I had to prove who I am, I had to go through court, I had to go through grand jury, I had to give testimony. I am very fortunate in my case that I had someone to point to. Sometimes, people aren't as fortunate.[6]

Krebs's story is not unusual, and it is a stark example of how challenging it can be for an individual to redress identity theft, even in a case where it is clear that financial data has been breached and that someone is using that data fraudulently. In Krebs's case, the authorities never discovered how the identity thief had first accessed Krebs's personal information, but the two—victim and thief—lived in neighboring towns, so perhaps the information was accessed from a retail outlet or other physical place where Krebs had used a credit card.

After first learning of the identity theft from a credit card company alert, Krebs attempted to check her credit reports to gauge the extent of the damage. She could initially only access the report from one of the three major credit agencies (Equifax, Experian, and TransUnion), because the identity thief's information had effectively overwritten Krebs's information in two of

Our Data and Our Money

the agencies' databases. Krebs learned of the misconduct around six months after her information was first misused—and by that time, the wrongdoer had attempted to open more than fifty credit accounts in her name, mixing Krebs's identity with her own so that any online aggregations of information about Krebs did not refer to a single real person, but rather to a pastiche of Krebs's and the thief's information.[7]

Krebs placed fraud alerts on all her credit cards and soon was receiving multiple calls daily about fraudulent activity involving her credit. Krebs notes that it is particularly easy for identity thieves to infiltrate credit if they have access to your social security number, so it is a good idea to protect that information better than we often do.

One of the more significant issues facing victims of identity theft and related fraud is knowing where to turn to redress any injuries sustained—financial and psychological. That may be one of the major downsides of America's sectoral approach to safeguarding privacy. Different government departments deal with different aspects of identity breaches, which leaves victims with the responsibility for following up with all relevant departments on their own time. As Krebs notes, "The government isn't much help either. You're bounced from agency to agency to agency: If you're an identity theft victim, here are the 400 steps you have to do."[8]

The United States does have federal laws against identity theft, but they are largely criminal laws that are not of great use to victims of identity theft. They require criminal action to be taken against the wrongdoer, and a court to actually pass a meaningful sentence, which may or may not deter the criminal from engaging in identity theft in the future. The Identity Theft Enforcement and Restitution Act of 2008 does allow victims to claim restitution for expenses related to the value of the time they reasonably spent trying to repair their credit and other aspects of their identity. But this is a drawn-out process, requiring both those meticulous records Krebs mentioned and also a court agreeing to value a victim's time in a meaningful way.

And like many digitally enabled crimes, vulnerable populations can be at the greatest risk as targets of identity theft. In 2019, five people were indicted for engaging in a major identity theft program that preyed on veterans, many of whom were elderly and/or disabled. The information pertaining to thousands of veterans and senior military members was taken from a computer screen at a U.S. Army base in South Korea and used in rerouting millions of dollars in disability benefits and other payments due to the veterans.[9]

A CONSTITUTIONAL RIGHT TO FINANCIAL PRIVACY?

In the absence of an all-encompassing federal privacy law or constitutional right, Congress has stepped up to create privacy rights in particular areas, including education, health, and financial privacy (we discussed education and health in chapters 6 and 9, respectively). The Right to Financial Privacy Act was implemented in 1978 and creates a Fourth Amendment-like right to privacy in certain financial records. We will look at the Fourth Amendment in more detail in chapter 11, but basically, that is the section of the Constitution that prevents searches and seizures of individuals and their property without due process. If you watch a lot of police procedurals, you have likely heard the characters talk about "probable cause" or "needing warrants" to search premises and records for evidence of wrongdoing. The law related to government searches of individuals and their property, including their data/records, derives from the Fourth Amendment. The constitutional bar on governmental authorities being able to search you or your property or records without due process is a form of privacy right: it creates a limited constitutional form of privacy against illegal government searches.

In 1976, the Supreme Court was asked to consider whether this Fourth Amendment privacy right applies to a person's bank records. In *United States v. Miller*, the Court held that bank records are outside the scope of the Fourth Amendment—in other words, there is no Fourth Amendment privacy protection of bank records against governmental searches. There were a number of legal reasons for this result, including the fact that the bank records were not regarded as belonging to the individual, but rather as being the property of the bank that created the records. The records don't "belong" to the account holder, and the Fourth Amendment doesn't prevent the government from making inquiries about an individual outside of his or her own property. In constitutional law terms, this is often referred to as the third-party doctrine: the Constitution does not generally protect records about you created by someone else from a warrantless search. The third-party doctrine is discussed in more detail in chapter 11, with respect to cell site location records, in particular.

In *Miller* there was also some discussion about whether the individual in question had a "reasonable expectation of privacy" in records generated and maintained by his bank. The Court ultimately held that a bank's customer has no reasonable expectation of privacy in these kinds of records created and maintained by the financial institution in the ordinary course of the banker-customer relationship.

Of course, Fourth Amendment issues arise only in situations where the *government* is investigating an individual, typically in the area of criminal law (discussed in more detail in chapter 11). The *Miller* case involved an investigation by the Treasury Department's Bureau of Alcohol, Tobacco, and Firearms about possible tax evasion by a distillery in Georgia. The bureau wanted to search bank records in the context of that investigation.

The result of the case, holding that the Fourth Amendment did not protect the privacy of the bank records, led to the enactment of the Right to Financial Privacy Act. This law created a Fourth Amendment–like right in financial records. Congress intended to create new protections for bank records that would

+   require notification of the customer before records were disclosed to the federal government;

+   allow customers to challenge the release of their records to the government; and

+   require government agencies to produce an audit trail documenting all disclosures of relevant information to the government (including transfers between government agencies).

The law applies only to *federal* government requests for information, although some states followed suit and implemented their own law to much the same effect. The Right to Financial Privacy Act requires a federal government agency requesting financial information to give the customer advance notice of the requested disclosure so that the customer has an opportunity to challenge the request. The law also prevents a federal government agency from accessing or copying financial records unless either the customer has authorized the access or the request is supported by a subpoena, summons, warrant, or appropriate written request from an authorized government agency.

As with many laws related to financial institutions and financial records, the question of whom the law applies to is rather broad. "Financial institutions," for the purposes of the law, include virtually any entity that issues credit, including retailers and merchants who issue credit cards, banks and credit unions, money-order businesses, traveler's check issuers, the U.S. Postal Service, casinos, and others. There is still some uncertainty about precisely which organizations fall within the definition of "financial institution" under the law, especially with respect to travel and entertainment cards that do not permit deferred payments. If the law is strictly interpreted, credit card issuers are usually those who extend credit, meaning that payments can be deferred if the customer pays interest. Some travel and entertainment cards do not fit that bill.

The law also only protects private individuals or partnerships with five or fewer individuals from disclosures of financial records. This limitation makes sense if we assume that the idea is to create individual privacy rights based largely on the notion of the due process rights in the Constitution, which had their genesis in the idea of personal protection against government interference.

PRIVACY NOTICES

As this chapter has demonstrated, financial privacy involves a delicate balance of rights created by Congress to protect confidentiality of some information while still enabling law enforcement officers to do their jobs, especially with respect to major crimes like terrorism, drug trafficking, and associated money laundering. Congress has also implemented laws that protect your privacy more generally in financial records, at least by requiring notice to be provided about what is being done with your personal financial information.

The GLBA attempts to balance a customer's right to privacy with a financial institution's need to share information for normal business purposes. The information held by a financial institution can include personally identifying information (name, address, phone number, etc.) as well as details about your

SUSPICIOUS CUSTOMERS AND TRANSACTIONS: WHEN A BANK MUST DISCLOSE INFORMATION

While most of this chapter is about ways to protect the privacy of your financial and credit information, there are some situations when a financial institution is *required* to share your personal financial information with the government without your authorization. Most, if not all, laws that provide a degree of privacy in financial information also make exceptions for disclosures required for legal and judicial purposes, including investigations of crime. The American banking system in particular is required to comply with a set of laws that require disclosures of financial information to the government, notably in the context of concerns about money laundering and drug trafficking.

For example, under the Bank Secrecy Act, financial institutions must file Suspicious Activity Reports with the Financial Crimes Enforcement Network (FinCEN) if they discover or suspect illegal activity involving abuse of a financial institution. These reports are kept highly confidential, and the subject of the activity is not notified of the report being filed. Also under the Bank Secrecy Act, financial institutions must compile other information on customers with a view to preventing and reporting suspicious activity. These procedures vary from institution to institution, but you will often see them referred to under the acronyms CID and CDD: Customer Identification Program and Customer Due Diligence. This is all part of a "know your customer" initiative that was beefed up after the 9/11 terrorist attacks to ensure that financial institutions, again fairly broadly defined, effectively know who they are dealing with as customers, and can flag any suspicious customers or accounts.

credit, income, and assets. Some financial institutions like to share this information with other businesses for targeted marketing purposes, for which they may be paid in return. Some people love targeted ads and some hate them, but many people would like to have a greater sense of who can access their information and for what purposes. Many would also like to have more control over that access, either for a sense of security and privacy in the information or simply to prevent unsolicited junk mail, spam, and the like. See chapter 4 for a refresher on the benefits and downsides of targeted marketing.

The GLBA requires each financial institution to let its customers know what kinds of personal information it collects and the types of businesses with which it might share that information.[10] This disclosure is made in a **privacy notice** and is supposed to help customers decide how comfortable they are with the arrangements their financial institution proposes. The privacy notice must be provided every time a new account is opened, and it must give you a chance to opt out of information sharing outside the institution's own corporate family.

So if ABC Bank tells me that it wants to share my information with Hypothetical Retailer, it has to tell me this when I open my account and give me the opportunity to opt out of the information sharing. Even if I decide not to become a customer, or my application for an account is rejected, or if I am a customer but decide to close my account, my opt-out request is supposed to stay in effect. It can be hard for an individual to monitor whether an opt-out request is being honored or not, because it is so difficult to pinpoint the source of a lot of the targeted marketing we face in our daily lives, but this is at least the theory of how opt-out notices are supposed to work.

The privacy notice that the financial institution gives me should also explain in simple terms how it will protect the confidentiality and security of my personal information. Granted, not many of us actually ever read these privacy notices, but if you want to try to opt out of information sharing, it is a good idea, when you open an account, to make your preferences on that score known.

You cannot opt out of the bank's sharing of information that it needs to conduct normal business operations or to prevent fraud and unauthorized transactions. As we have seen earlier in this chapter, there are other laws that require disclosure of your information in particular circumstances, such as investigating crime or complying with a court order. There are also exceptions for "joint marketing arrangements" in which a financial institution and, say, an insurance company decide to jointly offer or endorse particular products or services. The opt-out provisions will not apply to those kinds of initiatives.

It is also worth noting that you can opt out at any time *after* you open your initial account, but a later opt-out request will only cover future disclosures of information by the financial institutions and will not undo past disclosures. To opt out of information sharing, you will have to follow the procedure the financial institution gives you in its initial privacy notice, which may differ between institutions and could require a phone call to a particular number or mailing something in writing to a particular address. While this may seem unwieldy, the requirement allows financial institutions to avoid confusion about how their procedure works and hopefully helps them keep easier track of customers who have attempted to opt out of information sharing.

Other than the initial privacy notice the financial institution has to give you, it also has to provide **annual privacy notices** for customers who have an ongoing relationship with them (e.g., who have opened and continue to hold accounts with them). Also, if the institution changes its privacy policy, it must send a revised privacy notice. The institution may also ask customers to agree to electronic delivery of notices and, if you accept electronic notification, it is no longer obliged to send paper notices in the mail. Notices can be sent with bank or credit card statements or mailed separately, provided they are sent at the appropriate time.

PRIVACY TIPS AND TRICKS

This chapter has highlighted the privacy protections currently in place for financial and credit information, which are largely piecemeal and have lots of gaps. It is very difficult for any of us to maintain a complete picture of what financial institutions and credit agencies are doing with our financial and associated information. It is also impossible for us to take much action to prevent data breaches when our information is in the hands of banks, financial service providers, credit agencies, and associated businesses. However, as with all of our information, there are some steps we can take, both before providing financial data to businesses and with respect to concerns about data breaches and errors in our financial records. Here are some good practices in relation to financial information that you may want to consider:

+ If a business asks you for sensitive information, including financial information and notably your social security number, ask them why they need the information. In some cases, you will find that they do not need the information or that they need only some of it.

+ If you are concerned about credit fraud and identity theft (or if you have already been a victim), consider implementing a fraud alert and/or credit freeze as discussed in this chapter. In the case of a data breach of a financial institution that holds your records, the institution itself might offer to implement a credit freeze or fraud alert for affected customers.

+ Regardless of specific concerns about identity theft, it is a good idea to regularly monitor your credit, including credit card statements, alerts issued by your credit providers, and annual checks of your credit report.

+ Close any unused credit cards and financial accounts in your name if you are not planning on using them again.

+ It can be a good idea to consider registering for a post office box to avoid sensitive documents waiting in your mailbox, where identity thieves could find them.

+ Regularly check the Federal Trade Commission (FTC) and IRS websites for updates on concerns about consumer or financial fraud and tax fraud.

+ If you are a victim of identity theft, you can create an identity theft report online with the FTC (https://www.identitytheft.gov/).

+ If you suspect or know that you have been a victim of identity theft or fraud, take meticulous notes of all the steps you take to repair your credit, including when you speak to government departments like the FTC. This will help if you are asked to produce relevant information later in the process and, in particular, if the wrongdoer is ever apprehended and your testimony is needed in court.

+ Use strong passwords and encryption on digital devices you use to access sensitive financial information. Change passwords regularly.

Our Data and Our Money

+ Make sure you lock your devices (computers, cell phones, tablets, etc.) when you are not using them, so that no one can obtain accidental access to your sensitive information.

+ Be cautious about unsolicited emails from banks, credit companies, and financial institutions. If in doubt, call or email the business in question at an authentic contact number or address that you have obtained directly from their website. Do not rely on contact information in suspect emails.

+ Make sure that the antivirus and antimalware software on your personal devices is up-to-date.

+ Make sure you attempt to read and understand the privacy notices sent to you by your financial institution(s). If you have any concerns, contact the institution via the contact details included in the notice. If you still have concerns, consult the guide released by the FTC (https://www.consumer.ftc.gov/articles/0222-privacy-choices-your-personal-financial-information).

+ Some private companies offer credit monitoring and identity monitoring services. Further information about these services is available in a research brief from the Center for Victim Research (https://ncvc.dspacedirect.org/bitstream/item/1228/CVR%20 Research%20Syntheses_Identity%20Theft%20and%20Fraud_ Brief.pdf).

+ Some private companies also offer identity theft insurance (although this is usually limited in coverage) and identity restoration as well as reputation protection services. Some of these approaches are also outlined in the research brief from the Center for Victim Research cited above.

CHAPTER ELEVEN

Our Data and the Government

+ The Fourth Amendment and due process
+ Limitations on Fourth Amendment privacy protections
+ Foreign Intelligence Surveillance Act
+ Use of facial recognition technology in government investigations
+ Mass surveillance by the government

In January 2019, Robert Williams was arrested—accused of stealing almost $4,000 worth of watches—after facial recognition technology was used by the Detroit police to match surveillance footage to his driver's license photograph. Several months later, the same technology wrongly identified Michael Oliver in a larceny case. The misidentifications were not necessarily surprising, as both Williams and Oliver are African American, and the technology in question was known to have a record of racial bias, often misidentifying people of color, notably women.

Concerns about the use of facial recognition technologies have led a number of cities and states across the country to restrict the use of the technology to varying degrees. Some cities, like Portland, Oregon, have banned the use of this technology from all government and commercial use, while others have simply limited what can be done with the technology. Two of the latter, Detroit and New York, have limited the government's use of facial recognition technology to police investigating various kinds of crime.

In June 2020, during the widespread Black Lives Matter protests after the killing of George Floyd by police officer Derek Chauvin, a number of corporations announced publicly that they would not sell, or would stop selling, facial recognition services and products to police departments. IBM, Amazon, and Microsoft announced that they would refrain from selling these services to police departments until there was appropriate federal regulation put in place to govern the use of the technology.

Of course, these announcements do not mean that those companies cannot change their minds. They also do not mean that other companies will not sell services and products that seriously undermine personal privacy and security to the government. For example, the technology company Clearview AI boasts that it sells facial recognition technology to private industry and the government, and that its database contains well over three billion facial images that it has scraped from the internet, social media sites, and other sources.

There is an argument that scraping this information from the internet is not an infringement of anyone's privacy because the information is publicly available, although this statement probably does not give many of us much comfort. As previous chapters have demonstrated, we have little control over what photographs and video of us appear online.

Throughout this book, we have talked about ways in which private companies gather information about us and share it with others, often for a profit, without our consent. We have noted how few laws effectively protect our privacy against aggregation and sharing of our personal data, whether the data is shared with private companies for targeted marketing purposes, or with potential employers, educational institutions, health providers, or realtors. This chapter focuses more squarely on what happens when our personal information is shared with, or sought by, government agencies.

Obviously, police use of personal information has been a major concern of lawyers and legal scholars, especially when the technologies employed produce significant racial and gender biases. Personal information (facial recognition and other biometric information like fingerprints and DNA samples) is also used by U.S. Immigration and Customs Enforcement to track undocumented immigrants, by the FBI in investigating crime at the federal level, and by U.S. Customs and Border Protection, which has partnered with a number of airports and airlines to monitor passengers entering the country.[1] The Department of Homeland Security has also planned to employ facial recognition technologies widely at airports across the country, without significant vetting or any regulatory safeguards.[2]

A lot of this technology involves intelligent surveillance cameras that scan people's faces at the border, in airports, and so on. There is an

THE PRIVACY ACT OF 1974

Despite its name, the federal Privacy Act of 1974 does very little to actually protect our privacy. This law only requires government agencies to publish information about their practices in relation to the collection, maintenance, use, and dissemination of records about people maintained by the agency, and to correct mistakes in those records. It does not deal with the possibility of the government using information from private sources to investigate criminal activity, nor does it deal with information systems that are not maintained by a government agency.

argument, of course, that we have no expectation of privacy in public spaces, but there is also the question of what is done with that information. Does our understanding that we may not have privacy in public spaces (like airport terminals) extend to understanding how information from public surveillance cameras may be used behind the scenes by various government departments?

This is the traditional "Big Brother is watching you" question translated into the digital age. The idea that government agents could be sitting behind computer screens matching your face or voice or retinal scan with that of a person suspected of a crime was once in the realm of science fiction. Now, there is a very real possibility that your personal biometric information is included in databases accessed by the government in investigating numerous activities, and the major problem is that we have no comprehensive federal legislation to regulate how those technologies are used, and little understanding of how accurate those technologies may be.[3]

This chapter considers the limited protections that the U.S. Constitution, notably in the Fourth Amendment, gives us against government action, and the current debates about the need for greater protections. The main areas of the Constitution that give us some protection from government intrusion into our private lives are the First Amendment (which protects our freedoms of speech and association from government intrusion) and the Fourth Amendment (which protects us from unreasonable government

Our Data and the Government

FACIAL RECOGNITION TECHNOLOGY AND
THE PARADE OF HORRIBLES

In a *New York Times* article of May 14, 2019, Kate Conger, Richard Fausset, and Serge F. Kovaleski reported on a vote of 8–1 by San Francisco's Board of Supervisors to ban the use by city agencies of a particular facial recognition tool that was being used by many police forces around the country. The article cites myriad concerns, including the potential for development of a Chinese-style surveillance state, the error rate of the technology, the secrecy with which government agencies often employ it, and the difficulty, for individuals, of finding out whether they were misidentified through the use of an error-prone system. The reporters also noted a lack of standardized regulatory practices in relation to the use of the technology, and concerns about placing too much discretion over its use in the hands of private companies and individual government departments with little or no meaningful oversight.

Facial recognition technology, as an aspect of general surveillance, also raises significant First Amendment concerns related to the constitutional rights to speak and associate with others free of government interference. If people are constantly being watched, or unsure whether they are being watched, the result is that they may be chilled from exercising their constitutionally protected rights to gather and protest, among other activities. While the First Amendment is not specifically *about* privacy, it is about liberty—and, without privacy and autonomy from prying government eyes, it can be incredibly difficult to exercise constitutionally protected rights and freedoms without fear of retribution.

searches and seizures). Both provisions were obviously included in the Bill of Rights well before the advent of digital technology, and neither has been interpreted particularly consistently by the Supreme Court in recent years. In other words, there is still a lot of wiggle room for government actors to intrude into your personal life, despite the constitutional protections.

We will also look at current practices in government surveillance and laws that regulate, or to some extent arguably fail to regulate, those practices. Notably, in the wake of the 9/11 terrorist attacks in 2001, a number of federal laws were updated to allow for greater government surveillance not only of terror suspects, but of regular Americans going about their business. Some of the banking regulations we considered in chapter 10 were strengthened at the time, requiring more rigorous record keeping by banks about their customers and more robust reporting to the government of suspicious customers and/or transactions.

A PRIMER ON THE FOURTH AMENDMENT

In a *New York Times* op-ed in 2019, Professor Josephine Wolff clearly articulated why our Fourth Amendment rights fail to give much comfort in a digitally interconnected world:

> At any given moment, I'm usually carrying at least three different devices that track my location: a phone, a laptop and a Garmin watch. I carry these by choice, of course, and am well aware that they track my location in a variety of ways, including GPS satellites, wireless access points and cellphone towers, so I don't expect my location to be secret when I have them on me.
>
> Mostly, that just seems like the way the world is today, but I also find it unsettling: I'm worried by the fact that I don't expect my location to be private, and I'm also worried about the question of what that means in a country where legal protections for our data are predicated on the notion of a "reasonable expectation of privacy."[4]

Wolff points out that the Fourth Amendment relates to our reasonable expectations of privacy, but questions the extent to which any of us reasonably expect privacy in our daily activities to a significant extent in a digital world. She goes on to note that in the early part of the twentieth century, American courts (including the Supreme Court) slowly embraced Fourth Amendment protections even in some public settings, such as private conversations in a public phone booth, but then began to change course.

This course change happened in several ways. Wolff notes the rise of the "third-party doctrine" in Fourth Amendment law, which we touched on briefly in chapter 10 when dealing with financial information. The third-party doctrine fundamentally suggests that if a person hands over information to a third party (like a telephone company or a bank or even a social media service), there is no reasonable expectation of privacy in that information. We look at that doctrine in a little more detail in the following discussion, but remember the *Miller* case in relation to bank records from chapter 10? That was the case in which the Supreme Court said that a bank customer did not have a reasonable expectation of privacy in bank account records because the bank created and maintained those records itself, as a third party. We saw that Congress remedied that situation in the banking context by enacting the Right to Financial Privacy Act, but that law is very specific to financial institutions. What about all those other third parties that develop or maintain records about us, like cell phone service providers and EZ Pass/tollway payment systems?

As communications and surveillance technologies became more developed and more prevalent, our reasonable expectations of privacy may be eroded in other ways, too. For example, in the days before telephoto camera lenses, a person may have had a reasonable expectation of privacy on the balcony of their tenth-floor apartment. That may no longer be the case once the technology is commonly available.

A deep dive into the intricacies of criminal procedure and associated legal rules is beyond the scope of this chapter. However, American courts have developed sophisticated rules related to expectations of privacy in a person's home, garden, office, car, or other spaces to determine whether a police search complies with the Fourth Amendment and parallel state constitutional requirements. Many of these rules have to do with the circumstances under which police need a warrant to search people or premises and to seize property relevant to a criminal investigation. There are also rules about how specific the warrant has to be in terms of what the police are allowed to search for.

For any constitutional law geeks reading this, the actual text of the Fourth Amendment reads:

> The right of the people to be secure in their persons, houses, papers, and effects, against unreasonable searches and seizures, shall not be violated, and no Warrants shall issue, but upon probable cause, supported by Oath or affirmation, and particularly describing the place to be searched, and the persons or things to be seized.

From this language (even if you don't love reading old-fashioned wording), you can immediately see why courts have focused so much on developing rules about how specific a warrant needs to be to justify particular investigations. The Constitution itself requires a warrant to "particularly describe" what is to be searched and who or what can be seized. This was all well and good in 1791, when the amendment was added to the Bill of Rights (even then it was somewhat controversial), but how do you apply such an old-fashioned rule to twenty-first-century digital developments? Is a social media website a "place" that can be searched? What if it is password protected? Is there a reasonable expectation of privacy?

The word *privacy* does not appear in the Fourth Amendment, nor does the notion of a "reasonable expectation" of privacy. Those ideas have been read into the section by lawyers and courts. What happens in practice, when courts apply the Fourth Amendment to work out whether a particular government search is consistent with constitutional requirements, is that the judges ask whether the individual in question had an objectively reasonable expectation of privacy in the particular place or item.[5] A person in a public restroom or a public fitting room probably expects (reasonably) not to be spied on by surveillance cameras. A person carrying a leather bag on a bus probably reasonably expects the contents of the bag to be free from prying eyes. On the other hand, a person who walks down the street toting a gun, or drives a car with a gun visible on the passenger seat, probably doesn't have a reasonable expectation of privacy in relation to the weapon.

THIRD-PARTY DOCTRINE AND CELL SITE LOCATION INFORMATION

Let's turn back to the third-party doctrine for a moment. Remember, that's the doctrine courts have developed to effectively say that Fourth Amendment protections do not apply to personal data that is voluntarily in the hands of a third party—such as cell phone provider logs of what phone numbers you have called or texted. Sometimes Congress steps in and extends a privacy right to information that would otherwise not be protected because of the third-party doctrine. We saw in chapter 10 that the Right to Financial Privacy Act creates a Fourth Amendment–like privacy right in bank records.

One of the more problematic areas of the third-party doctrine in recent years is related to cell phone location data, often called **cell site location information**. This data is obtained from cell phone service providers from cell sites (i.e., radio antennas that connect to cell phones to provide coverage). Prior to the widespread use of cell phones, it was generally assumed that individuals have a reasonable expectation of privacy in their physical movements. While the case law was not 100 percent consistent on this point, some rights to privacy were considered to exist in relation to records of places we go in the course of our lives.

Current law is a little unsettled about the extent to which newer technologies impact our reasonable expectations of privacy. For example, courts in the past have weighed in on the extent to which GPS satellite tracking of individuals counts as a Fourth Amendment "search" and, if so, whether tracking devices amount to an "unreasonable" search in particular circumstances. Tracking devices have been attached by police to criminal suspects' vehicles to monitor their movements, and people convicted of certain crimes (e.g., some sex offenses) have been required to wear trackers on their bodies. American judges have varied in their views on how to apply Fourth Amendment principles to these different contexts.

Enter the cell phone, which allows a person's whereabouts over the course of a given period to be triangulated from the cell sites her phone pings, at least while she is carrying the phone. In other words, cell phones can be used very much like tracking devices, given the way the current system works. While courts have previously held that we do not have a reasonable expectation of privacy in records of, say, phone numbers that we have called or texted, because those records are maintained by the phone company with our knowledge and consent, a 2018 Supreme Court case said the same is not necessarily true of data about our location obtained from cell towers.

In *United States v. Carpenter*, the Court surprised a lot of people by saying that a suspect in a criminal investigation had a reasonable expectation of privacy in records of his movements over a period of time gathered through cell phone location data. The result of the case was that the third-party doctrine did not excuse the warrantless search, and the police should have obtained a warrant to comply with the due process requirements of the Fourth Amendment.

However, the *Carpenter* decision is narrowly limited to the context of the case. In fact, in handing it down, Chief Justice Roberts noted specifically that the *Carpenter* decision was intended to be "a narrow one" and that the Court was not weighing in on other surveillance techniques or tools (like security cameras) or other business records that might reveal a person's location.[6] He also noted that the decision was not to be read as impacting location techniques involved in foreign affairs or national security.[7] Quoting a mid-twentieth-century Supreme Court decision, he stated that when considering new innovations, the Supreme Court must tread carefully so as not to "embarrass the future."[8]

MASS GOVERNMENT SURVEILLANCE

The Fourth Amendment definitely applies to police and other government agencies and departments investigating particular individuals. Government agencies are supposed to obtain a warrant for a search or seizure of places, persons, or property when a reasonable expectation of privacy exists. While government practices vary from context to context, and there is no doubt that illegal searches and seizures take place all the time in practice, we know how the Fourth Amendment is supposed to play out in these contexts.

What about a situation where the government (or a government department) engages in general surveillance of the population when it is not investigating a particular crime or other regulated activity? As we move into a more digitally interconnected world, it is easier for governments to routinely spy on residents through technology like surveillance cameras, many of which now have built-in artificial intelligence that can take note of unusual patterns of behavior; and intelligence satellites, predominantly used by the military, that can record phone calls and other electronic communications.

IS MASS GOVERNMENT SURVEILLANCE UNCONSTITUTIONAL?

Edward Snowden thought so. If you've followed the news over the past decade—or saw the movie *Snowden* (starring Joseph Gordon-Levitt) or read his memoir, *Permanent Record*—you'll have some idea why. Snowden worked for the CIA and was subcontracted to the National Security Agency (NSA), where he discovered that the NSA, with the cooperation of various private telecommunication companies, was engaging in mass surveillance of electronic communications without any kind of warrant. He leaked thousands of classified documents providing evidence of the surveillance and fled to Russia, where he is now a permanent resident. The U.S. Department of Justice has charged him with various crimes, including violations of the federal Espionage Act and theft of government property.

Meanwhile, a number of cases have made their way through American courts on the legality of the surveillance programs in question. In one case, *Jewel v. NSA*,[9] on appeal to the Ninth District Court in California at the time of this writing,[10] the pro bono Electronic Frontier Foundation (EFF) is pursuing a class action against the NSA on behalf of a group of AT&T customers for infringements of their privacy rights under federal law, notably the Electronic Communications Privacy Act that we discussed in chapter 3. The lower court had initially dismissed the action because of concerns about disclosing government secrets in court. Snowden provided some testimony in the case.

Court of appeals judges in another case, *United States v. Moalin*,[11] noted that the government surveillance in question was illegal, but the illegality did not affect the outcome of the underlying issue, which was the conviction of four Somali citizens on charges related to terrorist financing. The court held that the government may have violated the Fourth Amendment, and did violate the Foreign Intelligence Surveillance Act, when it collected metadata related to millions of Americans' communications. However, the court held that, with respect to the Somali defendants, the role of the telecommunications evidence was so insignificant that it did not affect the outcome of the case.

What can we take from these cases? Well, we don't know as yet if the government's mass surveillance of telecommunications is unconstitutional—despite, in some contexts, its infringing of specific provisions of particular federal laws like FISA and the Electronic Communications Privacy Act. Might it be possible to argue that no one really has a reasonable expectation of privacy in *any* telecommunications anymore, if we all know that the government is routinely spying on us?

Even if we have legal and constitutional rights to prevent the government from spying on us, they can be notoriously difficult—and expensive—

to pursue. The *Jewel* case may have proceeded only because the EFF coordinated the legal action. Even with the EFF bringing the action, the case has been going on for over ten years. The case involving Somali terrorist financing took seven years. The prospect of lengthy and expensive litigation is a challenge the average person likely cannot overcome. In a review of its 2020 efforts against mass surveillance, the EFF emphasized how long the cases take and how frustrating they can be, noting that the slow pace of the court battles "makes it clear that we need additional and real reform of the state secrets privilege as well as an overhaul of the NSA's activities."[12]

IS GOVERNMENT SURVEILLANCE ALL BAD?

While mass surveillance clearly raises privacy concerns and potentially forces us to rethink our entire concept of a "reasonable expectation of privacy," there are obvious arguments in favor of some surveillance, even large-scale surveillance. The obvious arguments have to do with national security. That is the reason the NSA records were used in the *Moalin* case described above: to prevent terrorist financing. In fact, the law that enables much of the government surveillance we have today, the Foreign Intelligence Surveillance Act, was originally intended to allow for the investigation of foreign powers and foreign agents that may be a threat to the United States.

Another argument that might support large-scale government surveillance is a deterrence argument: the idea that mass surveillance deters people from engaging in harmful and criminal activities. If people do not know when they are being watched, or if they assume they are being watched all the time, they are less likely to engage in dangerous or criminal behaviors, or so the argument goes. The more we know about what everyone is doing, the less likely people are to engage in criminal activities—and, conversely, the more likely the authorities are to catch criminals. Surveillance gives authorities both evidence of the crime and identifying evidence of the criminal.

One of the major problems in considering the pros and cons of mass surveillance is that there are no simple answers. The technology enables governments (and businesses, as discussed in previous chapters) to do a lot of beneficial things, from preventing terrorism to more effective policing, to monitoring and controlling pandemics through contact tracing. On the other hand, the loss of privacy and autonomy is hard to fathom as mass

THE PATRIOT ACT

Much of the legal justification for mass government surveillance in the United States over the past few decades derives from laws passed in the wake of the 9/11 terror attacks in 2001. Under the George W. Bush administration, a number of laws were updated to allow the government to take greater measures to surveil communications and transactions without specific consent or warrants. The legislative package known as the PATRIOT Act—formally, "Uniting and Strengthening America by Providing Appropriate Tools Required to Intercept and Obstruct Terrorism (USA PATRIOT) Act of 2001"—did a lot of things other than increasing the government's surveillance powers. It created a lot of new federal crimes related to terrorism and terrorism financing, as well as funds to assist victims of terrorism, and gave the government additional powers to track and seize money used by terrorist organizations. However, it also increased the government's ability to spy on regular Americans going about their daily business. There are obviously great benefits to laws that allow the government greater powers to investigate terrorism and pursue terrorist actors and those financing them, but the downside has been the loss of a significant amount of privacy, notably in relation to telecommunications.

surveillance becomes available on such a sophisticated scale. Additionally, First Amendment concerns may be implicated in terms of the freedom to assemble, protest, and simply speak in public, if all conduct is monitored by the government. There are no easy answers to these questions, and a perfect balance is not likely to be possible. The final chapter of this book considers concerns about the future of privacy and digital technology.

GOVERNMENT SURVEILLANCE OUTSIDE THE UNITED STATES

Of course, the United States is not the only country where government surveillance has raised media and public concern, especially in relation to the protection of personal privacy and autonomy. For example, several years ago,

GOVERNMENT SURVEILLANCE DURING A PANDEMIC

The COVID-19 pandemic has raised new concerns in relation to the use of government surveillance for contact tracing—tracking the spread of disease within the United States and entering from other countries. In April 2020, the Congressional Research Service released a paper outlining the privacy concerns related to contact tracing (https://crsreports.congress.gov/product/pdf/LSB/LSB10449). According to this paper, in the early part of 2020 the federal government and some state and local governments had already started to gather geolocation data voluntarily provided by mobile communication companies in order to track community movements during the pandemic. The idea was not necessarily to identify what individual people were doing, but rather to discern general community patterns of movement. The paper addressed Fourth Amendment concerns that could arise with telecommunication companies, and potentially other companies, reporting collective and individual movement data to the government, despite the likely beneficial aims.

As with the detection and prevention of terrorism, there are clearly benefits to preventing the spread of COVID-19, but there are associated privacy concerns. The Congressional Research Service noted that there may not in fact be a major Fourth Amendment problem with some of the activities in question because of the third-party exception to the Fourth Amendment. To the extent that data was collected from third parties that had developed and maintained the relevant records—communication and internet companies—the third-party exception may well avoid a constitutional argument that individual privacy rights were infringed.

The paper also discussed another legal guideline that can excuse warrantless surveillance, known as the "special needs" doctrine, which can arise in situations where public safety is implicated. The Supreme Court has noted that blanket searches in the absence of suspicions of actual wrongful conduct may be justified under circumstances of a substantial and real risk to public safety. A pandemic may qualify as such a risk.

The public does not yet have a clear answer about what the government may be doing in relation to contact tracing, in concert with private companies or otherwise, and we may never know for sure. It is also unclear whether, and to what extent, any surveillance in this context is illegal or unconstitutional. Again, the same murky issues arise in the COVID-19 context as for many other forms of government surveillance. It is difficult to know when and whether we are being spied on (and maybe we should simply assume a constant state of surveillance)—and, even if we did know, we might have very limited recourse to prevent unwanted surveillance.

the Chinese government equipped their police officers with facial-recognition sunglasses that operate in real time, matching faces against databases to identify criminal suspects and others the police believe to be acting suspiciously.[13] China has a long history of monitoring its people and limiting actions, and access to information, that oppose government policy.

From the earliest days of the popular internet, the Chinese government has implemented technology to control people's access to government-sanctioned websites. This censorship has long been colloquially known as the Great Firewall.[14] While censorship does not necessarily invade privacy in and of itself, it can certainly impact individual autonomy when citizens cannot access different perspectives on topics of interest and importance. Additionally, China's Great Firewall monitored people using the internet at the same time their access was limited.[15] This monitoring was achieved through a combination of laws and technological filters.

In an article in *Politico* in late 2020, Yaqiu Wang, a researcher with Human Rights Watch, noted the long-term effects on Chinese society of the continuous digital monitoring and surveillance of the population, suggesting that the generation that grew up with this surveillance has become more nationalistic and less tolerant of views opposing the government.

The United Kingdom has long held the record for the highest per capita number of closed-circuit television (CCTV) cameras in the world. In 2020, it was estimated that there were approximately 5.2 million CCTV cameras in the nation, which amounts to about one camera per thirteen people.[16] Many of these cameras are installed by private individuals or businesses to monitor their property. A number are also used by local governments and can be accessed in police investigations to identify suspects. Concerns have been raised periodically about the infringement of individual privacy and autonomy caused by the rise of these cameras, and many of the concerns have since been exacerbated, because the cameras can now incorporate facial recognition technology and be linked to massive databases. CCTV cameras are in use all over the world, but many of the debates have focused on the United Kingdom because of the prevalence of cameras there.

Legal regulation of CCTV cameras, especially those that are privately installed, have raised issues throughout the European Union. Cases have arisen questioning the extent to which certain uses of the cameras, and retention of video gathered by the cameras, may infringe provisions of the General Data Protection Regulation,[17] the comprehensive privacy law implemented throughout the European Union (discussed in chapter 8).

In the United States, CCTV cameras play a role in police investigations, along with private surveillance and security systems. In 2013, public surveillance camera footage played a significant role in the real-time identification and apprehension of the two suspects in the Boston Marathon bombing.[18] Wherever in the world these technologies are used, they raise the same concerns: balancing the public good (e.g., aiding in the detection and prevention of crime) against the loss of individual privacy.

There is likely no perfect balance, and no one-size-fits-all solution to the question of how to protect privacy while also protecting the public against crime, terrorism, and other hazards (like public health crises). However, it is important for the public to be involved in policymaking discussions, which has not necessarily been the case in the past in many countries. Hopefully, books like this one will help make people aware of the costs and benefits of surveillance technologies and practices, and of laws that enable government and private use of these technologies.

PRIVACY TIPS AND TRICKS

For this chapter, it is inherently difficult to write any meaningful "tips and tricks"—other than to read the news and be aware of government policies and practices on surveillance, to the extent they are made available to the public. Good sources of information about government actions and practices that are likely to impact privacy are the Electronic Frontier Foundation (https://www.eff.org) and the Electronic Privacy Information Center (https://epic.org).

Our final chapter will talk about privacy questions we may face in the future, both nationally and globally, as our world becomes increasingly digitally connected.

CHAPTER TWELVE

Our Data into the Future

Welcome to the last chapter of the book. If you've read this far, you probably have a lot of mixed feelings about our data, in terms of who should have access to it, under what circumstances, and what kind of control we should have over it. You should also realize that there are no easy solutions to privacy concerns in the United States or elsewhere. Many U.S. laws, in particular, were crafted well before the rise of digital technology, and technological innovation easily outpaces the ability of Congress and the courts to address new privacy concerns.

Countries with more comprehensive data protection laws, like those of the European Union, may have some advantages in terms of data protection, although the downsides of heavily regulating collection of, use of, and access to large amounts of data can lead to problems as well. Many corporations and other organizations in EU countries have struggled to comply with provisions of the General Data Protection Regulation (GDPR) and/or have complained about costs of compliance. Where compliance with data privacy laws raises significant resource issues, often those costs are passed on to consumers in the form of higher prices for goods and services.

A major challenge when thinking about data protection regulation is the fact that the notion of "data" comprises so many different things, from consumer information about past purchases and preferences, which can be used for targeted marketing, to the most sensitive health or genetic information, which may be used in employment and insurance decisions. Increasingly, unique identifying information can be used to compile digital dossiers about us, including faceprints (facial recognition technology), fingerprints, and even our DNA. In-home devices can collect data about our daily routines, the temperature of our houses, what shows we like to watch, and music we like to listen to. Despite the advent of comprehensive data protection laws like the GDPR in the European Union, it is virtually impossible to craft a law that will adequately balance privacy protections against other interests in personal information and that will stand the test of time against technological advances.

Does the complexity of crafting effective laws mean that it would make more sense to do away with the idea of data privacy altogether, and accept the arguably prophetic words of Sun Microsystems CEO Scott McNealy in 1999—"You have zero privacy anyway. Get over it"?[1]

Maybe.

But the amount of ink spilled on privacy questions over the intervening years suggests that enough people worry enough about privacy to make it worth at least pursuing further debates about the importance of privacy in a digital world. If we didn't care about our privacy, we wouldn't have been so concerned about the Cambridge Analytica scandal or the Edward Snowden affair. We may not care much about whether Netflix or Amazon collects our consumer spending profiles and targets more directed ads to us, but we may care very much if we are denied health insurance because of a predisposition to an illness evidenced in a DNA test. I may not care if my Facebook friends know what TV shows and movies I like, while I fiercely guard the privacy of my children to protect them from online predators.

If we accept a need for privacy protection, we may also have to accept a need for a granular approach that directs particular protections to specific circumstances. And if a granular approach is desirable, maybe the U.S. position is not as problematic as it is often portrayed to be. If privacy is protected on a sectoral basis—industry by industry and issue by issue—it may well be easier for Congress and the courts to respond to problems that predominantly affect, say, student information, financial information, or health information. On the other hand, a sectoral approach, like the one we have in the United States, may fail to acknowledge the need for privacy to be a more significant central concern for future lawmaking. Additionally, some troublesome conduct might fall between the cracks of sectoral regulations.

Because the legal issues, large and small, are not likely to be resolved in the near future, and probably will never be addressed in a way that satisfies everyone or even a majority of people, the most that a book like this can achieve is to make readers aware of the challenges in protecting their personal information and provide them with some tips for monitoring and controlling their information to the extent possible. Some of the strategies set out at the chapter ends are common sense, but they may not be things enough of us think about as consistently as we might.

We all know we should protect our online passwords, we should use difficult-to-guess passwords, and we should read the contracts we accept, or at least pay attention to the wording of the clauses likely to be of greatest concern to us. But how many of us take a comprehensive approach to these practices? How many of us regularly check our bank statements and electronic health records to ensure their accuracy? How many of us have conversations with our children about the dangers of sharing personal information online, and follow up by monitoring what our children are doing online periodically?

In the United States, we have never had—and likely will never have—strong legal privacy protections, but for those of us who care about protecting our personal autonomy and privacy, there are steps we could take in a more organized way to ensure at least some control over our digital data. For those of us who have not thought much about protecting personal data, or who assume that it is not worth thinking about because privacy protection is a losing battle, maybe some of the tips and tricks in this book will be helpful.

It is clearly not possible to read every contract in detail or to monitor every second of what our children are doing online—or to even be fully aware of what we ourselves are doing online at every moment. Do we always remember to shut off our devices' cameras and microphones when we're not using them? But maybe this book will give you an idea of how to sort out the data issues you are most concerned about and the best ways to protect the data you care about the most.

The future will unquestionably bring even more technological innovation, and this book has only scratched the surface of directions those innovations may take. We will likely welcome more and more digital devices into our homes (including entertainment, educational, and healthcare devices). The police in China have sunglasses that can identify people's faces by connecting to sophisticated facial recognition databases. How long before we all have that capacity?

In 1998, author David Brin, in his groundbreaking book *The Transparent Society*, painted a picture of a future in which low-cost surveillance technology and massive databases have eroded privacy rights and allowed people to know pretty much everything about everyone else. He suggested that social accountability could take the place of the need for legal regulation: maybe in a society where we can all read each other's lives freely, we will all respect each other and hold each other accountable, without the need to legislate privacy. Many of us may harbor doubts that twenty-first-century society is capable of living up to those ideals. Calls for privacy regulation have certainly continued, if not increased, in recent years.

Whether the answer is that we need to know everything about each other or that we need to know less about each other, the best way for individuals to think about privacy is, at least for now, at an individual level. The best advice I can give is to do some of the things suggested in this book for monitoring personal information flows and to try to remain educated and vigilant, to the extent possible, about new technologies, business processes, and government programs that may threaten the privacy of information you care about.

There are no easy answers, but staying informed and keeping track of your data to the best of your abilities is probably the most effective way forward if you're not ready to "get over" the lack of privacy our modern world has created.

ACKNOWLEDGMENTS

This is the second opportunity I have had to work with the team at the University of California Press, notably with editor Naomi Schneider, who is the best partner an author could hope for as a mentor and collaborator in the process of translating often complex legal concepts for a more general readership. The UC Press marketing, publicity, and general team are amazing, and I would especially like to thank Teresa Iaofolla, Katryce Lassle, and Ramón Smith for all their help and support on my first book and for welcoming me so heartily to the UC Press family.

As always, I would like to thank my agent, Jane Dystel, who took me on for the previous book and not only stuck with me through this one, but championed and supported it and helped me develop a proposal for it that highlighted the need to speak to everyday Americans about digital privacy issues. Digital data privacy is a complex topic, especially in a country like the United States that has such powerful traditions related to free speech, but historically less focus on elevating rights to privacy and personal autonomy in a way that protects individual privacy.

When I was first mulling over whether the idea for this book would even be worth sharing with anyone, I discussed various visions for it with my favorite writing crew, the Sassy Djerassis, who, over a workshop week at the Highlights Foundation, not only convinced me that it could work, but gave me invaluable insights about how to do it. My special thanks to Amelinda Bérubé, Bree Barton, Tamara Mahmood Hayes, Catie Miller, TJ Ohler, Melissa Mazzone, Wendy McKee, Rachel Sarah, Alison Cherry, Shellie Faught, and special thanks to Nova Ren Suma for bringing us all together. And extra-special thanks to one of my major critique partners for many years (and agency sibling) Rebecca Barnhouse for the continued help and encouragement over these years and particularly these two book projects.

On the law school front, my heartfelt thanks go to Carina Mendola, who worked tirelessly as a research assistant on this project, especially with researching so many of the cutting-edge areas of digital technology like biometric and health information and machine learning. Thanks also to Dean Amy Wildermuth and Vice Dean Haider Hamoudi at the University of Pittsburgh School of Law for making funding available for Carina to help, and thanks also to Associate Dean Deborah Brake for her tireless support of all faculty work, including this project. (And a quick nod of thanks to Professor Ann Bartow at the University of New Hampshire School of Law with respect to the title of this book—she knows why!)

Obviously, I wrote this book from the perspective that we should think more seriously about privacy as an important aspect of our lives. Not everyone will agree with, or even be sympathetic to, that position. Even for those who are sympathetic to the idea, or concerned about better protecting our personal privacy, it may be that the digital age ultimately poses too many challenges for effective protection of our private lives. Nevertheless, the aim of the book is to give readers some tools for better monitoring the digital flows of their personal information and at least being more aware of what is being done, or may be done, with personal data.

And while I'm talking about the importance of privacy, I am typically a relatively private person about my family life, but the biggest thanks go to my husband and children for all their help and support as I tried to carve out time and space (especially during a pandemic when we're all stuck in a house together) to write these pages. Thank you from the bottom of my heart to Patrick, Sean, Brianne, and Megan, as always.

INTRODUCTION

1. Associated Press, *Judge Approves $650M Facebook Privacy Lawsuit Settlement,* Feb.26,2021,https://apnews.com/article/technology-business-san-francisco-chicago-lawsuits-af6b42212e43be1b63b5c290eb5bfd85.

2. Kashmir Hill, *How Target Figured Out a Teen Girl Was Pregnant before Her Father Did,* Forbes, Feb. 16, 2012, https://www.forbes.com/sites/kashmirhill/2012/02/16/how-target-figured-out-a-teen-girl-was-pregnant-before-her-father-did/#4311964d6668.

3. For a discussion of DNA due process concerns, see Scarlett L. Montenegro, *Criminalizing Asylum: DNA Testing Asylum Seekers Violates Privacy Rights,* 29 American University Journal of Gender, Social Policy & the Law 123 (2020); Antony Barone Kolenc, *"23 and Plea": Limiting Police Use of Genealogy Sites after Carpenter v. United States,* 122 West Virgina Law Review 53 (2019); Peter Aldous, *This Genealogy Database Helped Solve Dozens of Crimes. But Its New Privacy Rules Will Restrict Access by Cops,* BuzzFeed News, May 19, 2019, https://www.buzzfeednews.com/article/peteraldhous/this-genealogy-database-helped-solve-dozens-of-crimes-but.

4. For those who may not recall the report, it was the result of a Special Counsel investigation by Robert Mueller into claims of Russian interference in the 2016 presidential election. A copy of the report is available at https://www.justice.gov/storage/report.pdf.

5. Samuel Warren and Louis Brandeis, *The Right to Privacy,* 4 Harvard Law Review 193 (1890).

6. Bernard Marr, *The Complete Beginner's Guide to Big Data Everyone Can Understand,* Forbes, Mar. 14, 2017, https://www.forbes.com/sites/bernardmarr/2017/03/14/the-complete-beginners-guide-to-big-data-in-2017/#61d232807365.

7. Ibid.

8. Ibid.

9. See, for example, Lior Strahilevitz, *Privacy versus Antidiscrimination*, 75 University of Chicago Law Review 363 (2008), https://papers.ssrn.com/sol3 /papers.cfm?abstract_id=1003001.

10. See, for example, David Brin, *The Transparent Society: Will Technology Force Us to Choose Between Privacy and Freedom?* (New York: Basic Books, 1998); Lior Strahilevitz, *Reputation Nation: Law in an Era of Ubiquitous Personal Information*, 102 Northwestern University Law Review 1667 (2008), https://papers.ssrn.com/sol3 /papers.cfm?abstract_id=1028875.

CHAPTER ONE. WHO OWNS OUR DATA?

1. For those contract aficionados among us, the American law of contract formation generally requires "consideration"—an exchange of benefits or promises—for a contract to be enforceable.

2. Google Privacy Policy, January 22, 2019, https://policies.google.com /privacy#footnote-chrome-sync.

3. Ibid.

4. Ibid.

5. April Falcon Doss, *Cyber Privacy: Who Has Your Data and Why You Should Care* (Dallas, TX: BenBella Books, 2020), 67.

6. For a survey of state laws and proposed laws, see Cynthia J. Larose and Christopher J Buontempo, U.S. State Privacy Law Update—June 11, 2021, National Law Review, Aug. 21, 2021, https://www.natlawreview.com/article/us-state- privacy-law-update-june-11-2021.

7. State of California Department of Justice, California Consumer Privacy Act (CCPA), https://oag.ca.gov/privacy/ccpa (last accessed Aug. 21, 2021).

8. A highwater mark was the 1984 Supreme Court decision in *Ruckelshaus v. Monsanto*, 467 U.S. 986 (1984), where the court considered whether various iterations of the Federal Insecticide, Fungicide, and Rodenticide Act—requiring corporations to disclose ingredients of pesticides to the Environmental Protection Authority (EPA) and allowing the EPA to make use of the information in relation to other companies' applications for registration of their products—offended the "takings" clause of the Constitution. This is the clause that requires the government to provide fair and just compensation if it "takes" someone's property. The case revolved around whether trade secrets were property in the federal "takings" context.

9. For example, Amazon's Internet-Based Ads Policy, as communicated by the company to a customer on May 14, 2019, https://www.amazon.com/gp/help /customer/display.html?nodeId=202075050: "We do not provide any personal information to advertisers or to third-party sites that serve our interest-based ads. However, advertisers and other third parties (including the ad networks,

ad-serving companies, and other service providers they may use) may assume that users who interact with or click on a personalized ad or content are part of the group that the ad or content is directed towards (for example, users in the Pacific Northwest who bought or browsed for classical music). Also, some third parties may provide us information about you (such as the sites where you have been shown ads or demographic information) from offline and online sources that we may use to provide you more relevant and useful advertising."

10. See Michael Wines, *2020 Census Won't Have Citizenship Question as Trump Administration Drops Effort*, New York Times, July 2, 2019, https://www.nytimes.com/2019/07/02/us/trump-census-citizenship-question.html.

CHAPTER TWO. OUR DATA AT HOME

1. Reed Albergotti, *How Nest, Designed to Keep Intruders out of People's Homes, Effectively Allowed Hackers to Get In*, Washington Post, Apr. 23, 2019, https://www.washingtonpost.com/technology/2019/04/23/how-nest-designed-keep-intruders-out-peoples-homes-effectively-allowed-hackers-get/?utm_term=.51a46a32041a.

2. Restatement of the Law, Second, Torts, §652B.

3. Privacy Statement for Nest Products and Services, last updated Sept. 24, 2018, https://nest.com/legal/privacy-statement-for-nest-products-and-services/; Privacy Policy for Nest Websites, https://nest.com/legal/privacy-policy-for-nest-web-sites/.

4. See https://www.eff.org.

5. See https://epic.org.

6. Betsy Schiffman, *Facebook Is Always Watching You*, Wired, Dec. 4, 2007, https://www.wired.com/2007/12/facebooks-is-al/; Alexia Fernández Campbell, *Facebook Allowed Companies to Post Job Ads Only Men Could See. Now That's Changing*, Vox, Mar. 21, 2019, https://www.vox.com/2019/3/21/18275746/facebook-settles-ad-discrimination-lawsuits.

7. Hayley Peterson, *Whole Foods Shoppers Blast Amazon's Prime Member Discounts as the Company Announces Its Slashing Prices*, Business Insider, Apr. 6, 2019, https://www.businessinsider.com/whole-foods-shoppers-blast-amazons-prime-member-discounts-2019-4.

8. Cecilia Kang, *F.T.C. Approves Facebook Fine of about $5 Billion*, New York Times, July 12, 2019, https://www.nytimes.com/2019/07/12/technology/facebook-ftc-fine.html; Federal Trade Commission, *Equifax Data Breach Settlement*, July 2019, https://www.ftc.gov/enforcement/cases-proceedings/refunds/equifax-data-breach-settlement.

9. Jayne Ponder, *GAO Report Calls for Federal Privacy Law*, Covington Blog, Feb. 24, 2019, https://www.insideprivacy.com/data-privacy/gao-report-calls-for-federal-privacy-law/.

CHAPTER THREE. OUR DATA AT WORK

1. See Trent Gillies, *Why Most of Three Square Market's Employees Jumped at the Chance to Wear a Microchip*, CNBC Money, Aug. 13, 2017, https://www.cnbc.com/2017/08/11/three-square-market-ceo-explains-its-employee-microchip-implant.html.

2. See discussion in Andrew Keshner, *States Are Cracking Down on Companies Microchipping Their Employees—How Common Is It?*, Marketwatch, Feb. 4, 2020, https://www.marketwatch.com/story/states-are-cracking-down-on-companies-microchipping-their-employees-how-common-is-it-and-why-does-it-happen-2020-02-03.

3. Tracy Jan and Elizabeth Dwoskin, *Facebook Agrees to Overhaul Targeted Advertising System for Job, Housing and Loan Ads after Discrimination Complaints*, Washington Post, Mar. 19, 2019, https://www.washingtonpost.com/business/economy/facebook-agrees-to-dismantle-targeted-advertising-system-for-job-housing-and-loan-ads-after-discrimination-complaints/2019/03/19/7dc9b5fa-4983-11e9-b79a-961983b7e0cd_story.html.

4. See Nutrien Employee Privacy Policy, https://www.nutrien.com/employee-privacy-policy (last accessed Mar. 15, 2020).

5. Ibid.

6. Ibid.

CHAPTER FOUR. OUR DATA ON SOCIAL MEDIA

1. See Lauren Schenkman, *Why We Fall for Phishing Emails—and How We Can Protect Ourselves*, Ideas.Ted.com, Jan. 30, 2020, https://ideas.ted.com/why-we-fall-for-phishing-emails-and-how-we-can-protect-ourselves/#:~:text=Who%20fell%20for%20the%20phishing,susceptible%20than%20any%20other%20group (last accessed July 14, 2020).

2. At the federal level, the relevant law is the Identity Theft Act of 1998, which is enforced by both the Department of Justice and the Federal Trade Commission. All states have some form of identity theft law as well. These state laws are summarized by the National Conference of State Legislatures at https://www.ncsl.org/research/financial-services-and-commerce/identity-theft-state-statutes.aspx (last accessed June 14, 2020).

3. See Clause 11 (Privacy Violations and Image Privacy Rights), Facebook Community Standards, https://www.facebook.com/communitystandards/safety (last accessed June 2, 2020).

4. See Clause 9 (Bullying and Harassment), Facebook Community Standards, https://www.facebook.com/communitystandards/bullying (last accessed June 2, 2020).

5. Facebook, Terms of Service, https://www.facebook.com/terms.php (last accessed June 2, 2020).

6. The FTC press release providing details of the settlement is available at https://www.ftc.gov/news-events/press-releases/2019/09/google-youtube-will-pay-record-170-million-alleged-violations (last accessed June 6, 2020).

7. See, for example, FTC press release, *FTC Announces Settlement with Bankrupt Website, Toysmart.com, Regarding Alleged Privacy Policy Violations*, July 21, 2000, https://www.ftc.gov/news-events/press-releases/2000/07/ftc-announces-settlement-bankrupt-website-toysmartcom-regarding (last accessed June 14, 2020).

8. Lily Hay Newman, *Hacks, Nudes, and Breaches: It's Been a Rough Month for Dating Apps: Trouble at OkCupid, Coffee Meets Bagel and Jack'd Have Made February a Bad Stretch for Romantics Online*, Wired, Feb. 15, 2019, https://www.wired.com/story/ok-cupid-dating-apps-hacks-breaches-security/.

9. Anna Moore, *'There's No End and No Escape. You Feel So, So Exposed.' Life as a Victim of Revenge Porn*, The Guardian, Sept. 22, 2019, https://www.theguardian.com/lifeandstyle/2019/sep/22/theres-no-end-and-no-escape-you-feel-so-so-exposed-life-as-a-victim-of-revenge-porn.

10. Ibid.

11. Ibid. See also Cyber Civil Rights Initiative, *2017 Nationwide Online Study of Nonconsensual Porn Victimization and Perpetration: A Summary Report*, June 2017,https://www.cybercivilrights.org/wp-content/uploads/2017/06/CCRI-2017-Research-Report.pdf.

12. Carmel Abramov, *Revenge Porn: 21st Century Love*, Los Angeles Times, May 22, 2018, https://highschool.latimes.com/calabasas-high-school/revenge-porn-21st-century-love/.

13. For instructions, see https://m.facebook.com/help/mobile-basic/148233965247823?helpref=faq_content (last accessed June 14, 2020).

CHAPTER FIVE. OUR CHILDREN'S DATA

1. danah boyd [*sic*] et al., *Why Parents Help Their Children Lie to Facebook About Age: Unintended Consequences of the 'Children's Online Privacy Protection Act,'* First Monday, Oct. 21, 2011, https://journals.uic.edu/ojs/index.php/fm/article/view/3850/3075.

2. Federal Trade Commission, *Complying with COPPA: Frequently Asked Questions*, https://www.ftc.gov/tips-advice/business-center/guidance/complying-coppa-frequently-asked-questions#General Questions (last accessed June 19, 2020).

3. See Article 8(1) of the General Data Protection Regulation; and Article 6(1)(f), which also allows the interests of a child to override needs for which any entity can process personal data.

4. See Article 12(1) of the General Data Protection Regulation.

5. See Office of the Privacy Commission (Canada), *Privacy and Kids*, https://www.priv.gc.ca/en/privacy-topics/information-and-advice-for-individuals/privacy-and-kids/ (last accessed June 28, 2020).

6. Josh Constine, *Facebook 'Messenger Kids' Lets Under-13s Chat with Whom Parents Approve*, TechCrunch, Dec. 4, 2017, https://techcrunch.com/2017/12/04/facebook-messenger-kids/.

7. See https://meganmeierfoundation.org/suicide (last accessed June 28, 2020).

8. See https://tylerclementi.org (last accessed June 28, 2020).

CHAPTER SIX. OUR DATA AT SCHOOL

1. Emily L. Mahoney, *Florida Launches School Security Database, with Student Discipline, Health, Social Media Info*, Tampa Bay Times, Aug. 2, 2019, https://www.tampabay.com/blogs/gradebook/2019/08/02/florida-launches-school-security-database-with-student-discipline-health-social-media-info/.

2. Ibid.

3. Ibid.

CHAPTER SEVEN. OUR DATA IN THE DIGITAL MARKETPLACE

1. See, for example, Michael Hill and Dan Swinhoe, *The 15 Biggest Data Breaches of the 21st Century*, CSO, July 16, 2021, https://www.csoonline.com/article/2130877/the-biggest-data-breaches-of-the-21st-century.html (last accessed July 22, 2020); Michael Novinson, *The 10 Biggest Data Breaches of 2020 (So Far)*, CRN, June 26, 2020, https://www.crn.com/slide-shows/security/the-10-biggest-data-breaches-of-2020-so-far- (last accessed July 22, 2020).

2. See N. Cameron Russell et al., *APIs and Your Privacy*, CLIP at Fordham Law School, Jan. 2019, https://www.fordham.edu/download/downloads/id/12352/CLIP_UMSI_APIs_and_Your_Privacy__FINAL_.pdf.

3. Makena Kelly, *The US Government Is Considering a TikTok Ban, Says Secretary of State*, The Verge, July 7, 2020, https://www.theverge.com/2020/7/7/21316062/tiktok-ban-app-mike-pompeo-government-china-bytedance-communist-party.

4. Louise Matsakis, *The WIRED Guide to Your Personal Data (and Who Is Using It)*, Wired Business, Feb. 15, 2019, https://www.wired.com/story/wired-guide-personal-data-collection/.

5. For a more detailed examination of these uses of collated personal data, see Steven Melendez and Alex Pasternack, *Here Are the Data Brokers Quietly Buying and Selling Your Personal Information*, Fast Company, Mar. 2, 2019, https://www.fastcompany.com/90310803/here-are-the-data-brokers-quietly-buying-and-selling-your-personal-information.

6. Ibid.

7. Douglas MacMillan, *Data Brokers Are Selling Your Secrets. How States Are Trying to Stop Them*, Washington Post, June 24, 2019, https://www.washingtonpost.com/business/2019/06/24/data-brokers-are-getting-rich-by-selling-your-secrets-how-states-are-trying-stop-them/.

8. See Matsakis, *WIRED Guide to Your Personal Data*.

CHAPTER EIGHT. OUR DATA ACROSS THE POND

1. General Data Protection Regulation, Article 15(1)(h).

2. See, for example, Rowena Mason, *Right to Be Forgotten: Wikipedia Chief Enters Internet Censorship Row*, The Guardian, July 25, 2014, https://www.theguardian.com/technology/2014/jul/25/right-to-be-forgotten-google-wikipedia-jimmy-wales.

3. Sarah Marsh, *'Right to be Forgotten' on Google Only Applies in EU, Court Rules*, The Guardian, Sept. 24, 2019, https://www.theguardian.com/technology/2019/sep/24/victory-for-google-in-landmark-right-to-be-forgotten-case.

4. Joseph Lazzarotti, *National Biometric Information Privacy Act, Proposed by Sens. Jeff Merkley and Bernie Sanders*, National Law Review, Aug. 5, 2020, https://www.natlawreview.com/article/national-biometric-information-privacy-act-proposed-sens-jeff-merkley-and-bernie.

CHAPTER NINE. OUR DATA AND OUR HEALTH

1. See discussion in April Falcon Doss, *Cyber Privacy: Who Has Your Data and Why You Should Care* (Dallas, TX: BenBella Books, 2020), 26–28.

2. Megan Molteni, *What the Golden State Killer Tells Us about Forensic Genetics*, Wired, Apr. 24, 2019, https://www.wired.com/story/the-meteoric-rise-of-family-tree-forensics-to-fight-crimes/.

CHAPTER TEN. OUR DATA AND OUR MONEY

1. G. Dautovic, *Top 25 Financial Data Breach Statistics for 2020*, Fortunly, July 2, 2021, https://fortunly.com/statistics/data-breach-statistics/#gref.

2. Ibid.

3. The law actually distinguishes between "customers" and "consumers" with respect to the notice requirements. Under the law, *consumers* is a subset of *customers*. Anyone who submits an application for an account is a consumer, but a "customer" has an ongoing relationship with the financial institution. The notice requirements are sufficiently similar for the two categories to consider them together for the purposes of this chapter. Even a consumer whose application for credit is unsuccessful is owed an initial privacy notice under the law, although customers are entitled to annual notices.

4. For example, under the Gramm-Leach-Bliley Act, different agencies are contemplated as regulators for different categories of financial institutions. The regulators include the Office of the Comptroller of Currency, the Board of Governors of the Federal Reserve System, the Federal Deposit Insurance Corporation, the Office of Thrift Supervision, the Securities and Exchange Commission, the National Credit Union Administration, and the Federal Trade Commission. In terms of consumer complaints about financial institutions' practices, most would go directly to the FTC.

5. Scott Steinberg, *The Latest Ways Identity Thieves Are Targeting You—And What to Do if You Are a Victim*, CNBC, Feb. 27, 2020, https://www.cnbc.com/2020/02/27/these-are-the-latest-ways-identity-thieves-are-targeting-you.html.

6. Laura Shin, *"Someone Had Taken Over My Life": An Identity Theft Victim's Story*, Forbes, Nov. 18, 2014, https://www.forbes.com/sites/laurashin/2014/11/18/someone-had-taken-over-my-life-an-identity-theft-victims-story/?sh=1d1ff42925be.

7. Amy Krebs, *Know Your Own Data*, AKAJANEDOE Blog, Jan. 23, 2019, https://www.akajanedoe.com/blog (last accessed Nov. 30, 2020).

8. Shin, *Someone Had Taken Over*.

9. Neil Vigdor, *5 Indicted in Identity Theft Scheme That Bilked Millions from Veterans*, New York Times, Aug. 21, 2019, https://www.nytimes.com/2019/08/21/us/military-identity-theft-scheme.html.

10. As already noted, the law distinguishes between "customers" and "consumers" for notice purposes—although each group is entitled to an initial set of privacy notices as soon as an application for credit is made. Again, customers are those consumers who engage in an ongoing relationship with a financial institution and are entitled to periodic additional notices in that capacity.

CHAPTER ELEVEN. OUR DATA AND THE GOVERNMENT

1. Kate O'Flaherty, *Facial Recognition at U.S. Airports. Should You Be Concerned?*, Forbes, Mar. 11, 2019, https://www.forbes.com/sites/kateoflahertyuk/2019/03/11/facial-recognition-to-be-deployed-at-top-20-us-airports-should-you-be-concerned/?sh=7ffa25bb7d48.

2. Ibid.

3. These technologies also raise significant concerns about profiling (racial, religious, or otherwise). See, for example, Amna Toor, *"Our Identity Is Often What's Triggering Surveillance": How Government Surveillance of #BlackLivesMatter Violates the First Amendment Freedom of Association*, 44 Rutgers Computer & Technology Law Journal (2018); Katelyn Ringrose, *Religious Profiling: When Government Surveillance Violates the First and Fourth Amendments*, 1 University of Illinois Law

Review (2019), https://www.illinoislawreview.org/wp-content/uploads /2019/03/Ringrose-1.pdf.

4. Josephine Wolff, *Losing Our Fourth Amendment Data Protection*, New York Times, Apr. 28, 2019, https://www.nytimes.com/2019/04/28/opinion /fourth-amendment-privacy.html.

5. There are many live debates about whether the Fourth Amendment protects "places" or "people," and those debates are beyond the scope of this book, but, again, it is important to note that this chapter merely introduces the basic tenets of the Fourth Amendment and its limitations. Reading it will not make anyone a constitutional law or criminal procedure expert!

6. *Carpenter v. U.S.* 138 S. Ct. 2206, 2220 (2018).

7. Ibid.

8. Ibid., citing *Northwest Airlines Inc. v. Minnesota*, 322 U.S. 292, 300 (1944), per Justice Frankfurter.

9. Seehttps://www.eff.org/document/jewel-v-nsa-amicus-brief-free-speech-coalition-et-al-support-petition-rehearing.

10. Cindy Cohn, *Litigation against Mass NSA Surveillance: Year in Review 2020*, Electronic Frontier Foundation, Jan. 1, 2021, https://www.eff.org/deeplinks /2020/12/litigation-against-mass-nsa-surveillance-year-review-2020 (last accessed Feb. 26, 2021).

11. Full text available at https://law.justia.com/cases/federal/appellate-courts/ca9/13-50572/13-50572-2020-09-02.html (last accessed Jan. 17, 2022).

12. Cohn, *Litigation against Mass NSA Surveillance.*

13. Christina Zhao, *Chinese Police Using Facial-Recognition Sunglasses to Instantly Find Criminals in Crowds*, Newsweek, Feb. 9, 2018.

14. Yaqiu Wang, *In China the 'Great Firewall' Is Changing a Generation*, Politico, Sept. 1, 2020, https://www.politico.com/news/magazine/2020/09/01/china-great-firewall-generation-405385.

15. Ibid.: "China's internet censorship system, colloquially known as the Great Firewall, has existed since 2000, when the Ministry of Public Security launched the Golden Shield Project, a giant mechanism of censorship and surveillance aimed at restricting content, identifying and locating individuals, and providing immediate access to personal records."

16. IFSEC Global, *Role of CCTV Cameras: Public, Privacy and Protection*, Jan. 1, 2021, https://www.ifsecglobal.com/video-surveillance/role-cctv-cameras-public-privacy-protection/ (last accessed Feb. 4, 2021).

17. Adam Bannister, *GDPR Breaches Rife among CCTV Deployments, Investigation Finds*, IFSEC Global, Aug. 14, 2019, https://www.ifsecglobal.com/video-surveillance

/gdpr-breaches-rife-among-cctv-deployments-investigation-suggests/ (last accessed Feb. 4, 2021).

18. IFSEC Global, *Role of CCTV Cameras*.

CHAPTER TWELVE. OUR DATA INTO THE FUTURE

1. Polly Sprenger, *Sun on Privacy: "Get Over It,"* Wired, Jan. 26, 1999, https://www.wired.com/1999/01/sun-on-privacy-get-over-it/.

For those interested in more detail on the issues presented in this book, I offer the following suggestions.

GENERAL RESOURCES

April Falcon Doss, *Cyber Privacy: Who Has Your Data and Why You Should Care* (Ben-Bella Books, 2020).

Woodrow Hartzog, *Privacy's Blueprint: The Battle to Control the Design of New Technologies* (Harvard University Press, 2018).

Sarah E. Igo, *The Known Citizen: A History of Privacy in Modern America* (Harvard University Press, 2018).

Bruce Schneier, *Data and Goliath: The Hidden Battles to Collect Your Data and Control Your World* (W.W. Norton, 2016).

Shoshana Zuboff, *The Age of Surveillance Capitalism: The Fight for a Human Future at the New Frontier of Power* (PublicAffairs, 2020).

Ari Ezra Waldman, *Privacy as Trust: Information Privacy for an Information Age* (Cambridge University Press, 2018).

CHAPTER ONE. WHO OWNS OUR DATA?

Ann Bartow, *Our Data, Ourselves: Privacy, Propertization and Gender*, 34 University of San Francisco Law Review 633 (2000).

Jessica Litman, *Information Privacy/Information Property*, 52 Stanford Law Review 1283 (2000).

Jeffrey Ritter and Anna Mayer, *Regulating Data as Property: A New Construct for Moving Forward*, 16 Duke Law & Technology Review 220 (2018).

CHAPTER TWO. OUR DATA AT HOME

Bert-Jaap Koops, *Privacy Spaces*, 121 West Virginia Law Review 611 (2018).

Branden Ly, *Never Home Alone: Data Privacy Regulation for the Internet of Things*, University of Illinois Journal of Law, Technology & Policy 539 (2017).

Anna O'Donnell, *Why the VPPA and COPPA Are Outdated: How Netflix, Youtube and Disney+ Can Monitor Your Family at No Real Cost*, 55 Georgia Law Review 467 (2020).

CHAPTER THREE. OUR DATA AT WORK

Devasheesh Bhave, Laurel Teo, and Reeshad Dalal, *Privacy at Work: A Review and Research Agenda for a Contested Terrain*, 46 Journal of Management 127 (2019).

FindLaw, *Privacy at Work: What Are Your Rights?* (June 25, 2019), https://www .findlaw.com/employment/workplace-privacy/privacy-at-work-what-are-your-rights.html.

Tom Spiggle, *Employee Data Privacy Lawsuits: A Growing Trend*, Forbes, Apr. 22, 2021, https://www.forbes.com/sites/tomspiggle/2021/04/22/employee-data-privacy-lawsuits-a-growing-trend/?sh=3faa2a1e3555.

Wes Turner, *Chipping Away at Workplace Privacy: The Implantation of RFID Microchips and Erosion of Employee Privacy*, 61 Washington University Journal of Law & Policy 275 (2020).

CHAPTER FOUR. OUR DATA ON SOCIAL MEDIA

Victoria Cvek, *Policing Social Media: Balancing the Interests of Schools and Students and Providing Universal Protection for Students' Rights*, 121 Penn State Law Review 583 (2016).

Stephen E. Henderson, *Expectations of Privacy in Social Media*, 31 Mississippi College Law Review 227 (2012).

Brian Mund, *Social Media Searches and the Reasonable Expectation of Privacy*, 19 Yale Journal of Law & Technology 238 (2017).

CHAPTER FIVE. OUR CHILDREN'S DATA

Julia Jacobson and Heather Egan Sussman, *Protecting Children Online: New Compliance Obligations for Digital Marketing to Children*, 57 Boston Bar Journal 17 (Summer 2013).

Ariel Fox Johnson, *13 Going on 30: An Exploration of Expanding COPPA's Privacy Protections to Everyone*, 44 Seton Hall Legislative Journal 419 (2020).

Anna O'Donnell, *Why the VPPA and COPPA Are Outdated: How Netflix, YouTube, and Disney+ Can Monitor Your Family at No Real Cost*, 55 Georgia Law Review 467 (2020).

Chrissie N. Scelsi, *Recent Developments in Online Privacy Laws*, 90 Florida Bar Journal 72 (2016).

CHAPTER SIX. OUR DATA AT SCHOOL

Kitty L. Cone and Richard Peltz-Steele, *FERPA Close-Up: When Video Captures Violence and Injury*, 70 Oklahoma Law Review 839 (2018).

Lynn M. Daggett, *FERPA in the Twenty-First Century: Failure to Effectively Regulate Privacy for All Students*, 58 Catholic University Law Review 59 (2008).

Zach Greenberg and Adam Goldstein, *Baking Common Sense into the FERPA Cake: How to Meaningfully Protect Student Rights and the Public Interest*, 44 Journal of Legislation 22 (2017).

U.S. Department of Education, Family Educational Rights and Privacy Act (FERPA) website, https://www2.ed.gov/policy/gen/guid/fpco/ferpa/index.html.

U.S. Department of Education, Protecting Student Privacy website, https://studentprivacy.ed.gov/.

Jennifer C. Wasson, *FERPA in the Age of Computer Logging: School Discretion at the Cost of Student Privacy?*, 81 North Carolina Law Review 1348 (2003).

CHAPTER SEVEN. OUR DATA IN THE DIGITAL MARKETPLACE

Ken Dai and Jet Deng, *Big Data and Antitrust Risks in Close-Up: From the Perspective of Real Cases*, 30 Competition 36 (Fall 2020).

Dan Feldman and Eldar Haber, *Measuring and Protecting Privacy in the Always-On Era*, 35 Berkeley Technology Law Journal 197 (2020).

Adam J. Levitin, *Pandora's Digital Box: The Promise and Perils of Digital Wallets*, 166 University of Pennsylvania Law Review 305 (2018).

Adam B. Thimmesch, *Transacting in Data: Tax, Privacy, and the New Economy*, 94 Denver Law Review 145 (2016).

CHAPTER EIGHT. OUR DATA ACROSS THE POND

Elizabeth Feld, *United States Privacy Law: The Domino Effect after the GDPR*, 24 North Carolina Banking Institute 481 (2020).

Blake Klinkner, *Understanding the Changing Landscape of Data Protection Laws*, Wyoming Lawyer 44 (Feb. 2019).

Mark Peasley, *It's Time for an American (Data Protection) Revolution*, 52 Akron Law Review 911 (2019).

Jacob M. Victor, *The EU General Data Privacy Regulation: Toward a Property Regime for Protecting Data Privacy*, 123 Yale Law Journal 513 (2013).

CHAPTER NINE. OUR DATA AND OUR HEALTH

Emily DeCiccio, *Privacy Laws Need Updating after Google Deal with HCA Healthcare, Medical Ethics Professor Says*, CNBC, May 26, 2021, https://www.cnbc.com/2021/05/26/privacy-laws-need-updating-after-google-deal-with-hca-healthcare-medical-ethics-professor-says.html.

David M. Parker, Steven G. Pine, and Zachary W. Ernst, *Privacy and Informed Consent for Research in the Age of Big Data*, 123 Penn State Law Review 703 (2019).

Samantha Singer, *'The Greatest Wealth Is Health': Patient Protected Health Information in the Hands of Hackers*, 31 John Marshall Journal of Information Technology & Privacy Law 657 (2015).

Charlotte A. Tschider, *The Consent Myth: Improving Choice for Patients of the Future*, 96 Washington University Law Review 1505 (2019).

CHAPTER TEN. OUR DATA AND OUR MONEY

Consumer Financial Protection Bureau (CFPB), Consumer Resources, https://www.consumerfinance.gov/consumer-tools/.

Consumer Financial Protection Bureau (CFPB), Credit Reporting Requirements, https://www.consumerfinance.gov/compliance/compliance-resources/other-applicable-requirements/compliance-resources/.

Consumer Financial Protection Bureau (CFPB), Privacy Notices (GLBA), https://www.consumerfinance.gov/compliance/compliance-resources/other-applicable-requirements/privacy-notices/.

Federal Deposit Insurance Corporation (FDIC), Financial Privacy . . . Our Answers to Your Questions, https://www.fdic.gov/consumers/privacy/faqs/.

Federal Deposit Insurance Corporation (FDIC), Privacy Program, https://www.fdic.gov/policies/privacy/index.html.

Federal Trade Commission (FTC), Financial Privacy: Protecting Consumers' Privacy, https://www.ftc.gov/news-events/media-resources/protecting-consumer-privacy/financial-privacy.

CHAPTER ELEVEN. OUR DATA AND THE GOVERNMENT

Jennifer M. Bentley, *Policing the Police: Balancing the Right to Privacy against the Beneficial Use of Drone Technology*, 70 Hastings Law Journal 249 (2019).

Sarah Brayne, *Predict and Surveil: Data, Discretion, and the Future of Policing* (Oxford University Press, 2020).

Evan H. Caminker, *Location Tracking and Digital Data: Can Carpenter Build a Stable Privacy Doctrine?*, 2018 Supreme Court Review 411 (2018).

Harvey Gee, *Last Call for the Third-Party Doctrine in the Digital Age after Carpenter?*, 26 Boston University Journal of Science & Technology Law 286 (2020).

Chadwick Lamar, *The Third-Party Doctrine at the Crossroads: Rules and Direction for a Tech-Savvy Fourth Amendment*, 39 Review of Litigation 215 (2019).

Tamar Megiddo, *Online Activism, Digital Domination, and the Rule of Trolls: Mapping and Theorizing Technological Oppression by Governments*, 58 Columbia Journal of Transnational Law 394 (2020).

Christopher Slobogin, *Privacy at Risk: The New Government Surveillance and the Fourth Amendment* (University of Chicago Press, 2007).

John Taschner, *Era of Accelerating Digital Convergence: Security, Surveillance, Data, Privacy, Big Tech, and Politics*, 36 American University International Law Review 773 (2021).

Amna Toor, *"Our Identity Is Often What's Triggering Surveillance": How Government Surveillance of #BlackLivesMatter Violates the First Amendment Freedom of Association*, 44 Rutgers Computer & Technology Law Journal 286 (2018).

Jesslin Wooliver, *Want to Know a Secret . . . ? Electronic Surveillance, National Security, and the Role of the Foreign Intelligence Surveillance Act*, 61 Boston College Law Review (E-Supplement II) 393 (2020).

CHAPTER TWELVE. OUR DATA INTO THE FUTURE

Christopher Bret Alexander, *The General Data Protection Regulation and California Consumer Privacy Act: The Economic Impact and Future of Data Privacy Regulations*, 32 Loyola Consumer Law Review 199 (2020).

Annie Brown, *AI's Role in the Future of Data Privacy*, Forbes, July 2, 2021, https://www.forbes.com/sites/anniebrown/2021/07/02/ais-role-in-the-future-of-data-privacy/?sh=4759c4d318c0.

Peter H. Diamandis and Steven Kotler, *The Future Is Faster Thank You Think: How Converging Technologies Are Transforming Business, Industries, and Our Lives* (Simon & Schuster, 2020).

Philip Kushmaro, *The Future of Data Privacy Consent: Are Brands Ready for a National Privacy Law?*, CPO Magazine, July 9, 2021, https://www.cpomagazine.com/data-protection/the-future-of-data-privacy-consent-are-brands-ready-for-a-national-privacy-law/.

California, 4, 49, 57. *See also* Consumer Privacy Act (California, 2018)

Cambridge Analytica, 21–22, 72, 115

Canada, 27, 91–92

cancer, 7, 14, 15

Care-O-bot 3, 152

CCTV, 192–93

celebrity health information, 142. *See also* health information

cell lines, ownership of, 14, 15

cell site location information, 10, 185–87

censorship, 138

Chauvin, Derek, 62, 179

Child Pornography Prevention Act, 82

children's data and privacy: COPPA and, 73–74, 75–76, 81–90; cyberharassment, 8, 84, 89; schools and, 97–107. *See also* bullying and harassment; data ownership

Children's Online Privacy Protection Act. *See* COPPA

China, 81, 115, 182, 192, 197, 209n15

choice of law clauses, 35

ChoicePoint, 28

CIA (Central Intelligence Agency), 187

CIPA (Children's Internet Protection Act, 2000), 83, 84, 97

The Circle (Eggers), 9

citizen journalism, 63

CJEU. *See* European Court of Justice (ECJ)

Clearview AI, 180

Clementi, Tyler, 84, 105

click-through advertisement, 71–72

clickwrap agreement, 34

common law, defined, 34

Communications Decency Act (CDA, 1996), 82, 83

computer fraud, 122. *See also* hacking; identity theft

Computer Fraud and Abuse Act (CFAA, 1986), 121

confidentiality, 56, 68, 87, 100, 105, 151, 156–59

Congressional Research Service, 191

consent: contracts and, 6–7, 18–20; defined, 70–71; employee privacy and, 47–50, 53, 60–61; health information and, 14–15; for schools and data sharing, 101–4; verifiable parental, 88. *See also* contracts and contract law; terms of service (TOS)

constitutional rights, 4–5, 10, 26–27, 34. *See also* U.S. Constitution

Consumer Privacy Act (California, 2018), 22, 42, 52, 118, 129, 138

Consumer Privacy Bill of Rights, 139

consumer reporting agency, 164, 165, 166, 167

contact tracing, 3, 140, 189, 191–92

contracts and contract law, 18–20, 33, 38–39, 73–74, 105. *See also* consent; terms of service (TOS)

cookies, 90, 112, 114, 125

COPA (Child Online Protection Act), 82, 85

COPPA (Children's Online Privacy Protection Act, 2000), 75–76, 81–90

copyright law, 12–13, 14, 22–25

coronavirus. *See* COVID-19 pandemic

Court of Justice of the European Union (CJEU). *See* European Court of Justice (ECJ)

covered entities, 145, 153

COVID-19 pandemic, 3, 81, 102–4, 148, 159, 165, 191–92

credit card fraud, 3, 122. *See also* financial information

credit freeze, 123, 124, 126, 168. *See also* financial information

credit information, 7, 58–60, 119, 123–24, 163, 164. *See also* data breaches; financial information

credit score, 167

crime and Big Data, 7. *See also* police

cyber attribution, 66

cyberbullying and harassment, 8, 77–79, 84, 89–91, 105

data aggregation, 3, 6, 85, 111–16, 117, 120. *See also* Big Data; data processing

Database Directive (EU, 1996), 13, 17–18, 23

data breaches, 2, 3, 79, 110–11, 119–24, 144–45, 151–53, 154, 161–62. *See also* hacking; identity theft

data breach fatigue, 161
data brokers, 116–19
data ownership: contract law and, 18–22; copyright and, 22, 23–24; by government, 26–27; by individual, 13–15; privacy tips on, 29–30, 43, 60–61, 79–80, 93–94, 108–9; by private companies, 15–18; regulation of, 27–29; third party sharing and, 24–26, 37–38, 70–72, 175; trade secret law and, 22–23. *See also* children's data and privacy; data breaches; data privacy protection; property rights
data privacy protection: of children's data, 73–74, 75–76, 81–90; data sharing and, 24–26, 101–4; in Europe, 4, 33, 42, 60, 90–93, 127–38; Google's policy on, 19–21; by hired experts, 140–41; in the home, 31–33, 42–43; legal background of, 4–6; regulation of, 27–28; by schools, 97–107; technology and, 6–11; tips and tricks for, 29–30, 43, 60–61, 79–80, 93–94, 108–9, 124–26, 159–60; of video rentals, 113, 115. *See also* data breaches; data ownership; financial information; health information
data processing, 91. *See also* Big Data; data privacy protection
Data Protection Directive (1995), 4
Data Protection Offices (EU), 27
dating websites, 76–77, 78
Deal v. Spears, 53–54
defamation law, 33, 34
Department of Health and Human Services (DHHS), 145
Department of Homeland Security, 180
Department of Justice, 188
digital databases, 25
directory exception, 101
discrimination and Big Data, 7–9
disease and Big Data, 7, 15. *See also* health information
DNA testing, 3, 116, 140, 147, 156–60. *See also* genetic information
Docusearch, 117
domain name ownership, 12–13

Donor Sibling Registry, 157
Doss, April Falcon, 21
doxing (or doxxing), 35, 36, 38, 78, 119. *See also* harassment
Drew, Lori, 105, 121
due process, 34, 45, 46, 57, 163, 171, 173, 186. *See also* Fourth Amendment, U.S. Constitution

Economic Espionage Act, 188
ECPA (Electronic Communications Privacy Act), 52–55, 59
educational institutions. *See* schools
educational records, 100. *See also* children's data and privacy
eHarmony, 76
election hacking, 2, 3, 21, 62, 63, 72. *See also* hacking
Electronic Communications Privacy Act (1986), 188
Electronic Frontier Foundation (EFF), 42, 43, 188–89
Electronic Privacy Information Center, 42, 43
emergency exemption, 103
emotional trauma, 78–79
Employee Polygraph Protection Act (1988), 52, 58
employers: COVID and, 149; discrimination by, 7–8, 9, 45, 55; HIPPA and, 56, 147; monitoring by, 48, 50–52. *See also* workplace privacy
employment discrimination, 9, 45
Equifax, 2, 3, 58, 110, 119, 164, 165
E-rate program, 97
EU Directives and Regulations, 17
European Convention on Human Rights (ECHR), 4, 45, 60, 131
European Court of Justice (ECJ), 17, 127–28
European Union: Brexit, 72; children's privacy in, 90–93; database directive in, 13, 17; GDPR, 4, 42, 60, 91–92, 99, 131–34, 138; privacy laws in, 3, 4, 33, 127–38; workplace privacy in, 60. *See also* United Kingdom
Experian, 58, 164, 165

Facebook, 64; apps for children, 93; authentication options of, 80; class action settlement of, 1; data harvesting by, 1, 2, 16; dating services by, 76–77; ECPA and, 53; employment discrimination by, 45–46; fines imposed on, 81; hacking of, 67; hate speech algorithms of, 120; Ireland, 128; legal resources of, 34; targeted marketing by, 63; terms of service of, 68, 71, 86; use of FRT, 1, 69

faceprint, 1

facial recognition technology (FRT), 1, 3, 69, 179–80, 182, 192. *See also* artificial intelligence (AI)

Fair Credit Reporting Act. *See* FCRA

false light publicity, 38

Family Educational Rights and Privacy Act. *See* FERPA

FCC (Federal Communications Commission), 32

FCRA (Fair Credit Reporting Act, 1970), 52, 58, 60, 118–19, 122, 135, 162, 163, 164–67

FDA (Food and Drug Administration), 152

FDIC (Federal Deposit Insurance Corporation), 28

Federal Trade Commission. *See* FTC (Federal Trade Commission)

Federal Trade Commission Act (1914), 74–75

Feist v. Rural Telephone Service, 23

Feminist Women's Health Center v. Jenkins, 49

FERPA (Family Educational Rights and Privacy Act, 1974), 97, 98, 99–105

filtering technologies, 82–83, 97

Financial Crimes Enforcement Network (FinCEN), 174

financial information: constitutional right to privacy of, 171–73; credit, 7, 58–60, 119, 123–24, 163; credit card fraud, 3, 122; credit freeze, 123, 124, 126; ownership of, 15, 28; privacy tips and tricks of, 176–78. *See also* data breaches; data ownership; data privacy protection; FCRA

fingerprinters, 114

fingerprints, 140, 180, 195

First Amendment, U.S. Constitution, 4–5, 11, 22, 66, 181

Florida, 96, 106

Florida v. Jardines, 41

Floyd, George, 62, 179

Foreign Intelligence Surveillance Act (FISA), 128, 188

forum selection clauses, 35

Fourth Amendment, U.S. Constitution, 10, 40–41, 163, 171–72, 181, 183–88, 191, 209n5. *See also* due process

fraud alerts, 123, 124, 126, 168

freedom of speech, 4–5, 11, 22, 66

FRT. *See* facial recognition technology (FRT)

FTC (Federal Trade Commission), 21, 27–28, 32, 39, 72, 85; health information and, 153

gender discrimination, 7, 8, 16, 179

General Data Protection Regulation (GDPR), 4, 60, 91–92, 99, 131–34, 138

genetic information, 52, 55–58, 142, 143, 144, 148, 154–60. *See also* DNA testing; GINA; health information

genocide, 130

Germany, 130

GINA (Genetic Information Nondiscrimination Act, 2008), 52, 55, 56, 143, 154–56. *See also* genetic information

GLB Act. *See* Gramm-Leach-Bliley Act (1999)

González, Mario Costeja, 135, 137

Google, 19–21; class action lawsuits against, 54, 75–76, 95, 96; fines imposed on, 28, 81, 88, 90; hate speech algorithms of, 120; Home device, 32; legal resources of, 34; Nest Cam and, 31–32; right to be forgotten and, 135, 137; Spain, 135

government ownership of data, 26–27. *See also* data ownership

government surveillance, 5, 40–41, 180–84, 187–93

Gramm-Leach-Bliley Act (1999), 28, 162, 163, 173–75, 207n3 (ch. 10), 208n4
Great Firewall (China), 192, 209n15

hacking: of elections, 2, 3, 21, 62, 63, 72; overcriminalization of, 121. *See also* data breaches
harassment, 8, 77–79, 84, 89–91, 104–6, 108. *See also* doxing (or doxxing)
hate speech algorithms, 120
health and safety emergency exemption, 103
health entities, 145
health fraud, 3
health information: antidiscrimination law and, 57; data breaches of, 151–53, 154; disclosures of, 146–49; genetic, 52, 55–58, 142, 143, 144, 148, 154–58; healthcare robots and, 152; ownership of, 12, 15, 116; PHI, defined, 146; privacy tips and tricks on, 159–60; public health and Big Data, 7, 11; telehealth and, 154; workplace privacy and, 55–58. *See also* data privacy protection; GINA; HIPPA
HeLa cell line, 15
HIPPA (Health Insurance Portability and Accountability Act, 1996), 52, 55–56; data breaches and, 123, 144–45; employers and, 56, 147; individual rights under, 149–50; privacy rule of, 150–51. *See also* health information
home security, 31–32, 35, 38–39
housing discrimination, 7, 9
human body parts and property rights, 14, 49
Human Rights Watch, 192
hunger prevention and Big Data, 7

IBM, 179
IDEA (Individuals with Disabilities Education Act), 100
idea/expression dichotomy, 24
identity theft, 3, 66, 122–24, 161, 167–71, 177. *See also* data breaches; data privacy protection; financial information

Identity Theft and Assumption Deterrence Act (1998), 66, 122, 204n2 (ch. 4)
Identity Theft Enforcement and Restitution Act (2008), 170
identity trackers, 114
Illinois, 1, 52, 69, 95, 140
The Immortal Life of Henrietta Lacks (book and movie), 15
information gathering. *See* data aggregation; data processing
Instagram, 64
International Covenant on Civil and Political Rights (ICCPR), 130
Internet Bill of Rights, 139
intrusion into seclusion, 35, 36–37, 59

Jackson, Michael, 142
Jewel v. NSA, 188, 189
Johns Hopkins Hospital, 15
Joy for All Companion Pets, 152

keystroke monitoring technology, 114
KFC, 22–23
King, Ruth, 77–79
Krebs, Amy, 169–70
Kyllo v. United States, 40–41

labor theory (Locke), 16, 23
Lacks, Henrietta, 15
land ownership, 14, 16
legislation, defined, 34
LGBTQIA+ community, 8
libraries, 83, 97
Locke, John, 16
Lohr, Steve, 48
Lyft, 6

machine learning, 8, 120
marijuana growing and privacy case, 40–41
Marjory Stoneman Douglas High School, 96, 106
marketing. *See* targeted marketing
Marr, Bernard, 6, 7
Match, 77
Match Group, 77
Matsakis, Louise, 114, 116

third-party doctrine, 171, 183–84, 185–87
Third Restatement on Torts, 35
thisisyourdigitallife (app), 72
threat assessment databases, 106–7
TikTok, 81, 115
Tinder, 77
tort laws, 5, 34–38, 59
TOS. *See* terms of service (TOS)
tracking technology, 10, 185–87
trademark law, 14
trade secret law, 18, 22–23
transparency, 9
The Transparent Society (Brin), 198
TransUnion, 164, 165
Treasury Department, 172
trespass, 34
Trump, Donald, 62–63, 72, 83, 138
23andMe, 116, 157
Twitter, 62, 63, 64, 138
Tyler Clementi Foundation, 94

Uber, 6, 28
United Kingdom, 33, 72, 79, 90, 192
United Nations Declaration of Human
    Rights (UNDHR), 130–31
United States Patent and Trademark
    Office, 25
United States v. Carpenter, 186–87
United States v. Miller, 171–72, 184
United States v. Moalin, 188
USA PATRIOT Act (2001), 190
U.S. Constitution, 26; First Amendment,
    4–5, 11, 22, 66, 181; Fourth Amend-
    ment, 10, 40–41, 163, 171–72, 181,
    183–88, 191, 209n5

U.S. Customs and Border Protection, 180
U.S. Immigration and Customs Enforce-
    ment, 180

verifiable parental consent, 88. *See
    also* children's data and privacy;
    consent
Verizon, 10
veterans, identity theft scheme against,
    170–71
Video Privacy Protection Act (VPPA,
    1988), 113, 115
Virgin Mobile, 37
virtual school. *See* schools

Walmart, 16
Wang, Yaqui, 192
Warren, Samuel, 5
wearable medical devices, 154
website ownership, 12
Whole Foods, 42
wire fraud, 122
Wiretap Act (1968), 53. *See also*
    Electronic Communications
    Privacy Act (1986)
workplace discrimination, 7–8, 9, 45,
    55, 57
workplace privacy, 44–46; consent and,
    47–50; employee monitoring, 48,
    50–52; federal laws on employee
    privacy, 52–60
World War II, 130

YouTube, 21, 28, 63, 64, 75–76, 81, 88, 90.
    See also Google

Founded in 1893,
UNIVERSITY OF CALIFORNIA PRESS
publishes bold, progressive books and journals
on topics in the arts, humanities, social sciences,
and natural sciences—with a focus on social
justice issues—that inspire thought and action
among readers worldwide.

The UC PRESS FOUNDATION
raises funds to uphold the press's vital role
as an independent, nonprofit publisher, and
receives philanthropic support from a wide
range of individuals and institutions—and from
committed readers like you. To learn more, visit
ucpress.edu/supportus.